The Care Maze

*The law and your rights
to community care
in Scotland*

Colin McKay
*Solicitor, Legal & Policy Adviser,
ENABLE*

Hilary Patrick
*Solicitor, Legal Adviser,
the Scottish Association for Mental Health*

ENABLE

Scottish Association
for Mental Health

Published by: ENABLE   Scottish Association for Mental Health
               6th Floor   Atlantic House
               7 Buchanan Street   38 Gardner's Crescent
               Glasgow GI 3HL   Edinburgh EH3 8DQ

Distributed by   ENABLE, 6th Floor, 7 Buchanan Street, Glasgow GI 3HL

First published 1995

British Library Cataloguing in Publication Data. A catalogue record for this book is available from the British Library.

ISBN 1-874004-06-4

Designed by The Graphics Company, Edinburgh.
Cover illustration by David Sim.
Printed by L & S Litho Printers/Designers Limited, Glasgow.

Contents

The law and your rights to community care

RESIDENTIAL CARE

The law and your rights to community care

HELP FROM OTHER AGENCIES

COMMUNITY CARE AND CITIZENSHIP

The law and your rights to community care

IF THINGS GO WRONG

Stop press

Assessing a person's need for services

(page 23)

When Gloucestershire County Council had a cut in its funding, it withdrew certain welfare services provided under the Chronically Sick and Disabled Persons Act. Three pensioners took the local authority to court. In a linked case, a man from Islington complained because the care he received was not consistent. If his carer was ill or on holiday, the social services department did not provide any cover.

The Queens Bench Division said that Gloucestershire County Council had acted unlawfully. It should not have withdrawn services without reassessing the claimants' need for services and carrying out a new community care assessment under the NHS & Community Care Act. (See page 15, *Reviewing your assessment*.) However the court said that Islington Council had not acted illegally by failing to provide a continuous and regular service.

The court also looked at how a local authority should decide what services you *"need"* under the Chronically Sick and Disabled Persons Act. They said a local authority can take resources into account both when it works out what you need and when it decides whether to make arrangements to meet your needs. However, if you are at risk of physical harm, the local authority must arrange help for you.

The court confirmed that once a local authority decides that you *"need"* something under the Chronically Sick and Disabled Persons Act, it must make arrangements for help to be provided. Shortage of resources is no defence.

The cases are going to be appealed.

R v Gloucestershire County Council, ex parte Mahfood. Times Law Report 21/6/95.

Local authorities and residential care

(page 26)

The Court of Appeal in England has looked at the duty of local authorities to provide residential care homes. Some people feel that there should always be some residential care homes directly run by the local authority, but the Court said that local authorities do not have to provide residential care homes themselves; they can make arrangements for voluntary or independent organisations to run homes.

The wording of the English statute is similar, but not identical, to the Scottish statute. This case would not be binding on a Scottish court, but they would take it into consideration.

R v Wandsworth London Borough Council, ex parte Beckwith. Times Law Report 29/6/95.

Temporary residents in residential care

(pages 36 and 53)

From April 1995, there is a new concession for people who enter residential care for a trial period. For up to 13 weeks, they can still get Income Support or housing benefit to pay for their housing costs. This is in addition to the existing rules for temporary residents (which may still be more beneficial for some people).

Welfare Rights Bulletin April 1995 page 9.

Paying for residential care: value of occupational pensions

(page 48)

The Government has announced that it will change the rule whereby the local authority can take into account the whole of a spouse's occupational pension when he or she goes into residential care. From April 1996, local authorities will only be able to take account of half of the spouse's occupational pension when they fix the charge for services. A similar change will be made for people who were in residential care on March 31 1993 and have preserved rights to higher levels of Income Support.

"Changes to residential care rules gives partner half of pension." *Guardian* 22/6/95.

Reform of social work complaints

(page 126)

The Scottish Office has issued a consultation paper on changes to the Social Work Complaints Procedure Directions and Guidance.

NHS & Community Care Act 1990, *Local Authority Complaints Procedures*, Draft circular 30/6/95.

NHS complaints and the Health Service Ombudsman

(pages 133-134)

The Scottish Office has promised to introduce a simplified complaints procedure for all NHS complaints by April 1996. There will be a review procedure for dissatisfied complainants. Also the health service ombudsman will have new powers to consider clinical complaints and complaints against GPs.

"Scottish Office responds to NHS complaints review", *Scottish Office News Release* 22/3/95 (0340/95).

The Accounts Commission

(page 136)

Since April 1995, the Accounts Commission has also become responsible for monitoring the financial affairs and value for money of health boards and NHS Trusts.

NHS & Community Care Act 1990 (Commencement No. 11) (Scotland) Order 1994. SI 2658/1994.

Suing local authorities

(page 151)

The House of Lords has given its decision on the case of the children who alleged that they had suffered because they were not properly protected against child abuse.

The Lords refused to allow their cases to go ahead. The Lords said that many people were involved in child protection cases; police, social workers and psychiatrists. It would be wrong to hold any one group legally liable. Child protection work was complex and sensitive. To allow children and parents to bring claims might make it more difficult for the authorities to protect children at risk. This case is likely to be appealed to the Court of Human Rights in Strasbourg.

In a linked case, two men with dyslexia complained that their needs had not been properly recognised by their schools. Their careers and prospects had suffered as a result. Another man with special educational needs, who had been expelled from school, sued because he was not provided with the education he needed.

The Lords said that these cases should go ahead. If a local authority offered a service, like an educational psychology service, to the public, the professionals involved should exercise their skills carefully and could be liable in law if they did not. A headmaster advising parents on the education their children needed should act carefully and responsibly.

House of Lords cases, even when they deal with English law, are taken into account by Scottish courts. This case would be very important if you decided to sue because of a negligent community care assessment or a failure of a local authority to assess your needs properly. We believe that such a claim would be closer to the educational cases, which the House of Lords did allow to go ahead, than to the Lords decision on the child abuse cases, which probably failed for public policy reasons.

X (minors) v Bedfordshire County Council and others. Times Law Report 30/6/95.

Acknowledgements

We are very grateful for the support and patience of ENABLE and the Scottish Association for Mental Health. They continued to have faith in us while all about were losing theirs.

Many people read earlier drafts of this book or part of it and made helpful comments and suggestions. We are very grateful to them all. Among them were Liz Sutherland, Alison Petch, Jim Gray, Kate Fearnley, Ann Marie Mullaney, Derek Munn, Tom Mullen, Susan McPhee, Mark Brough, Paul Dumbleton and Hector Mackenzie. Any mistakes in the book are, of course, our own.

The production of the book is in large part due to the editorial skills of Val Tough. We are also grateful for the support and assistance of Hugh Stewart, Linda Kerr and Elinor Paul of ENABLE and Claire Walker of SAMH, and for the design skills of Michelle Cosgrove of The Graphics Company.

Finally we thank our partners, Allison and Bruce, and our children, Alexander and Lucy, Ruth, Catherine and Robert. Without them the book would surely have been finished many months ago.

Colin McKay
Hilary Patrick
June 1995

The law and your rights to community care

Foreword

AIM OF THIS BOOK

This book explains the law relating to community care in Scotland. It looks at the law and the guidance from the Government on good practice and tries to indicate how community care should work. It also looks at problems which are already arising and tries to suggest solutions.

This book is aimed at everyone who may be involved in community care: those who are providing or arranging services, social workers, care managers and planners, doctors and health board staff, and, most importantly, people who will use community care and their families, carers and friends.

We hope this book will be useful for everyone who might need help living in the community. Because we hope that it will also be helpful to advice workers and advocates, it contains full footnotes and references.

The book explains how community care works. It describes what legal rights people have to insist on getting help. It looks in some detail at how the Government wants community care to work. It has suggestions of what to do if things go wrong, where to complain, and how to take matters further.

It assumes no prior knowledge, and we hope it will be useful to people who need an introduction to community care as well as those who feel they are already familiar with how it works.

The law is stated as at 1 January 1995.

DIFFERENT RULES APPLY TO ENGLAND

A great deal of what has been written about community care has been written about the system in England and Wales.

Whilst many of the principles are the same, the actual law is very different and people in Scotland can become extremely confused if they read these English guides. The law is different and what you can do if the law is not complied with is different too.

Whilst warning our readers to be careful about English guides, therefore, we would not want to put off potential English readers. To you we recommend this book as a useful comparative exercise!

OUTLINE OF THE BOOK

In the **Introduction** we look at the structure of the community care system, explain who care in the community is for and who is responsible for providing it.

The first section looks at the duties of the social work department. We explain the assessment of needs, which is the central part of community care, and the legal duties of the social work department to provide services. We look at the situations when you will be asked to pay for services and we explain the rights of carers and the special rules relating to respite care.

The second section looks at residential care, your rights to choose what care you need and the complex rules for paying for care.

The third section looks at what help other agencies can provide. We look at the duties of the National Health Service (NHS), housing authorities, and the education and employment services.

The fourth section looks at your rights as citizens. It explains your rights to access to information, to confidentiality and to non-discriminatory services. We suggest ways in which a person who feels unable to speak for themselves can get representation. We talk about some of the things to look out for before you sign any agreements for community care. We look at ways for you to become involved in deciding how community care is provided and what opportunities there are for consultation about community care plans.

The final section looks at what to do if things go wrong. We look at the complaints mechanisms built into the system and try to indicate when you should consider getting a lawyer involved. We aim to help you choose the best remedy for your complaint.

A word of warning! Some of this book is difficult. It is not always as straightforward as we would like, because the law itself is sometimes quite complex.

Whilst we have tried to avoid technical legal language, we have felt it important to try to look at some complex questions and suggest answers.

We urge readers who find any parts difficult to skip them. Come back to them if you need to. This is not a book which has to be read from cover to cover: we hope it will also be used as a reference for people who have specific points to clarify.

CHANGES IN LOCAL GOVERNMENT LAW

The Government is proposing big changes in the way local government is organised in this country. From April 1996 each area will have one local authority which will be responsible for all the work which is now done by the district councils and the regional councils. So housing and social work will both be the responsibility of the new councils (as well as education, leisure and so on).

The new councils will still have the same legal duties as the old ones but the change will obviously have quite an impact on the way community care is delivered to people. Some of the councils will be much smaller than the current regions and they may have to "buy in"

services from elsewhere, or they may join together to form joint committees or joint boards. At the moment no-one really knows how it will work.

For readers after April 1996

If you are reading this book after the local government changes, remember that the legal duties of the councils will be the same. References to regional councils and district councils in the book will apply to the new councils.

There are some minor exceptions:

- Councils will not be legally required to have a social work committee. Most will have one, but some might join up different services (for example, social work and housing) into a single committee.

- Councils will not have to have a Director of Social Work with a social work qualification. However they will have to have a senior social work official who will have legal responsibility for some aspects of the social work service. Where we talk about the social work department in this book, what we say will apply to the department in the new council which provides social work services.

- Social work departments will no longer be legally required to consult housing departments in assessments (see Chapter 2) and community care plans (see Chapter 24). This is because they will be part of the same council.

Introduction to community care

In this chapter we look at what care in the community is and how it came about, who it is for and how to find out about it.

WHAT IS CARE IN THE COMMUNITY?

Basically it means looking after people who are disabled, people who have special needs, and people who need help because of old age in their own homes rather than in large institutions like hospitals. Even if people need to move out of their own homes into some sort of sheltered housing, this should be in as homelike surroundings as possible.

Need for reform

A lot of people have been saying for a long time that there are many people living in hospitals or other large institutions who could have a much better quality of life if they could live in smaller, more family-type accommodation in the community. Often they are living in hospital only because there is no suitable housing or support for them in the community.

Vast sums of money are tied up in these institutions, which not only deprive society of the resources to develop viable local alternatives, but also do not always give their residents the quality of life which they deserve.

And of course there already *is* care in the community. The hospital population is only a fraction of those elderly, ill or disabled people who need help or care. The vast majority are already living at home, cared for by family or friends, or living alone, in many cases not receiving the help they need. Adequate resources are not available to help people living in the community; too much of the money available goes to the expensive institutions.

Meanwhile the Government had become concerned by a different development; the rising cost of residential care for elderly people.

Under the old system, a person going into residential care who needed help with the fees could automatically obtain help from the Department of Social Security (DSS) if their income and savings were below a certain limit. As the number of people going into residential care increased, the money the DSS had to provide also increased dramatically.

The Government wanted to be able to control this development, which was costing it a vast amount of money and yet gave it no influence on what kind of services were developed. It believed that some people were going into residential care because there was no alternative, and not because they wanted or needed to. It wanted to be able to influence how care was provided and what kind of care was available.

So it commissioned the former chairman of Sainsbury's, the late Sir Roy Griffiths, to look into this. He produced his first report in 1988[1]. The Government adopted the majority of his proposals[2] in their White Paper, *Caring for people: community care in the next decade and beyond*[3]. In 1990 they passed the National Health Service and Community Care Act, which set the framework for their model of community care.

The Government's aims

In *Caring for People*, the Government set out six principles which would be the basis of community care. These were:

- to encourage the development of services to help people to **live in their own homes** wherever possible

- to give high priority to the needs of **carers**

- to establish proper **assessment of need** and good **case management**

- to promote the development of a **strong independent sector** along with good quality public services

- to **clarify the roles** of the various agencies and improve their **accountability**

- to introduce a **new system of funding** for community care[4]

The law and your rights to community care

Changes introduced by the legislation

The community care legislation of 1990 introduced four major changes in the way social work departments would plan and supply community care services:

- **Money to pay for new places in residential care and nursing homes was transferred from the Department of Social Security to social work departments.**

  A person moving to residential care or a nursing home after 1 April 1993 who cannot pay the fees no longer has their full fees paid by the DSS. The DSS pay part of the fees, but most is paid by the social work department.

  Unlike the old system, payment is not made automatically if a person's income and savings are below a certain level. The social work department will first "assess" the person's needs and decide whether it considers residential care is the best alternative (see Chapter 2)[5].

- **A change in the role of social work departments.** Instead of being mainly concerned with *providing* services, they will start to spend more time *working out* what people need and *organising* who is to provide this.

  The Government wants to encourage a split between the purchasers of services and the people who provide services. Social work departments will be encouraged to buy services on behalf of their clients from a whole range of suppliers: from voluntary and private sector agencies and from statutory services such as the National Health Service.

- **Social work departments will be encouraged to develop services to enable people to remain in their own homes wherever this is feasible.**

  The kind of services which are needed will include domiciliary, or home based, services, such as home helps and help with home-making, respite care schemes to give people a break and day services such as drop in centres or lunch clubs.

  Efforts to move people out of institutions into more homely surroundings in the community will continue, but people should not be moved out of hospital until proper services are available in the community (see Chapter 16).

- **All local authorities must prepare comprehensive community care plans saying how they will provide community care.**

  The plans are public documents and there is extensive consultation on them. Users of services are thus to help shape the plans for the future (see Chapter 24).

This book looks at how the new arrangements for providing and paying for community care are intended to work.

WHO IS COMMUNITY CARE FOR?

The right to community care services under the new legislation is not available to everyone. Community care is for people who:

- are elderly and in need of help (whether because of dementia, illness or otherwise)
- have a disability
- are experiencing or have had mental health problems
- have learning disabilities
- are having problems with drugs or alcohol or
- are living with HIV or AIDS

On the whole the new community care rules do not apply to children. There are separate rules for them (see below).

There are other people who may be entitled to help under the law but who do not fall within one of the recognised community care groups. In this section we look at how the law affects:

- people who are ill
- homeless people
- offenders
- children and young people

(The law is very complicated here. Unless it is relevant to you, you may want to skip this section.)

The NHS and Community Care Act says you are eligible for help under community care if you *"appear to be in need of"* community care services[6].

These are defined[7] as services (other than services for children) which the social work department can or must provide under Part II of the Social Work (Scotland) Act or ss7–11 of the Mental Health (Scotland) Act. The Mental Health (Scotland) Act covers services for people with learning disabilities and for people who are experiencing or have had mental health problems, who are, therefore, entitled to community care services.

Part II of the Social Work (Scotland) Act looks at the social work department's duties to children (who, as we have said, are excluded from community care) and also to persons in need. Persons in need are people who:

- need care and attention because of infirmity, youth or age
- suffer from illness or mental disorder or are substantially handicapped by disability
- are in need of care and attention because of drug or alcohol dependency or release from prison or other form of detention[8]
- are listed in orders made by the Secretary of State (To date no such order has been made)

If you are a person in need you may have a right to community care. If you feel you need help, you should apply to the social work department. If you ask for help and are refused, you should seek advice (see page 162).

How do these rules about persons in need work in practice? Let us look at some of the groups of people who might be affected.

People who are ill

If you are ill you are a person in need. The law does not say how ill you have to be. There is no list of illnesses which qualify and those which do not. You might feel you need temporary help from the social work department during an acute illness or you might ask for more permanent help if you have a progressive illness such as multiple sclerosis. **If you are ill and you think you need help from the social work department, you should ask for a community care assessment (see Chapter 2).**

Homeless people

If you are a homeless person, you do not necessarily need help from the social work department[9]. What you need is a house. But if you have other needs as well, or are vulnerable because of youth or age or for some other reason, it might be helpful for the social work department to be involved and you might receive some community care help[10].

If you are homeless and you are also a person in need, you have a legal entitlement to a community care assessment.

You might qualify because you are young and vulnerable. The social work department might be able to give you home-making help, counselling or help in finding daytime activities. If you are vulnerable because you are old or ill the social work department might be able to offer you help.

People leaving prison or other detention

The law says that people leaving any form of detention are "persons in need". Part II of the Social Work (Scotland) Act says that the social work department must give help to offenders and ex-offenders who are being supervised by the department. Yet people leaving prison are not mentioned in any of the literature about community care services.

This appears to be because the funding for social work services for people leaving detention is to be organised separately from the general community care funding. Services for ex-offenders do not have to be included in community care plans. Separate plans will be produced[11].

Be that as it may, if you have been in prison or some other form of detention and need help from the social work department, you have the right to ask them for community care help. If you are refused help, you should seek advice (see page 162).

Children and young people

Services for children are not part of community care. The Government argues that children's needs are different from those of adults and they should be treated separately. They have tried to do this in the community care legislation. Unfortunately the law is extremely complicated. It will be changed again when the Children (Scotland) Bill, introduced to Parliament at the end of 1994, becomes law.

The law says that community care services are services *other than services for children* which the social work department provides under the Social Work (Scotland) Act or the Mental Health (Scotland) Act[12]. In this section we look at what this means in practice for different groups of children and young people.

Children under 16

It is the Government's intention that children under 16 should not come into the community care system. They are not entitled to ask for a community care assessment.

This may have little practical effect on what help the child or young person receives. It is mainly a question of how they get the help they need. However a young person under 16 does not have the right to ask for a formal community care assessment of needs.

(Children who have special educational needs will have a Future Needs Assessment before they reach 16: see page 17.)

If a child or young person is chronically sick or disabled, has mental health problems or a learning disability, there are some services to which they are entitled. These are listed below.

Children of any age who are chronically sick or who have a disability

A child of any age who is chronically sick or disabled is entitled to a disabled person's assessment. There are no age limits in the Chronically Sick and Disabled Persons Act (see page 21).

Children with mental health problems

A child or young person who has mental health problems is entitled to after-care from the social work department whatever their age, even if they are under 16 (see page 24).

A child with mental health problems is also entitled to a disabled person's assessment (see page 14).

Children or young people with learning disabilities

They are entitled to after-care from the social work department, whatever their age (see page 24). A child with a learning disability has the same right to a disabled person's assessment as a child with a physical disability (see page 14).

Young people with learning disabilities who are over 16 are entitled to training and occupation provided by the social work department (see page 25). They are also entitled to a disabled person's assessment (see page 14).

Young people over 16

At what age does a child or young person become old enough to qualify for community care help?

One of the problems is that the Social Work (Scotland) Act does not say what it means by a "child". It does not say whether a child is someone under 16, 18, or 21. Instead the Act requires social work departments to provide services for children and young people. Some services are provided until a child reaches 16, others until he or she is 18 and a few until 21.

But generally, the Act sees 16 as a watershed. The services available for the over-16s are generally for young people who have already been in contact with the system, either through a children's panel or through being in care.

If you are over 16 and you need more help, it is our view that you should be able to apply for a community care assessment if you are a person in need (see page 3). You will be asking the social work department to assess your need for community care services, not "*services for children*". The fact that you are already receiving other children's services from the social work department should not stop you getting community care help.

(For instance, you might have left care and still be getting some help from the social work department[13]: this should not stop you getting a community care assessment if you need it.)

The law about who qualifies for community care is very complicated. It is particularly unclear about the rights of 16–18 year olds. If you feel you need community care help and are not sure whether you qualify, you should apply for help anyway. If you are refused help, you should get advice on what to do next. See Helpful names and addresses, *page 160*.

All the remedies we discuss in Chapters 25 and 26 apply to children. In particular, the social work department complaints procedure is not just for community care, but includes children as well.

FINDING OUT ABOUT COMMUNITY CARE LAW

Acts of Parliament

In this section we list the main Acts of Parliament relating to the community care system and try to explain how they fit in with each other. Other important acts are noted on page 177 (Table of Statutes). The main community care acts are:

- **National Health Service & Community Care Act 1990.** The major piece of legislation introducing community care in Scotland (and England). It also introduced the NHS reforms, such as NHS Trusts[14].

- **Social Work (Scotland) Act 1968.** The law which sets out the main duties of social work departments. The NHS & Community Care Act inserted the community care provisions into this Act (see table on page 5).

- **Chronically Sick And Disabled Persons Act 1970.** A major piece of legislation advancing the rights of disabled people. In 1972 the Chronically Sick and Disabled Persons (Scotland) Act was passed and the Act came to Scotland. It was further amended by the 1986 Disabled Persons Act (see below).

- **Disabled Persons (Services, Consultation and Representation) Act 1986.** Sometimes known as the Tom Clarke Act because he introduced it into Parliament. It introduced

Changes to Social Work (Scotland) Act 1968 by NHS & Community Care Act 1990

Section in NHS & Community Care Act	New provision in Social Work (Scotland) Act	What it did
s51	s5	Gave the Secretary of State the power to issue "directions" to local authorities on how they should exercise their functions
s52	s5A	Local authorities to publish community care plans
s52	s5B	Improved complaints procedure for social work departments
s53	s6	Added powers to Scottish Office to inspect care facilities
s54	s6A	Secretary of State may hold public enquiry into social work functions
s55	s12A	Assessment of needs
s56	s13A	Social work department given power to pay for nursing home places
s56	s13B	Gave local authorities power to provide after-care, to help prevent illness and to care for ill people[15]
s57	s6A	Stopped the DSS from paying for people in registered homes after 1.4.93
s58	s92A	Established new Mental Illness Specific Grant for new projects for mental health, dementia and head injury

an impressive scheme for advocacy and representation for people dealing with social work departments. Unfortunately major sections of it have never been implemented. The Government says that full implementation is no longer necessary because of community care, but many disabled people do not agree.

- **Mental Health (Scotland) Act 1984.** The main piece of legislation dealing with hospital care and guardianship for people with mental health problems or learning disabilities. It set up the Mental Welfare Commission (see page 134).

- **National Assistance Act 1948.** This mainly applies to England but in Scotland it is the legal basis for charging for residential care.

- **Health and Social Services and Social Security Adjudications Act 1983.** It gives local authorities extra powers to charge for services they provide.

Although these statutes set out the framework, we do not suggest that you rush out and buy copies. This is because these acts are all very substantially amended from time to time, and so the version you get from HMSO may not be up to date[16]. If you want to find out what parts of a statute are up to date at any particular time, you really have to go to a law library or one of the organisations listed on pages 160-162, and ask them to help you.

Other sources of law

As well as the law in statutes there are other legal rules to consider. These include:

Statutory Instruments

These are rules made by the Secretary of State for Scotland under a power given to him in a statute. (For example s68 of the Social Work (Scotland) Act deals with the registration of residential homes. It gives the Secretary of State for Scotland the power to make rules about appeals on registration. He issued a statutory instrument setting out the detailed rules[17].)

Directions by the Secretary of State

He is given the power to direct how social work departments are to operate community care[18]. He may issue directions either to individual local authorities or to them collectively. If he issues a direction, they *must* comply with it. So when trying to work out the duties of the local authority you have to check whether there are any directions. A direction imposes a legal duty on the local authority.

The law and your rights to community care

Directions are usually issued as appendices to circulars from the Scottish Office. A list of directions issued so far is on page 166. So far, the Secretary of State has not issued individual directions to any local authority.

As well as his power to issue directions to social work departments, the Secretary of State also has the power to issue directions to health boards[19]. Again, these may be general directions or directions issued to a specific health board. He can also issue directions to the new NHS Trusts on a variety of matters[20]. If he issues a direction to health boards or to an NHS trust, they must do what the direction says.

Scottish Office circulars

One of the main features of community care has been the vast number of circulars which the Scottish Office has issued to social work departments on how to implement community care. A list of circulars to date is on pages 164-165.

The circulars contain "guidance" from the Secretary of State to social work departments. He has the power to give "general guidance" to social work departments[21] and they have to carry out their duties under this general guidance.

Guidance is not as strong as a direction. Local authorities do not have to follow it to the letter. However if they paid no attention at all to guidance, they would be breaking the law. If a local authority does not comply with guidance, you would have good grounds for making a complaint (see Chapter 25). We discuss guidance in more detail on page 145.

If guidance which affects you is not complied with, you could:

- complain to the social work department (see Chapter 25)

- write to the Secretary of State asking him to issue a direction to the department involved

- take legal proceedings for **judicial review** against the local authority (see Chapter 26).

NOTES

1 *Community care: agenda for action.*

2 But not all, and most notably, perhaps, not the suggestion that there be a Minister for Community Care.

3 1989 Cm 849.

4 See para 1.11 of *Caring for people.*

5 But these changes will not affect people who were living in residential care at April 1 1993, even if they are not now receiving help from the DSS with the fees (see Chapter 12).

6 Social Work (Scotland) Act 1968, s12A.

7 In s5A(4) of the Social Work (Scotland) Act 1968.

8 s12(6). Added by the NHS & Community Care Act 1990 Sched 9, s10(5).

9 Homeless people were, in fact, specifically removed from the list of "people in need" when housing departments took over new responsibilities for homelessness under the Housing (Homeless Persons) Act 1977. (Now contained in the Housing (Scotland) Act 1987.)

10 A briefing paper, *Homelessness and community care*, produced by the Scottish Council for Single Homeless in February 1994, looks at some of the issues on this important topic.

11 See first circular on *Community care planning*, (Circular SW1/91) para 3.2.

12 See Chapter 3.

13 Under s12 of the Social Work (Scotland) Act 1968 (see page 20).

14 See Chapter 15.

15 Previously in s27 of the National Health Service (Scotland) Act 1947.

16 This is particularly true of the Social Work (Scotland) Act 1968.

17 Registration of Establishments (Appeal Tribunal) (Scotland) Rules 1983 SI 1983/71.

18 s5(1A) of Social Work (Scotland) Act 1968, inserted by s51 of the NHS & Community Care Act 1990.

19 Under s2(5) of the National Health Service (Scotland) Act 1978.

20 For the detail see the NHS & Community Care Act 1990, Sched 6, s6(1) and 6(2).

21 Social Work (Scotland) Act 1968, s5(1) .

Who does what in community care?

What kind of help is available to people who need care in the community? And who provides it? We have listed some of the types of help that the different agencies provide or can arrange for you.

The social work department

The social work department is part of the regional council. It is responsible for making community care work. If you need help to carry on living at home or if you think you may need to move to somewhere which can give you more help, you should get in touch with the social work department.

It can arrange a wide range of services. It can also get in touch with other organisations and ask them what help they can offer. If you have complicated needs, it will arrange a care plan for you and co-ordinate your care.

Section One looks at the social work department's role in community care.

If you need any of the following kinds of help, you should contact the social work department. They may be able to arrange it.

- personal care at home

- help with housework, shopping or preparing meals

- respite breaks for carers

- somewhere to go during the day, such as a day centre or lunch club

- training or education for someone with learning disabilities

- help in household budgeting or home-making

- telephone

- special equipment or adaptations in your home to make it more convenient or accessible

- an alarm system to get help

- holidays

- residential care or supported accommodation

- welfare rights advice

- information about services available in your area

- protection of your property if you go into hospital or care

- support after you leave hospital

- help with parenting

- help if someone is being financially exploited or abused

- guardianship: a way of helping someone who is unable to cope

You may have to pay for some of these services.

Help from the NHS

The NHS can offer help in hospital but it is also developing its community services. It may be able to offer you help so you can stay at home rather than go into care. The kind of help which you might need could be:

- GP services

- nursing

- physiotherapy

- occupational therapy

- community psychiatric nurses

- help with bathing

- speech therapy

- chiropody

The first place to go would normally be your GP. He or she can arrange for help with other services. If you don't have a GP and find it difficult to get one, contact your local health board. They will allocate you a GP.

The social work department may get in touch with the health service for you when they arrange your community care to discuss what medical help you may need.

Chapters 15 and 16 look at the duties of the health service under community care.

Medical services from the NHS are free.

The housing department

The housing department is part of the district council. It provides housing and housing advice. If you are disabled, the housing department may able to help with a grant to adapt your house. They also provide specialised housing for disabled and elderly people.

You can contact the housing department yourself or get the social work department to do it for you as part of community care.

Chapter 14 looks at housing and community care.

The education department

The education department is part of the regional council. It organises education in schools and community education such as evening classes and leisure classes. It used to organise further education colleges but now the colleges are run by Boards of Management, appointed by the Secretary of State for Scotland.

Chapter 17 looks at education and community care.

Voluntary organisations, housing associations and independent providers

Many community care services are run by voluntary organisations, housing associations and independent providers.

Voluntary organisations/charities

Voluntary organisations are usually charities set up to benefit a particular group of people, such as people with learning disabilities or mental health problems, or people who are elderly or who have physical or sensory disabilities. They use volunteers in some way, either working on their projects or running their Management Committee.

Voluntary organisations are not run for profit. As well as providing services they may campaign for changes in the law or for extra resources to help the people they represent.

Housing associations

Housing associations are non-profit making bodies which provide affordable housing for a wide variety of people. It is often housing of very high quality. They receive money from the Government, through a body called Scottish Homes, to help build and run new housing. They also convert and modernise older housing.

Housing associations have been encouraged by the Government to develop housing for people with special needs and they now run a variety of schemes, such as sheltered housing for elderly people and supported accommodation for people with mental health problems or learning disabilities. They have also been at the forefront of developing barrier-free housing for people with physical disabilities.

Housing associations are listed in the *Yellow Pages*. There is also a national *Directory of Housing Associations*, which lists housing associations and says what kind of housing they provide. It is free from Scottish Homes, Thistle House, 91 Haymarket Terrace, Edinburgh EH12 5HE. (Tel: 0131. 313 0044.)

Independent providers

Independent providers have always been important in providing residential care homes and nursing homes. They are now moving into domiciliary care, providing services for people in their homes.

Independent providers may be private limited companies or private individuals, and they are businesses, run for profit.

Housing projects run by voluntary organisations, housing associations and private providers will usually be registered with and inspected by the social work department. We look at this on page 39.

There is no similar procedure for registering and inspecting care services provided in the home. If care services are paid for by the social work department, the department may have the right to inspect them under the terms of their contract with the provider.

If you pay for home care services yourself, you might want to check whether the person providing them is a member of the United Kingdom Home Care Association (UKHCA).

The UKHCA sets standards for care provided in the home, including home nursing services. All members have to agree to keep to the UKHCA Code of Practice. It has a complaints panel which will investigate complaints about services provided by members. The United Kingdom Home Care Association is at 42 Banstead Road, Carshalton Beeches, Surrey SM5 3NW. (Tel: 0181. 770 3658.)

②

Social work services: assessment of needs

INTRODUCTION

So far as individual users of services are concerned, the biggest single change introduced by the NHS & Community Care Act is the requirement for local authorities to carry out a formal assessment of needs before providing a community care service. The idea was to get away from the situation where people were fitted into the service which happened to be available, and where the service people got depended more on who they spoke to than what would be best for them. Assessment was seen as part of the move towards a system of care management which gave more choice and power to service users. It was also intended to be a better way to identify unmet need, so that future services would be better planned.

Assessment is not new. Some kind of judgement has always had to be made about a person's needs. What is new is that social work departments now have legal duties to assess needs in a certain way. People have rights based on these duties and may also have rights (legitimate expectations) based on the policies of the local authorities or the Government.

The assessment introduced by the NHS & Community Care Act is not the only type of assessment required by law. Disabled people have a right to an assessment under s4 of the Disabled Persons (Services, Consultation and Representation) Act 1986 (for convenience, we refer to this as a **disabled persons's assessment**). Children with **Records of special educational Needs** leaving school have a right to a **future needs assessment**.

People being discharged after a long stay in hospital should get a clinical assessment that they are fit to be discharged. This is discussed in Chapter 16.

COMMUNITY CARE ASSESSMENT

When is an assessment done?

If you want community care from the social work department, you should ask for an assessment. The law states that **a local authority must carry out a community care assessment where it appears to them that a person who is eligible to receive community care services may need such a service**[1]. (See pages 2-4 for descriptions of who may be eligible for community care services and what these services include).

The service user does not have to ask specifically for an assessment. The person's possible need for a service can come to the attention of the social work department by any route (eg a request by a carer, or referral by a GP). If the person appears to be covered by the above duty, the assessment must be carried out.

Some assessments will be simpler than others but, as we go on to explain, there are some things that should always be done.

Can the social work department refuse to do an assessment?

The social work department may decide not to carry out an assessment if they do not think the person fits into any of the categories of people who may be eligible for community care services; that is, they are not a **person in need** (see pages 2-4). If the person is eligible, the local authority then have to decide if it appears that the person "*may be in need*" of a community care service.

The precise effect of this is not completely clear. It seems that a local authority would be within their rights to refuse an assessment if there was absolutely no evidence that the person was a person in need. However, if there is some evidence that the person is a person in need, then it would seem to be almost inevitable that that person may need a community care service, so an assessment must be carried out.

Scottish Office guidance on assessment[2] states that *"there should be an initial screening process to verify that the presenting problems lie in the field of community care"*. It is not clear whether this screening process is to take place as part of a community care assessment or to rule out some people who will not then get a community care assessment.

In our view, it is legitimate for a social work department to check to see if a person counts as a person in need. If they accept that someone appears to be a person in need, we do not think they can consider whether or not a person gets a service without doing a community care assessment. Some community care assessments will be simpler than others but the rules and guidance we discuss below apply to them all. A system which said that people who appeared to be low priority should not get community care assessments would not be lawful. Another practice which would be legally dubious is "screening" by people like receptionists.

The local authority cannot refuse to carry out an assessment because they do not believe they can offer a service to meet your needs or wishes. Also, they cannot refuse an assessment because they feel you have not co-operated with them now or in the past.

What if I don't want an assessment?

Strictly speaking, you have no right to refuse a community care assessment if the social work department think one is needed. A carer, friend or professional could ask the social work department to carry one out and they would have to decide whether you needed one, even if you didn't want it.

On the other hand, you do not have to co-operate with the social work department, and you would not have to accept any service they offered (unless there was some other legal measure in force, like **mental health guardianship**)[4].

In practice, social work departments will probably be reluctant to force assessments on people, but they do have to bear in mind what a person might need, not just what they say they want.

Sometimes carers do not want the social work department involved. Again they have no right to refuse a community care assessment of the person they care for, but they don't have to participate themselves.

Which social work department do I see?

Normally, you would ask the social work department where you live to do the assessment. If specialised services were needed which could only be provided by another social work department, it would be up to your "home" department to try to arrange this[3].

Sometimes it is not easy to work out which social work department is responsible for someone's care. This can happen with people who are homeless, or who may already be living in institutions away from their family. The law says it is up to the social work department where the person is *"ordinarily resident"* to pay for the services. It does not clearly say that it has to be that social work department that does the assessment, although it normally would be.

Periods spent in hospital are ignored in working out where you are ordinarily resident. If there is any argument, the Secretary of State can be asked to decide.

The law on assessment does not talk about ordinary residence but about whether a person might need a service from a social work department. Therefore we think that you could ask a social work department to do an assessment if:

- you live in their area

- you are moving into their area

- you came from their area and want to go back

- you come from their area and have been in institutional care

- the department has a special type of service that you think you need

However, if the assessment is to lead to actual services, that will mean working out who is to pay for them – which means trying to decide where you are ordinarily resident. This phrase has quite a complex legal meaning and you may need to see a solicitor if you get nowhere with the social work department.

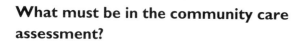

What must be in the community care assessment?

There are certain things which the local authority must consider as part of the assessment process. They are:

- the needs of the client
- consultation with other agencies
- possible right to disabled person's assessment
- the provision of services

Assessment of needs

The legislation does not say how detailed the assessment of needs must be. The Scottish Office has chosen not to prescribe in detail how assessment should be carried out[5] but has said that *"assessment should be needs-led, not service-led"*[6]. In other words, the assessment should look at the individual needs of the person, not simply how suitable they are for a particular service. This aim is reinforced by the fact that assessment is a two stage process, with the assessment of need coming before the separate decision about what services to provide.

There is concern that people carrying out assessments may be under pressure not to detail any need which cannot be met because it is too expensive, or the service is not available. These considerations would not be relevant in law and an assessment of need based on these considerations could well be unlawful (see Chapter 26).

Another concern is that assessment procedures will become too rigid and bureaucratic, and will not pick up people's unique circumstances. Clearly, local authorities must have systems of working. However, they must be flexible enough to take account of individual need. For example, if a person needed help in having things done at home and a holiday, but the assessment did not consider the need for the holiday, that would not only fall short of Government guidance but may make the assessment defective in law[7].

Consultation with other agencies

Legally, the primary aim of a community care assessment is to determine the needs that should be met by the social work department. However, one of the points underlying the original report by Sir Roy Griffiths[8] was that people's community care needs were linked to other needs, such as adequate health care and suitable housing. When the legislation was going through Parliament, there was strong pressure to have a "multi-disciplinary assessment" (meaning an assessment involving all the different professionals). The Government refused to say that all community care assessments should be multi-disciplinary, but tried to deal with this problem both in the legislation and guidance.

The law states that social work departments must consult with health boards, doctors and housing departments. Guidance makes it clear that there should be other types of consultation where relevant to the service user. This could include consulting with people involved in education, employment, leisure, etc.

Consultation – the legislation

Consultation with doctors

Social work departments can now fund places in nursing homes[9]. Before arranging for nursing care, the social work department must consult a medical practitioner[10]. This duty would apply to a place in a nursing home, but not a **residential care home** (see page 39 for an explanation of the difference).

The legislation does not specify who the medical practitioners should be, but it would presumably be the person's GP in most cases (sometimes it might be a hospital specialist like a geriatrician).

Although the social work department must consult with a doctor, the final decision is with the social work department, who are not bound to follow the doctor's advice. (Health boards may also place people in nursing homes. See page 41).

Consultation with health boards

If the social work department thinks a person being assessed may need any service from the National Health Service, they must notify the health board where the person lives, or where the person is likely to get a community care service[11].

The social work department does not have to carry out a full assessment of the person's health care needs but simply identify whether there is a possible need. The social work department must then ask the health board what services they are likely to provide and take this into account in completing their own community care assessment.

For example, the social work department might want to know what community psychiatric support would be available for a person with a mental health problem, so that this can be fitted into the overall **package of care**.

The NHS & Community Care Act does not actually spell out how health boards should co-operate in this process, but the Government expects them to do so[12]. Proper consultation should avoid both duplication of services and "passing the buck" between different agencies. (Health boards and social work departments also have a general duty to co-operate. See Chapters 15 and 16 generally for health board duties.)

Consultation with housing departments

Where the social work department thinks a person being assessed may have a housing need which could fall within the responsibilities of a district council housing department, they must notify the housing department. The procedure and responsibilities are basically the same as that detailed above for health boards.

As an example of how this might work, a social work department may want to establish if any special needs housing is available for a disabled person. If housing is available, the social work department may decide to provide a home help service. If it is not available, residential care may have to be considered as a way to meet the person's needs. (For details of housing departments' other responsibilities, including those to disabled people and homeless persons, see Chapter 14).

This duty does not apply to Islands Councils, where the housing department is part of the same local authority as the social work department. The duty will be abolished altogether in April 1996, when social work departments become part of the same councils as housing departments.

Consultation – the guidance

A number of other agencies may provide services which are relevant to the needs of a user of community care. These services may include financial assistance, education, leisure and recreation, transport and employment.

There is no specific legal duty on the social work department to involve these agencies in a community care assessment, but the Government's guidance states:

> "The local authority has the lead responsibility for securing the involvement of other agencies in the assessment procedure in order to decide what should be done, by whom, and for whom. Other agencies will have to make available the staff needed for assessment and will have to implement their own contribution to packages of care which they have agreed to deliver. All relevant agencies should be involved in the assessment and subsequent decision taking process before commitments are made".[13]

Education

Attempts were made when the NHS & Community Care Bill was in Parliament to oblige social work departments to involve education departments in community care assessments. The Government said this was not necessary because they were both part of the same local authority. The guidance states that "*social work departments should ensure that any apparent needs for education services which come to attention during a community care assessment are communicated to the education department*".[14]

Further education

Colleges of further education are no longer part of the local authority but are run by independent Boards of Management. Many offer courses for students with special needs and have links with social work departments. During the passage of the Further and Higher Education (Scotland) Act, 1992, the Minister, Michael Forsyth, promised to include a requirement for Further Education Colleges to co-operate with community care assessments, but this had to be dropped for technical reasons. However, both the Secretary of State and College Boards have a duty to "*have regard to the requirements of persons over school age who have learning difficulties*"[15]. This includes people with physical disabilities, mental health problems or other problems in learning, not just people with learning disabilities in the sense of having a mental handicap.

See Chapter 17 for more details on education.

Welfare Benefits

A person who needs community care may be entitled to particular welfare benefits such as Disability Living Allowance or a Community Care Grant. Carers may be entitled to Invalid Care Allowance. A community care assessment does not have to involve a benefits check. However, since local authorities may be charging for community care services, they often have to carry out a financial assessment. Some authorities, including Strathclyde, have decided to combine this with a benefits check to ensure that clients are receiving the maximum financial assistance. This helps the service user but may also mean there is more money to meet charges where the person uses services such as residential care.

It is a good idea that people who may need community care assessments get help to ensure they are getting all the benefits to which they are entitled. However, the assessment of need does *not* depend on what you can afford to pay (see page 30).

Employment

Many disabled people wish help into employment and this possibility should be looked at as part of a community care assessment (see Chapter 18 for more details).

Right to a disabled person's assessment

If a social work department is doing a community care assessment and it appears to them that the person concerned is a "disabled person", they must carry out a disabled person's assessment without being asked. They must also tell the person being assessed that this is being done and what their rights are under the Disabled Persons (Services, Consultation and Representation) Act 1986[16].

This is a very important right because the disabled person's assessment is for services to which people have strong legal rights.

At the time of writing this book, it seems that very few community care assessments are doing this properly. Anyone being assessed who is a disabled person should make sure this has happened. If it has not been done, the social work department have broken the law. (For a definition of disabled person, see page 157. For an explanation of the disabled person's assessment, see page 16).

Provision of services

Once needs have been assessed, the local authority must decide whether the needs call for the local authority to provide any community care services[17]. (This should form part of a care plan)[18]. The fact that a need has been assessed does not, in itself, give a person a right to have that need met. However, where a person may have a right to a service because of other legislation (see Chapter 3) the fact that the need has been established in a community care assessment will make it easier to enforce the existing legal right.

For example, an assessment might state that the person needs help in the home. If the person is disabled, they will have a right to that service under the Chronically Sick and Disabled Persons Act.

Legally, it is also relevant that a local authority must *"have regard to"* the assessment of need in deciding on what service, if any, to offer. This means that, even where the person does not have a strong legal right to a service, the social work department cannot simply refuse to provide a service out of hand. They must be able to show that they have taken account of the person's individual situation rather than making a

decision purely based on financial considerations or blanket policies (see page 144-149 *Judicial Review*)[19].

Remember, the actual services to be offered are only decided *after* the assessment, and should not affect how the person's *needs* are decided.

What about emergencies?

A local authority is entitled to provide community care without having done an assessment first if they think the person needs the services as a matter of urgency. They then have to do an assessment as soon as practicable afterwards[20]. This could allow, for example, an emergency admission to residential care where a carer has died.

Involving users and carers

The guidance states that local arrangements for assessment and care management should:

"give people a greater individual say in how they live and the services they need to help them to do so".[21]

"Assessment systems should ensure the participation of the individual and his or her carer. The wishes of both should be taken fully into account...Individual choice should be based on adequate information about the different forms of care which may be available...People with communication difficulties whether due to sensory impairment, mental incapacity, or other disabilities, should be able to participate in the assessment process. Assessment should also be accessible to people from minority ethnic backgrounds".[22]

In other words, although it is the social work department that finally decides what a person's needs are, that should only be done after the person has given their own views.

It is clear that it is not enough for a social worker to ask questions about a person's problems and fill in a form. Users should be asked what they want and be told what the possibilities are. If they need help in saying what they want, or want a friend or advocate to be involved, this should be allowed.

The best way to challenge a social work department if they do not consult the user or carer in an assessment will often be the statutory complaints procedure (page 126) or some of the other non-legal remedies in Chapter 25. However, if the local authority has not paid proper attention to Government guidance, it may have acted unlawfully. If there is a serious problem, Chapter 26 on legal remedies could also be relevant[23].

How long will an assessment take?

There is no specific time limit to complete an assessment. It will often depend on how complicated the case is. The time needed to carry out a full assessment should not delay services in urgent cases. Unreasonable delay may justify a formal complaint or a referral to the local government ombudsman (see Chapter 25). In extreme cases, legal action may be appropriate (see Chapter 26). If a decision takes too long, a court may decide that the social work department has not in fact taken a decision at all and so has not complied with its legal duty to carry out an assessment and then make a decision about services.

Telling you about your assessment

Strictly speaking, the law does not say that an assessment has to be written down. However, it is difficult to imagine how a local authority could comply with its obligations without writing down what needs had been assessed, and what decision had been taken about those needs. Government guidance states that:

"the outcome of assessment should be a clear decision about what services are required to meet needs and by whom they could be provided. This should be recorded in a systematic way".[24]

It also states that *"Users and carers should be informed of the conclusions of an assessment"* and a contact person's name should be given[25]. You may be asked to sign your assessment. Chapter 23 discusses this.

There has been controversy in England and Wales over a suggestion by the Social Services Inspectorate that users should not be told of any need found by the assessment which cannot be met[26] (or at least it should not be called "unmet need"). The aim seems to be to avoid service users getting ammunition for possible legal action against social services departments. There is no such suggestion in the Scottish guidance. People who feel that part of their assessment is being concealed should seek immediate expert advice.

Even in England and Wales, many people believe it would be unlawful to conceal unmet need from users. Apart from the principles of the community care legislation, an assessment would normally form part of a user's social work file. The user is entitled to access to this file except in certain clearly defined circumstances. The fact that you were, for example, considering legal action against the social work department would not be a good ground to deny you access to part of the file (see Chapter 21).

Reviewing your assessment

There is no specific period when an assessment must be reviewed. Guidance states that needs *"should be reviewed at regular intervals".*[27] The original assessment should indicate how and when review will take place[28], but a review should also take place if the person's needs or the department's policies have changed. Reviews should monitor the quality of the service. The user should be asked for their views on this and whether their preferences have changed since the last assessment. All those involved in the original assessment should be consulted[29].

A user cannot insist on a review at a particular time but, if a request is made, the authority would have to consider whether a review was appropriate, bearing in mind the Government's guidance.

Who does the assessment?

Because the community care assessment is a legal responsibility of the social work department, it will normally be an employee of the department who co-ordinates the assessment. It could be a social worker or someone like an occupational therapist. However, it is possible for the assessment (or parts of it) to be done by other people[30]. Sometimes, this is appropriate where a person has very specialised needs or there is a voluntary body with expertise with a particular client group (eg blind people). Whoever does the assessment, it will be the social work department which carries out the second part of the process – deciding what services to provide.

Assessment and carers

Government guidance states that local authorities should take carers' wishes fully into account in carrying out an assessment [31]. Often this is because the carer can speak up for the wishes of the user (although the person doing the assessment should always try to speak to the service user directly as well). In some cases, the carer's views may be different from the user's views. In that case, both views should be considered separately.

If the user is a **disabled person** (see page 21), there is also a legal requirement[32] for the local authority to have regard to the ability of the carer to continue caring. This means that the decision about services should be based not just on the needs of the disabled person, but must also take into account what help that particular carer needs. Any problems or special needs of that individual carer should be considered.

Sometimes a person who is a carer may be a person in need themselves, because of age or disability. Carers will be entitled to their own separate assessment for any community care services they may need in their own right. Guidance reminds local authorities to bear this possibility in mind when doing an assessment of the person being cared for, and to advise carers of this right[33].

Unfortunately, it is not clear whether **respite care** should be part of the assessment of the carer's needs or those of the person being cared for. If it has not been properly considered in the assessment of the person being cared for, the carer should request an assessment of their own needs.

This keeps the carer's options open. It may be possible to argue that the original assessment did not comply with s8 of the Disabled Persons (Services, Consultation and Representation) Act 1986 (at least if the person being cared for counts as a disabled person). It is also worth having a separate assessment of the carer's needs because this will give the carer a legal right to complain on their own behalf rather than on behalf of the person being cared for.

In early 1995, Malcolm Wicks, MP, introduced the Carers (Recognition and Services) Bill. The aim of this is to give all carers (not just those who count as persons in need) the right to request a formal assessment of their needs, to be considered alongside the needs of the person being cared for. The Government has said it will support this Bill. If it becomes law, it will greatly clarify the rights of carers.

Local procedure for assessment

The legislation, and even the guidance, leave a lot of the details of how the assessment is done to individual social work departments. General information about their assessment procedures should be contained in the authority's published **community care plans** or in other public information. The full procedures and copies of the forms may be available from the department or from local voluntary sector agencies.

It is worth finding out about local procedures for a number of reasons:

- knowing how the system works could help you to prepare for your own assessment

- if a council sets out a procedure then fails to apply it properly in a particular case, it would be good grounds for a complaint and possibly also for legal action under the principle of **legitimate expectations** (see Chapter 26)

- some procedures may be inconsistent with Government guidelines or even with the legislation. If so, action should be taken

- many councils are anxious to improve assessment procedures and would welcome comments from users and carers

DISABLED PERSON'S ASSESSMENT

The disabled person's assessment was created by s4 of the Disabled Persons (Services, Consultation and Representation) Act 1986. The aim was to strengthen the rights created by s2 of the Chronically Sick and Disabled Persons Act 1970 (see page 21). It is now basically part of the community care process. To understand how this came about, the history may help.

Under the 1970 Act, social work departments had to provide certain services if they decided the disabled person needed them. There was evidence that some local authorities avoided their duties by simply failing to make decisions about the individual needs of disabled people. To get around this, s4 of the 1986 Act says that the disabled person or the carer has the right to request the local authority to consider the person's needs for services under s2 of the 1970 Act, and the local authority must comply[34].

This should have greatly strengthened the rights of disabled people. If the local authority did not comply with a request, they would be acting unlawfully. It would also be unlawful for them to accept that the person needed services under s2 and refuse to supply them, or to deny unjustifiably that the person needed the services.

Unfortunately, few people were aware of their rights to an assessment of their needs under the Chronically Sick and Disabled Persons Act. This makes the change introduced by the NHS & Community Care Act particularly important. As we have seen (page 14), if the social work department are carrying out a community care assessment on a person who appears to be a disabled person, they must also do a disabled person's assessment without being asked. They must also tell the person being assessed of his or her rights under the Disabled Person's (Services, Consultation and Representation) Act 1986. This should ensure that specific consideration is given to the need for services under s2 of the 1970 Act, which must be provided where need exists.

FUTURE NEEDS ASSESSMENTS FOR YOUNG PEOPLE

Children with disabilities or learning difficulties often have a Record of Needs, setting out what educational help they require[35]. This ends when the child leaves school. To try to ensure a smooth transition to adult services, there is a future needs assessment which must be carried out before a child with a Record becomes 16. This involves the social work department[36].

It is the duty of the education department to consider what provision would benefit a Recorded child after he or she reaches 16[37]. The assessment has to be carried out between the ages of 14 years and 15 years and 3 months.

As part of the assessment, the education department must ask the social work department if the child is a disabled person (see page 21). In most cases, this should be a formality since the majority of children with Records of Needs are disabled.

If the child is a disabled person, the social work department must assess the needs of the child for social work help, including community care services. They must then make a report. This must be done within the same period as the education department's assessment.

The education department should then give at least 6 months notice to the social work department of the expected date when the young person will leave school. They should also send the full future needs assessment to the social work department and may also send it to the local health board or (with the consent of the parents or the young person) other agencies[38].

The full assessment only has to be carried out once. However, the education department and the social work department must keep the young person's case under consideration and review the reports when appropriate[39]. This is important because many children with special needs stay at school until 18 or even older, and reports done when a child was 15 may be of little use.

If the young person says he or she does not want the social work department involved in a future needs assessment, the social work department does not have to act. (For a child under 16 or a young person unable to make a request on their own, the parents can say if they do not want social work involvement)[40].

A future needs assessment is not a community care assessment. It is not clear whether young people leaving school who need community care services will always be expected to get a community care assessment as well as a future needs assessment. **In any case, disabled young people or their representatives are entitled to request a full community care assessment if the future needs assessment is out of date, or they are not happy with the service being offered.**

It is also important to remember that a young person may be entitled to community care services and a community care assessment while they are still at school (see pages 3-4 for how the law affects children).

The law and your rights to community care

SUMMARY – KEY POINTS

- People who may need social work services have a legal right to a community care assessment.

- A community care assessment should look at ALL the things the user might need or want from the social work department, and should involve other relevant services (especially health and housing).

- The user and carer should feel involved in the assessment and know the outcome.

- Carers' needs should be considered and the carer may be entitled to their own assessment. After the assessment, the user should be told what the social work department are offering.

- A disabled person must get a disabled person's assessment as part of a community care assessment. This is important because they may have a right to get the services they need from the disabled person's assessment.

- Assessments should be completed in reasonable time and should be reviewed when things change.

- In an emergency, a user can get a service before the community care assessment is finished.

- Children and young people with Records of Special Educational Needs will have a future needs assessment before leaving school. This involves the social work department but is not a community care assessment.

Getting an assessment – where to go and what to do

- If you want a community care assessment, or know someone who needs one, ask the social work department. Different councils have different systems. If you are not sure who to contact, write to the nearest social work office. You can get its address from the phone book or the local library.

- If someone from the social work department contacts you, ask them if they are doing a community care assessment and what the process will be.

- Before the assessment is done, it is a good idea to prepare. People often forget to mention things, or don't want to ask for too much. Remember it is important to give as full a picture as possible. One way to prepare is to try to write down all the different things you need help with or would like to do. Talk it over with someone who knows you to make sure you haven't missed anything.

- If at any stage you are not happy, check this chapter to see if things are being done properly. If the problem isn't sorted out, Chapters 25 and 26 give details of how to take things further.

NOTES

1 s12A of the Social Work (Scotland) Act 1968 (introduced by s55 of the NHS & Community Care Act 1990).

2 *Assessment and care management* (Circular SW11/1991), para 5.2.

3 Social Work (Scotland) Act 1968, s86. For the situation after local government reorganisation, see also s58 of the Local Government Etc (Scotland) Act 1994.

4 Blackie & Patrick *Mental health: a guide to the law in Scotland*, Chapter 3.

5 *Assessment and care management*, para 1.4. However, it has issued (jointly with the Social Services Inspectorate) a practitioners' guide and managers' guide to care management and assessment (both HMSO, 1991).

6 *Assessment and care management*, para 5.1.

7 There could be various legal reasons why this could be unlawful. An assessment which did not look properly at a person's needs might be judged not to be a community care assessment at all. Another argument might be that the local authority had failed to take all relevant circumstances into account in exercising its discretion. Finally, if the person was disabled, a holiday is one of the things which must be considered as part of the disabled person's assessment.

8 *Community care: agenda for action.*

9 s13A of the Social Work (Scotland) Act 1968, introduced by s56 of the NHS & Community Care Act 1990.

10 Social Work (Scotland) Act 1968, s12A(2).

11 Social Work (Scotland) Act 1968, s12A(3).

12 This is clearly implied in *Assessment and care management* eg, paras 12 & 13.

13 *Assessment and care management*, para 12.2.

14 *Assessment and care management*, para 12.3.

15 Further and Higher Education (Scotland) Act 1992, s1(2) and s12(3).

16 Social Work (Scotland) Act 1968, s12A(4).

17 Social Work (Scotland) Act 1968, s12(A)(1)(b).

18 *Assessment and care management*, para 6.1.

19 *R v Avon County Council ex parte M* [1994] 2 Family Court Reports 259 – discussed at page 146.

20 Social Work (Scotland) Act 1968, s12A(5) and (6).

21 *Assessment and care management*, para 3.1.

22 *Assessment and care management*, paras 5.3 to 5.6.

23 In one English case, a county council was held to have acted unlawfully because it failed to establish what the user wanted before making a decision – see *R v North Yorkshire County Council ex parte Hargreaves* Queens Bench Division 30/9/94. See page 146.

24 *Assessment and care management*, para 5.7.

25 *Assessment and care management*, para 5.9.

26 Social Services Inspectorate Circular CI (92) 33 *Implementing "Caring for people": assessment.*

27 *Assessment and care management*, para 19.1.

28 *Assessment and care management*, para 5.8.

29 *Assessment and care management*, para 19.3.

30 *Assessment and care management*, para 17.

31 *Assessment and care management*, para 5.3.

32 Disabled Persons (Services, Consultation and Representation) Act 1986, s8.

33 *Assessment and care management*, para 9.

34 s3 of the Disabled Persons (Services, Consultation and Representation) Act 1986 also contained a detailed procedure for carrying out assessments of the needs of disabled people. The Government has decided not to implement this section, on the grounds that it has been superseded by the community care reforms.

35 Education (Scotland) Act 1980, ss60-65 as amended by Education (Scotland) Act 1981. See *The law of the school* and *In special need* (HMSO).

36 s13 of the Disabled Persons (Services, Consultation and Representation) Act 1986 sets out the duties of the social work department.

37 Education (Scotland) Act 1980, s65B(1).

38 For example, the future needs assessment might be helpful to a careers adviser or further education college.

39 Disabled Persons (Services, Consultation and Representation) Act 1986, s13 (7).

40 Disabled Persons (Services, Consultation and Representation) Act 1986, s13 (8).

Social work services: the duty to provide services

INTRODUCTION

We have seen in the previous chapter that, although the social work department may assess a person as having certain needs, it may not have a legal duty to meet these needs if it does not have the resources. However there are some services which the social work department *must* supply by law.

These include:

- practical help for ill and disabled people
- home helps
- after-care for people with mental health problems
- occupation and training for people with learning disabilities
- information about local services
- residential accommodation for people in need

If a social work department does not supply these services it could be breaking the law. You might be able to take legal action to force it to provide the service. See Chapter 26. Or you might complain using one of the procedures in Chapter 25.

Also in this chapter, we look at the social work department's responsibility for setting up a register of blind people. While this is not a legal obligation, the Government has asked social work departments to do this, and if they did not, you might want to complain, using one of the procedures in Chapter 25.

We believe that it is very important that people become aware of their legal rights to community care services. And we hope that some people will be prepared to take legal action to enforce their rights if necessary.

As the new system comes into operation we believe that it is vital that people take a new look at the existing legislation, some of which has been around since the 1970s, and try to establish how best to use it for the people for whom they are caring or whom they are advising.

THE DUTY TO PROMOTE SOCIAL WELFARE

Social Work (Scotland) Act 1968, s12

The Social Work (Scotland) Act gives social work departments both the power and the duty to act for the good of the community. This is where they get their legal authority to act.

General duty to act for the common good

Under s12 of the Act, social work departments must:

> *"promote social welfare by making available advice, guidance and assistance on such scale as may be appropriate for their area...and provide...such facilities... as they may consider suitable and adequate"*[1].

They may provide the facilities themselves or arrange for other organisations, including voluntary organisations, to do so[2]. We saw on page 8 the sorts of services they provide.

What is the legal effect of this provision?

It works in two ways. It gives the social work department the *power* to promote social welfare, and also the *duty* to do so. They can do it and they must. However the section gives them a great deal of **discretion** on how to allocate their resources. They can decide what facilities are suitable and adequate for their area and it would only be in a very unusual case that the courts would interfere with their decision[3].

The local authority can decide how much of its budget to allocate to its social work department and this will influence what services are provided. What they decide to allocate will depend, at least partly, on their financial resources. The courts recognise this and will not criticise a local authority for not providing services under s12 if they do not have the money to do so.

Power to help people in need

The social work department can also give specific help to children or persons in need. (see page 3). The help can be practical help or cash. However cash can only be given in circumstances which amount to an emergency. In either case the social work department can only give help to adults if this would prevent them from having to spend more money later on[4].

Social work departments use s12 very widely to make emergency cash payments to people. But they can also give practical help in circumstances which do not amount to an emergency. They could, for example, buy someone a personal alarm or pay a bill or provide someone with meals.

The test is whether doing this would mean that the social work department would not have to spend more money at a later stage. For instance, if giving the help or paying the money would stop someone from having to go into residential care, the department could do this.

If you are a person in need and you need practical help or a cash payment, you should apply to the social work department.

It is up to the social work department to decide how to help you. They have a discretion[5]. They can decide what assistance is appropriate. If they were unreasonable in making a decision about offering you help you might have a legal remedy in judicial review (see Chapter 26).

Direct payments to service users

Many disabled people believe that the right way for community care to go forward is for them to be given their own money and budgets to enable them to employ their own personal carers. Independent living schemes have been set up to assist this process[6]. There have been attempts to use s12 to authorise social work departments to make financial payments directly to disabled people for independent living schemes.

It is not clear whether the section can be used in this way. The Government thinks it cannot be used in this way at present[7]. It may be that there are better ways of achieving the same results, such as grant-aiding voluntary organisations which arrange independent living schemes[8].

However, the Scottish Office has announced that it is now going to bring in a scheme to enable disabled people to buy their own care[9]. The new Independent Living Fund can also be used to buy care direct. See Chapter 4.

PRACTICAL HELP FOR ILL OR DISABLED PEOPLE

Chronically Sick and Disabled Persons Act 1970, s2[10]

Who qualifies for help?

You qualify if you are:

- chronically sick
- disabled
- a person with mental health problems *or*
- a person with a learning disability[11]

None of these terms is defined in the Act. It is for the social work department to decide if you qualify. If you disagree with their decision, you could go to court and they would decide. You do not need to be registered disabled to qualify.

The Chronically Sick and Disabled Persons Act lists welfare services which a social work department must supply to a person who needs them. **Once it has established that a person is in need of the services, it cannot argue it does not have the money.**

What services are available?

The services are listed as follows:

- practical help at home (eg help with dressing, cooking, getting out of bed, or a home help)
- radio, television, books or similar leisure facilities (such as talking books or a remote control device to help you use a television or radio)
- games, lectures, outings or similar recreational facilities or help in using educational facilities which may be available
- help with transport to local authority services, or similar services run by another organisation[12]
- home adaptations or other facilities which would improve the person's safety, comfort or convenience. (*This provision gives great scope for use. Traditionally it has been used for adaptations for physically disabled people, such as handrails, ramps and bath adaptations. It could also be used for help with an alarm, for a home extension or for extra heating. You might be able to think of other ways it could be used. See next page for problems with home adaptations.*)

- holidays[13] (which may be organised by the local authority, the person him or herself[14] or by a carer)

- meals at home or at a day centre

- telephone and equipment to help to use it

If the social work department decides that you need one or more of these services and that your needs will not be met unless it makes the necessary arrangements, it must make arrangements for the services to be provided to you. It can either do this itself or arrange for a voluntary organisation or similar body to do this[15].

Home adaptations

If you are chronically sick or disabled and the social work department decide that you need adaptations to your home, they must help you arrange this. They must also make arrangements to help provide you with the facilities which you need to improve your safety, comfort or convenience[16].

You might think this means that it is up to the social work department to carry out all the adaptations you might need to your home. But it is more complicated than that. The social work department may tell you home adaptations are not their responsibility. You may be entitled to a grant to help with the cost of repairs. The housing department can make an improvement grant if you are disabled and the repair is essential for your needs[17].

The Government has set out guidelines about who carries out which adaptations. Some adaptations are the responsibility of the health board and others are the responsibility of the local authority. These are summarised in the table above[18].

If you need equipment to help with a medical condition, the equipment should be provided by the health board. If you live in a council house, permanent alterations to your house will be carried out by your landlord, but if the equipment is removable, the social work department is responsible.

If you own your own house, the health board should supply medical aids. If you require permanent alterations you can apply to the housing department for a grant, but the social work department can also help. If you require less permanent facilities or equipment, this would be for social work to arrange.

It is important to remember that, whatever the Government guidelines say, it is the social work department which has the legal duty to help you adapt your home. They may decide that the health board should be involved or that you should contact the housing department because you could qualify for a grant. Or they may say this is something your local authority landlord should arrange, but they still have responsibility for helping you get the work done.

The social work department should assess your needs, and help co-ordinate your application. It is up to them to help you chase up the housing department if the grant application holds things up. If a health board is slow getting you what you need, ask your social worker or occupational therapist to ask what is going wrong. If delays are unacceptable, the social work department may be able to provide some temporary adaptations for you in the meantime.

If something is needed urgently, and it would take too long to apply for a grant or to get someone else to arrange it, the social work department could provide the item or the home adaptation for you. They would be entitled to charge you, according to your means (see Chapter 4). However, sometimes the social work department can be more flexible in looking at your financial resources than the housing department.

If you are having problems with home adaptations, you should get advice. You might want to complain, or go to the local government ombudsman. You may even want to take legal action. See Chapters 25 and 26.

Alterations required	If you live in local authority/public sector housing, the responsibility lies with	If you live in private housing, the responsibility lies with
Medical aids	Health board	Health board
Permanent alterations	Housing department or housing provider	Owner with grants or social work department if appropriate
Alterations for your special needs	Social work department	Social work department

How do you get an assessment under the Chronically Sick and Disabled Persons Act?

The Act does not say how the social work department decides whether you qualify for help. There are two ways in which your case may come to its attention:

- You, or your carer, may **request** the social work department to consider whether you could be helped by being provided with services under s2(1). If you do so, the social work department **must** consider your case[19] if you are one of the people who would qualify for help.

    The request could be verbal or in writing, although, if possible, you should write a short letter and keep a copy of it.

- When the social work department is carrying out a **community care assessment** for someone who appears to be disabled[20], it must also make an assessment of the person's needs under s2(1) and must also inform them that it is doing so[21]. See page 16.

Problems with s2

- **Deciding whether you "need" a particular service.** How does the individual social worker or occupational therapist who assesses you decide what you need? What if the department has told its staff that there is little money available for such services and they should keep the criteria high? How can they decide what "need" is? Some people might believe that every disabled person living alone needs a telephone. But the social work department may say otherwise. How should their staff decide?

    The question has to be a matter for the professional judgement of the staff member involved. They may be given guidelines by their management, but these should not be too restrictive. The person assessing your needs must look at all your circumstances, not just the general policy laid down by the department.

    A person assessing your needs who feels that his or her judgement about your need is conflicting with what their department told them should seek advice from their union or professional body. If the social work department act unreasonably in determining need, their decision could be challenged in the courts[22].

- **Deciding how to meet your need.** What if you disagree with the way the social work department says they will meet your needs? They may say they will take you in a social work bus to a day centre, but you would prefer to be given a bus pass so you could make your own arrangements. What could you do?

    You could ask the social work department to review their decision. If they do not change their mind, you could complain. But you would probably not have a legal remedy. The Act says they must make arrangements to meet the needs they decide you have. It does not say they have to meet your need in the way you would like them to.

- **Disagreement about what you need.** They say you do not need any of the services mentioned in s2; you disagree. What can be done?

    There is no formal right of appeal under the Act. The social work department could be asked to review their decision. If a review did not succeed, you could put in a formal complaint[23]. If you think that the department is not acting in accordance with its legal duties, you might be able to take further action. See Chapters 25 and 26[24].

- **No money to pay for services.** From time to time certain local authorities, faced with cash restraints or rate-capping, have announced in the press that they are unable to meet requests for special aids for a certain group, such as home adaptations for older people.

> **Social work departments cannot refuse to carry out their legal obligations under the Chronically Sick and Disabled Persons Act. If they do not have the money they have to find it elsewhere.**

If you think you have needs under the Act, you should ask for them to be met. If the social work department refuses you should seek advice. If you have a need covered by s2 which the department will not meet because of financial restraints, you have a good chance of winning a court case. Often the threat of legal action might be enough to get the service you need.

- **Delays**. You may be told that, although you need one of the services mentioned in s2, there is no money to pay for it or there will be long delays.

If you qualify for help under the section, then you should consider taking the matter further. In certain cases a delay can be so long that the courts would say that the social work department is breaking the law[25].

DOMICILIARY SERVICES (HOME HELPS)

Social Work (Scotland) Act 1968, s14[26]

Who qualifies for help?

You should be a person in need. See pages 2-3, *Who is community care for?*

The social work department has a legal duty to provide adequate domiciliary services for their area. These are to be supplied to households which need them because a person in need lives there or is proposing to live there. The social work department may supply the services themselves or may get someone else to supply them[27].

The new term *"domiciliary services"* was introduced by the NHS & Community Care Act. It is wider than the old concept of home helps which it replaces. Domiciliary services are defined as services provided in the home which appear to the social work department to be necessary to help a person to *"maintain as independent an existence as is practicable in his (or her) home"*.

This could include help with respite care and "home-making" as well as cooking, shopping, cleaning and the more traditional role of home helps.

Problems with s14

• **Not getting enough help.** You may feel you need a home help but are told that there are no helps available or not as much help as you need. The delay for getting a home help may be too long. Can anything be done?

It is not entirely clear how the courts would interpret the Act. It is rather strangely drafted. It does not say outright that every household in need should have domiciliary services but instead refers to providing them on a scale adequate for the area.

This may mean that the social work department does not have to supply services for every household in that area, only that they must have roughly the right number of home helps statistically. However it may mean that someone who was told that there was not enough money to give them a home help would have a good case.

We do not know, therefore, whether the courts would order a social work department to provide a home help to someone who needed one. We need a test case to establish what the law is. If you are not offered the help you need, you should get advice. See Chapters 25 and 26. If you qualify for help under the Chronically Sick and Disabled Persons Act, you might have a better case under that Act (see page 21).

• **Not getting the right kind of help.** Home helps have always helped with cleaning, but now there is a move to look at new kinds of care in the home. Some social work departments have said that the help they provide should concentrate more on "home care" and not so much on domestic tasks such as cooking and cleaning. Some social work departments are saying that they will not just provide cleaning on its own.

The Social Work (Scotland) Act says it is the duty of social work departments to provide help to allow you to live an independent life. Most people would agree that if you are not able to keep your house clean, you are not really able to live an independent life. **If you need help with cleaning, you should ask for it**[28].

If the social work department tells you they will not provide you with domestic assistance such as cleaning and you think this is what you need, you may want to ask them to review this. If they are unwilling, you could complain. This is also a matter you might want to take to the local government ombudsman or to judicial review[29]. See Chapter 25 and Chapter 26.

HELP FOR PEOPLE WITH MENTAL HEALTH PROBLEMS AND LEARNING DISABILITIES

Mental Health (Scotland) Act 1984, s8

Who qualifies for help?

You must have or have had a "mental disorder". This means a mental illness or a learning disability[30]. It includes someone with dementia.

It is the legal duty of the social work department to provide after-care for people who are or have been suffering from a mental disorder[31].

In providing after-care services, the local authority must co-operate with the relevant health board or boards and with relevant voluntary organisations[32].

This is a very important duty. It is a clear duty of the social work department. It is not subject to any limitations or qualifications. Its existence is one of the best kept secrets around[33].

This section gives very little discretion[34] to the social work department about who should receive after-care or how it should be provided. It *must* supply after-care for *anyone* who is or has been suffering from a mental disorder, whether or not they have been in hospital.

If people do not feel that they are receiving after-care from their social work department, or if voluntary organisations do not feel they are being adequately consulted about how after-care arrangements should be made, they should be taking further action. They could begin by asking questions, but might end up taking legal action. See Chapters 25 and 26.

What is "after-care"?

The term is not defined in the Act, so it is very hard to know what was intended[35]. It is hard to tell where after-care ends and where the longer term obligation of local authorities to provide day-care, training and occupation for people with learning disabilities[36] begins.

But that does not mean that the section is dead. At the very least the wording envisages that a person who has had mental health problems or who has a learning disability is entitled to some help from the social work department. This might include getting help with housing or in setting up home, advice on benefits or help to become established in the community again.

Anyone who feels they are not receiving adequate after-care from the social work department should seek advice. If the case came before the courts, they would decide what "after-care" means. They could decide whether what you said you wanted could reasonably be called after-care or whether it was something more than this.

How long should after-care be given for?

We do not know. The law does not say. A case has never come before the courts. If it did the courts would decide what was reasonable.

It is important to realise that if a case did come to court, even the fact that the social work department was short of funds would not necessarily be an excuse in the eyes of the law.

HELP FOR PEOPLE WITH LEARNING DISABILITIES

Mental Health (Scotland) Act 1984, s11

Who qualifies for help?

You qualify if you have a learning disability and are over school age. If you are living in hospital, you will not qualify until you move into the community.

The social work department has a legal duty to provide *"suitable training and occupation for people with learning disabilities who are over school age".* They can provide this themselves, through adult training centres or other day services, and they can also arrange for other organisations to provide services[37]. Many services are run by voluntary organisations.

The social work department must also make arrangements to ensure that there is adequate transport to take people to and from their places of training or day care.

If the local authority makes arrangements for a voluntary organisation to provide occupation and training, the Act gives it the power to make a contribution to the funds of the voluntary organisation[38].

Problems with s11

What is the scope of the duty under s11? Is it a duty to provide training and occupation for everyone with learning disabilities in the region? If you are not receiving adequate or suitable day-care, could you take the social work department to court to insist on receiving this?

If you do not have a place at a day centre and do not have any other training or meaningful occupation during the day, you may have a very good case for going to court.

If you have some training but do not think it is suitable, you might still have a case. This would be more difficult to prove. In this case you would be best to ask for a review of your case, or perhaps even put in a complaint before you took legal action. See Chapters 25 and 26.

INFORMATION ABOUT LOCAL SERVICES

Chronically Sick and Disabled Persons Act 1970, s1(2)(a)

Who qualifies for help?

Everyone is entitled to basic information. You qualify for more detailed information if you use any social work service, for example, a day centre or lunch club.

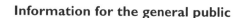

The law and your rights to community care

Information for the general public

The social work department must publish information about the services they provide[39]. They can decide how and when to publish the information. Some provide comprehensive and readable guides, others simply give out information to people who phone or write in.

If you get in touch with your local social work office, they ought to be able to tell you about services which might help meet your needs. When you have your community care assessment, you will have a better idea of what is available. (Although, as we have said above, you should tell them what you think you *need*, even if that kind of service is not yet available.)

Information for people using social work services

If you already use a social work service, the social work department is supposed to give you extra information.

Anyone who uses any social work service is entitled to be told by the social work department of any other services which the local authority provides which might be relevant to their needs. The department should also tell you about any other services which they know other organisations provide[40].

Every person attending a local authority day centre, therefore, should be given details of other services which might be helpful to them. This could include information about dental services, chiropody, meals-on-wheels or drop in centres run by local church or voluntary groups (provided the social work department knows about them). Someone living in local authority residential care should be told what else is going on in their neighbourhood. Someone who is getting respite care should be told of other services they might find helpful.

The law says that social work departments must *"ensure"* that people receive this information. (It would not be enough to put up notices on notice boards, as people might not read them.) This is a very clear cut duty on social work departments. Yet this is, unfortunately, not a law many people have heard of.

Does it matter? We believe it does. Imagine a situation where every user of services is given a personal folder, with information which is relevant to their needs, telling them about local services which they might find useful. Any one of the services could make a dramatic difference to the person's life. How different this would be from having to scan notice boards or find out by chance of a group which could offer support!

That is why this piece of legislation was introduced nearly 25 years ago and that is why users and carers who are not receiving this level of information, should ask why not. Remember though, you only have a legal right to insist on getting this information if you are already using a social work service.

THE DUTY TO PROVIDE RESIDENTIAL ACCOMMODATION AND NURSING HOMES

Social Work (Scotland) Act 1988, s59 and s56

Who qualifies for help?

You have to be a person in need. See page 3.

There is a legal duty on the social work department to provide and maintain an adequate number of residential and other establishments[41]. They may provide these themselves or jointly with another local authority or they can arrange for voluntary organisations or other bodies to provide them. The local authority can give grants to voluntary organisations to help them set up such accommodation[42].

Transport problems

One group who contacted us was experiencing difficulties with their transport to adult training centres. The buses run by the social work department were unreliable and often late. Trainees were late for classes and their carers' plans were disrupted.

The social work department has a legal duty to provide transport to training centres for people with a learning disability. If it does not provide a reliable service, the courts might say that the social work department is breaking the law.

We told them that it might be best to put in a formal complaint to the social work department before they took any legal action. If there was no improvement they might want to complain to the local government ombudsman. Legal action might be something they would consider as a final resort. (See Chapters 25 and 26.)

The social work department must also make arrangements for residential accommodation with nursing help for people who might need this in certain cases. They cannot provide this themselves but should make arrangements for voluntary organisations, nursing homes or private hospitals to provide the accommodation[43].

It is up to the social work department to decide what is an adequate and suitable provision for their area. It would be very difficult for an individual to challenge their decision, except in an extreme case, such as a council which refused to fund residential care for a whole group of people.

For further information on nursing homes and residential care, see Chapter 7.

HELP FOR PEOPLE WITH A VISUAL HANDICAP

Scottish Office guidance recommends that each social work department should keep a register of blind and partially sighted persons living in its area[44]. In much of Scotland, this is done for the social work department by local Societies for the Blind.

You do not need to register, but if you do, you will become entitled to certain important services from departments other than social work, such as free travel and income benefits. For further details, contact your local Society for the Blind.

Even if you do not put your name on the register, you are still entitled to social work services.

NOTES

1   s12(1).

2   s4.

3   See Chapter 26 for how the courts look at the discretion of local authorities.

4   Such assistance may be given *"where the giving of assistance in either form would avoid the local authority being caused greater expense in the giving of assistance in another form, or where probable aggravation of the person's need would cause greater expense to the local authority on a later occasion"*. s12(2).

5   See page 149.

6   For example, in Lothian, the Lothian Centre for Integrated Living facilitates such schemes for physically disabled people.

7   On 25/6/91, Michael Forsyth answered a written question in Parliament by saying that payments could be made only in an emergency.

8   Under s10 of the Social Work (Scotland) Act 1968. A voluntary organisation could be specifically set up for the purpose.

9   See *Ending discrimination against disabled people,* January 1995, para 8.4.

10 (Amended by Chronically Sick and Disabled Persons (Scotland) Act 1972 and Disabled Persons (Services, Consultation and Representation) Act 1986.)

11 Chronically Sick and Disabled Persons Act 1970, s29(2), as amended by s12 of the Disabled Persons (Services, Consultation and Representation) Act 1986.

12 But the local authority has the discretion to refuse to pay for transport to services which it does not provide itself or which it has not arranged.

13 See Chapter 6 for holidays and respite care.

14 See *R v Ealing London Borough Council ex parte Leapman* Times Law Report 10/2/84: the local authority cannot refuse to fund a holiday on the grounds that it has not arranged it.

15 Social Work (Scotland) Act 1968, s4.

16 Chronically Sick and Disabled Persons Act 1970, s2(1)(e).

17 Part XIII Housing (Scotland) Act 1987. The rate at which the grant can be paid is fixed by a statutory instrument called the Housing (Percentage of Approved Expense for Improvement Grants) (Disabled Occupants) (Scotland) Order 1982 SI 1982/1809. It is currently 75%.

18 The rules are in a Scottish Office circular: SDD 40/1985, *Provision of aids, equipment and house adaptations for disabled people living at home.* See also *Community Care: the housing dimension* (SW7/94) Annex 7.

19 Disabled Persons (Services, Consultation and Representation) Act 1986, s4.

20 For this purpose "disabled" means either "chronically sick" or "disabled" or a person with mental health problems or learning disabilities.

21 s12(4) of the Social Work (Scotland) Act 1968 (added by s55 of the NHS & Community Care Act 1990).

The law and your rights to community care

22 See Chapter 26.

23 See Chapter 25.

24 RADAR, the English national disability charity, is so concerned about the operation of s2 that it has set up a separate department to monitor its operation and to give advice to people wishing to enforce their rights. Unfortunately its remit extends only to England and Wales.

25 Delays are matters which can be investigated by the local government ombudsman. (See 128.)

26 (As amended by the NHS & Community Care Act 1990, Sched 9, para 10 (14)(b).)

27 NHS & Community Care Act 1990, Sched 9, para 10(3).

28 See RADAR's report *Disabled people have rights*, which looks at the working of s2 of the Chronically Sick and Disabled Persons Act 1970. On page 8 it considers the impact of the withdrawal of cleaning services.

29 If you are chronically sick or disabled you might want to go under s2 of the Chronically Sick & Disabled Persons Act 1970, as this contains a very clear duty on social work departments to provide *"practical assistance in the home"* to people who need it in s2(1)(a).

30 Mental Health (Scotland) Act 1984, s1(2).

31 Mental Health (Scotland) Act 1984, s8(1).

32 Mental Health (Scotland) Act 1984, s8(2).

33 At a recent conference a professional described the section as "dead"; meaning, presumably that nobody bothered about it. But it is not dead, only hibernating. It can be revived and used and acted upon by anyone with the will or energy.   ·

34 See 149.

35 s7 of the Disabled Persons (Services, Consultation and Representation) Act 1986 imposes a duty on social work departments to assess the needs of anyone who has been in a psychiatric hospital for 6 months or more. It has not been implemented.

36 Under s11 of the Mental Health (Scotland) Act 1984.

37 Mental Health (Scotland) Act 1984, s11(1).

38 Mental Health (Scotland) Act 1984, s11(3).

39 Chronically Sick and Disabled Persons Act 1970, s1(2)(a).

40 s1(2)(b) of the Chronically Sick and Disabled Persons Act 1970, as amended by s9 of the Disabled Persons (Services, Consultation and Representation) Act 1986.

41 Social Work (Scotland) Act 1968, s59.

42 Social Work (Scotland) Act 1968, s10(3).

43 Social Work (Scotland) Act 1968, s13A.

44 See Scottish Office Circular NHS 1986 (PCS) 35, / SWSG8/1986: *Certification of the blind and partially sighted*. In England there is a legal duty to do this under s29 of the National Assistance Act 1948.

Social work services: paying for services

INTRODUCTION

We saw in Chapter 1 that one of the major changes of the community care reforms is a shift from care in institutions to care in the community. What this means is a shift away from care provided by the NHS to care arranged or provided by social work departments.

However not many people realised when community care was introduced what the financial implications for people who used the new community care services would be. The effect has been to move people out of NHS care, which is free, to social work care, for which social work departments can make a charge.

So if you are living in the community, using home helps or other support services, the social work department has the right to charge you for this. What services they charge for, and how they charge is up to them. This process has only just begun. Most social work departments have traditionally charged a nominal amount for home helps and respite care. We are seeing moves in some departments to charge the full cost of care to people who can afford it.

We do not yet know how far this will go. What about a vulnerable person who is given support services and counselling? Will they be charged for this? Or if you are helped with home making and budgeting will a charge be made? Many groups are saying that it would be quite wrong for social work departments to charge for such services. But social work departments have the legal power to do this. There will be a lot of political campaigning ahead.

This chapter looks at the legal position. It deals with paying for social work services (other than residential care). Chapter 6 looks at paying for respite care. Chapters 9 to 13 deal with the complicated subject of paying for residential care.

THE RIGHT TO MAKE CHARGES

If the social work department supplies you with community care services, such as help in the home, adaptations to your house or other services under the Chronically Sick and Disabled Persons Act, they may make you pay for these. The law says that they may charge what they consider to be a reasonable amount for the services they provide[1].

Social work departments can also charge for after-care services for people with mental health problems or learning disabilities. But they do not have the power to charge for the day services for people with learning disabilities which they provide under s11 of the Mental Health (Scotland) Act (see page 25). Nor should they charge for any transport which they provide to these day services[2].

It is important to understand that there are no rules which cover the whole of Scotland on how departments should charge for the services they provide. This means that different people in different parts of the country may be paying different amounts for services which are very similar.

The Scottish Office is to issue guidance to social work departments on how they should charge for services[3]. But this general guidance will not specify rates for different services. The Government will leave this to the individual social work departments themselves to decide.

WAYS OF CHARGING

Many social work departments are currently involved in considering how to charge for their services.

Some are unwilling to charge for services at all, as this involves means testing, which is usually unpopular. They believe that charging stops people who need help from making contact with social work services.

Other departments are offering claimants detailed welfare benefits check-ups, to see if they are receiving all they should. People may then be better able to pay for the help they receive from social work.

Some departments are not charging people whose only income is Income Support but are charging people receiving Attendance Allowance or Disability Living Allowance, arguing that these benefits are intended to help pay for care.

YOUR RIGHTS

For the person being asked to pay, there are five important things to remember:

- **Your need for services should be assessed regardless of your ability to pay.** There should be two separate assessments: an assessment of your need for services and also a financial assessment[4].

- **There are some things the department must never charge for.** They must not charge you for making a community care assessment or for general help or advice.

- **Services which the local authority is under a legal duty to provide should be provided whether or not you can afford to pay for them. If you are later unable to pay, the services should not be withdrawn.**

  This is because the legal duty to provide services is not linked to the right to charge for them. In none of the cases mentioned in Chapter 3 does the law say that social work departments only have to provide the services if you can afford to pay for them.

- **You should not be made to pay more than you can afford.** If you cannot afford to pay the charges which the social work department has fixed, you can ask them to review the charges in your case[5].

  The authority must take your individual circumstances into account and see whether you can afford to pay. For instance, you might have debts to repay or extra expenses which make it difficult for you to pay the fees which the department has fixed. If you have a disability you may have extra expenses, such as laundry costs, the cost of a special diet, extra heating bills or extra wear and tear on clothing.

  You should write to the social work department saying that you cannot afford to pay the fees. It must then look into your case and decide whether it is *"reasonably practicable"* for you to pay anything, and if so, what.

- **Your relatives and carers should never be charged for the home care services you receive.**

  It is only the means of the person receiving the services that should be taken into account.

Charging: The right to an independent assessment

Essex County Council changed the way it charged for home helps. Some people who had not previously had to pay now had to. Some elderly people who could not afford to pay appealed to the social services department, asking them to consider whether it was practical for them to pay.

The appeals committee said that the charges should stand. The department had laid down guidelines for exempting people from charges and they did not fall within the guidelines. The people complained to the local government ombudsman. (See page 128.)

The ombudsman said that the appeals were not properly conducted. The appeal committee did not look properly at people's individual circumstances. The ombudsman asked the social services department to review their appeal procedure. They should reconsider whether the people could afford to pay for home helps. If they agreed they could not, the social services department should pay them compensation[6].

FINANCIAL LIMITS ON CARE AT HOME

Some people have become concerned that in some cases it might cost more to support a person properly in his or her home than if they were living in residential care. If a person had very complex needs and needed a lot of help from a number of different people, it might be cheaper if they lived in residential care. Are there any rules about this?

In England and Wales there have been suggestions from the Department of Health that if the weekly bill for a person's care was more than £500 – £600 a week, it would be preferable for that person to go into residential care. There have been no such suggestions from the Scottish Office.

There are no fixed limits on the amount of care that can be provided to a person living in the community.

It is up to individual social work departments to decide. Of course, they are constrained by their own budgets, and clearly if they are spending a great deal on one person, there will be less to spend on someone else. We will have to wait and see how this works out in practice.

GETTING HELP FROM THE INDEPENDENT LIVING FUND

In the past, one way people could be helped to stay in their own homes was by getting a grant from the Independent Living Fund. The Government set this up to help people with very serious disabilities stay at home, by providing them with the money they needed to buy care at home. However this fund was so successful that it stopped taking new applications in November 1992.

A new, more restricted, fund has now been set up. This is the Independent Living (1993) Fund.

Who qualifies ?

You need to be:

- aged 16 to 65
- getting the highest rate of Disability Living Allowance (care component)

- living alone or with people who cannot meet your care needs in full
- on a low income (Income Support or the equivalent)

Help will generally not be given to people who are terminally ill.

If you need help from the fund, you must do this through the social work department. They will assess your needs for residential or nursing care. If they find you could stay at home with support and you want to do so, they can involve the fund, provided the cost of paying for all the support you need is less than £500. The social work department has to agree that it will pay the first £200 worth of services you receive.

If you receive help from the fund (and you may not, even if you appear to qualify, because its funds may run out) you will receive up to £300 a week yourself. You can then buy the services you need. The amount you get will be reduced by the amount of any financial contribution you have to make. For instance, you may have to contribute up 50% of the care component of your Disability Living Allowance.

The Independent Living Fund is one of the few ways in which disabled people can be given money to buy care services for themselves. Many disabled people feel that this kind of approach allows a person more control over their own lives. You may need help managing your money and employing staff. The social work department should arrange this.

For a free booklet about the Independent Living (1993) Fund contact PO Box 183 Nottingham NG8 3RD. (Tel: 0115. 9428191).

NOTES

1   s87(1) of the Social Work (Scotland) Act 1968, added by s18 of the Health and Social Services and Social Security Adjudications Act 1983. As amended by the NHS & Community Care Act 1990, Sched 9, para 10(13).

2   Because while s87 of the Social Work (Scotland) Act 1968, as amended, gives them the power to charge for services provided under that Act and under ss7 and 8 of the Mental Health (Scotland) Act 1984, it does not give any power to charge for services provided under s11 of the Mental Health (Scotland) Act 1984.

3   The guidance will be in a Circular from the Social Work Services Group, entitled *Discretionary charges for adult day and domiciliary social work services.*

4   See *Assessment and care management* (Circular SW11/1991), para 11.

5   s87(1A). It is the local authority which has to decide whether it is reasonable for the person to pay and it also decides the amount. The courts would not overturn this decision on the grounds that they would have imposed a different sum: ie, there is no right of appeal against the size of the sum charged by the local authority. However **judicial review** may be available if the authority acted in an unreasonable way, for example by imposing a blanket policy on rebates which did not look at individual circumstances (and see case on page 30).

6   Report by the local government ombudsman into complaint No 90/A/2675, 2075, 1702 and others against Essex County Council.

❺
Carers

Carers are crucial to community care.
What do the rules say about carers' legal rights?
We look at getting help with caring and getting
help for yourself.

We saw on page 1 that practical support for carers was one of the six main aims of the Government's reforms. This chapter looks at carers' rights and Chapter 6 looks separately at respite care.

GETTING HELP FROM THE SOCIAL WORK DEPARTMENT

If you are a carer and you feel you need help with caring, you can, of course, arrange this yourself and pay for it privately. You may need no help at all from the social work department. But if you need help either arranging extra care or paying for it, you should contact the social work department.

You should ask the social work department to assess the needs of the person you are looking after (see Chapter 2). They must carry out an assessment if the person appears to be a person in need. See page 3.

Remember that the social work department can also help work out how to meet the person's other needs, such as needs for housing or medical services.

You should be fully involved in the assessment process and your views should be taken into account. If you feel that you and the person you are looking after want different things, you should ask to be seen separately from him or her. The social work department will have to try to help you work out something which will suit you both.

If the person you are looking after would qualify for help under the Chronically Sick and Disabled Persons Act (see page 21) their assessment should include an assessment of their needs under that Act. (If it doesn't, you have the right to insist the social work department look at those needs.) Remember that if the social work department believes the person needs one of the services listed in the Act, they must arrange this.

When making all these assessments, one of the crucial factors which the social work department will have to consider is your ability to care for the person in the future and what help you

may need to do this. The law says that when a **disabled person** is assessed for services the social work department must take into account whether their carer will be able to continue to look after them in the future[1]. Any problems or special needs which you have should be considered.

Plans for care for the person will need to be discussed with you to see how you think they will work. You need to be consulted both when the assessment is made and afterwards, when decisions are made about what services are going to be offered[2]. The care plans will also need to be discussed with the person you care for. Sometimes the person making the assessment may want to speak to them separately to try to find out what they want. For further details of the assessment process, see Chapter 2.

GETTING HELP FOR YOURSELF

If you have needs yourself which might mean that you should be receiving community care services in your own right, you are entitled to a community care assessment too. You might be a person in need yourself. The guidance to social work departments reminds local authorities to bear this possibility in mind when they do an assessment of the person being cared for, and to advise carers of this right[3].

Soon all carers may be able to get an assessment of their need for help. The Carers (Recognition and Services) Bill, now before Parliament, makes it the duty of social work departments to assess the needs of carers. The social work department will have to consider specifically what help a carer needs to help them carry on caring. The Government has said that it will support this bill, which means that it has a good chance of becoming law.

In Chapter 6 we look at respite care, which can be a way you can get a break from caring. The guidance does not make it clear whether respite care should be part of the assessment of the carer's needs or those of the person being cared for. If you are someone who may have community care needs and the question of respite has not been considered in the assessment of the

person you care for, you should ask for an assessment of your needs and mention your need for respite care.

SPEAKING UP FOR SOMEONE

Chapter 19 looks at how carers can speak up for people they care for, and Chapter 20 explains what happens when the person you care for cannot take their own decisions.

BENEFITS FOR CARERS

If you are under pension age, not working and are caring for someone for at least 35 hours a week, you may qualify for Invalid Care Allowance. The rate as at April 1995 is £35.25 a week. You will not have to sign on for work, and you will get National Insurance Contributions credited to your record.

If you are also claiming Income Support you will also get a carer's premium on top of your basic benefit.

For further information about these benefits, contact the Benefits Agency, a Citizens Advice Bureau or a welfare rights adviser.

COUNCIL TAX AND CARERS

In this book we have not said much about tax or welfare benefits. There are other very helpful books covering these areas. *(See Further Reading.)* However we have made an exception for a particular aspect of the Council Tax, because so few people seem to know about it. There is a reduction which some carers can claim.

Under the Council Tax, a person who is treated as living alone can claim a 25% discount. A house which is treated as empty gets a 50% discount[4]. Some people are "disregarded", which means they are not counted as living in the house. You can be disregarded if[5]:

- you are living with someone you care for (unless they are your husband or wife; someone living with you as if you were husband or wife[6], or your child under 18) *and*

- you care for the person for more than 35 hours a week *and*

- the person you care for gets the highest rate of Disability Living Allowance care component (or some other, less common benefits)[7]

There are a number of other special provisions in the Council Tax which benefit disabled people. See *Council Tax in Scotland: a guide for people who have special needs and their carers* for details[8].

Council tax and carers: Case study

A woman who lives with and cares for her elderly mother would be disregarded for council tax purposes. The mother would be treated as living alone and the household would get a 25% discount.

More than one carer can be disregarded. For example, a couple caring for their adult son with a severe learning disability could both be disregarded if they each cared for him for over 35 hours a week. (The son might also be disregarded on the grounds of "severe mental impairment".) This means that a house which actually had three people living in it could be treated as empty and get a 50% discount!

GIVING UP CARING

People give up caring for many reasons. Sometimes they can no longer cope, even with help. Sometimes the needs of the person being cared for grow too great. Sometimes, as with many young people with learning disabilities, the person being cared for would benefit from a new independent life.

Normally this change will involve a new community care assessment (see Chapter 2). Section Two explains about the different types of residential care and how to pay for it. Some parts are particularly important for carers.

Pages 48 to 49 explain how and when a carer might be asked to contribute to the cost of residential or nursing care. Pages 72 to 73 explain what happens if a carer is living in the house of someone who has gone into residential care.

CARERS AND COMPLAINTS

What do you do if you are not getting the help you need? What if staff are unhelpful? Can you complain? Chapters 25 and 26 deal with complaints and taking legal action, but there is one technical problem about carers making complaints.

The law and your rights to community care

The social work department complaints procedures (see page 126) provide for complaints to be made by people who receive community care services or people acting on their behalf[9]. They do not specifically provide for carers to make complaints on their own behalf.

This does not seem to be a problem in practice. Generally carers will be able to complain because they will be doing so on behalf of the person eligible for help. If you have asked for your own community care assessment, you will, of course, be able to make a complaint on your own behalf.

If you are a carer and you have problems in making a complaint, you should seek advice. See pages 160-162.

CAMPAIGNING FOR CHANGE

You may want to join a carers' group and campaign for better services in your area. (See pages 160-162.) These groups are valuable sources of information and help, too. Through them you could become involved in having your say about how community care will work in the future. See Chapter 24.

NOTES

1 Disabled Persons (Services, Consultation and Representation) Act 1986, s8.

2 In the Hargreaves case in England, (see page 146) the judge criticised the social services department for not having adequate discussion with the carer about the care they were planning to offer.

3 *Assessment and care management* (Circular SW11/1991), para 9.

4 Local Government Finance Act 1992, s11.

5 Council Tax (Discounts) (Scotland) Regulations 1992 SI 1409, amended by the Council Tax (Additional Provisions for Discount Disregards) (Amendment) Regulations 1994 SI 629.

6 A homosexual couple would not be treated as living together as husband and wife. They could claim the discount if they met the other criteria.

7 People getting one of the following benefits can also qualify:

   • an increase in disablement pension under s104 of the Social Security Contributions and Benefits Act 1992, provided they require constant attendance from their carer

   • an increase in constant attendance allowance under article 14(1)(b) of the Naval, Military and Air Forces etc. (Disablement) Pensions Order 1983;

   • an increase in constant attendance allowance under the proviso to article 14 of the Personal Injuries (Civilians) Scheme 1983.

8 This is published by the Scottish Office and should be available free in council offices and libraries.

9 Social Work (Scotland) Act 1968, s5B.

Respite care

WHAT IS RESPITE CARE?

Respite care is giving someone, or their carer, a break. A person may receive respite care in a hospital or nursing home, a residential home, or from one of the new respite services being organised by voluntary organisations and independent agencies. Or they may go to stay in another carer's home for a short time.

Most carers say that respite care is essential for them, and helps them to keep going. A change of scene may help the person you care for, too. But respite care services throughout Scotland are very patchy. Some areas have good provision, others not so good. It all depends on where you live[1].

ARRANGING RESPITE CARE

Getting an assessment of needs

If you or your carer think you need respite care, you will probably need to get in touch with the social work department. You may know what you need, but need help with the cost. Or you may have no idea where to turn. In either case, the social work department may be able to help.

The social work department will assess your needs and decide what respite care you need (see Chapter 2). Remember that if you need respite care urgently, perhaps because your carer feels they can no longer cope without a break, it can be arranged without an assessment (see page 14).

Your carer may have their own community care needs. In this case the social work department will assess the carer's needs (see page 15). As part of the assessment they might decide the carer needs a break.

How does the assessment work?

We saw in Chapter 2 that when the social work department assess your need for services they will meet both you and your carer. They will generally meet you together, but if you and your carer disagree about what you need they should meet you both separately. It is very important that they find out the wishes of both the carer and the person being cared for. (See Mr Hargreaves' case below, and on page 146.)

For instance, you may feel that you are fine where you are and not want to leave home, but your carer may feel they need a break. If you cannot agree, the social worker or person carrying out the assessment will have to try to help you work out what is for the best.

DO YOU HAVE A LEGAL RIGHT TO RESPITE CARE?

Although the social work department has a legal duty to assess people's needs for services such as respite care, it does not generally have the legal duty to provide what people might need. What they can actually provide depends on what funds they have. However, there are certain services which the social work department *must* provide if they decide you need them.

One of these is the right to a holiday. We have shown on page 21 that under the Chronically Sick and Disabled Persons Act, if the social work department decide you "need" a holiday, they must make arrangements for you to have one. They cannot argue that they do not have the funds.

A holiday is one way of giving you and your carer some respite care. The law says that if you are a **disabled person**, when the social work

A legal right to respite care?

Mr Hargreaves in Yorkshire sued his local social services department in the county court. They had agreed his sister needed respite care, but refused to pay more than £100 per week. The actual cost was £160.33. Mr Hargreaves read up the books and took out a writ against them. They had to pay him the £60.33 and he got a lot of publicity for his cause[3].

department decides what services you might need under the Chronically Sick and Disabled Persons Act, the person assessing you must bear in mind whether your carer will be able to continue to care for you on a regular basis in the future[2]. In other words, if giving you a holiday might help your carer to continue to look after you in the future, this would be a factor they should take into account.

So in certain cases you may be able to argue that you have a legal right to respite care. This has certainly been recognised in the courts in England.

PAYING FOR RESPITE CARE

What you pay for respite care will depend on where you go and how long your break lasts.

If you go to a hospital, it will be free. The National Health Service does not charge for its services. If you have nursing or medical needs, it could be quite reasonable for you to argue that you should receive respite care in hospital. If this is denied you, you might want to put in a complaint (see Chapter 25).

But generally you will go into some sort of residential care. You will normally have to make a contribution towards the cost of your care, if you can afford to do so. Exactly what you pay will depend on the social work department's policy and on how long you stay in respite care.

Some social work departments are able to arrange for someone to come into your home either on a regular basis or to give your carer a short break. If you receive this kind of respite care, the social work department can charge you for it according to your means. See Chapter 4 for the rules and for how you can ask to have your circumstances reviewed if you think you are being charged too much.

People in respite care for under 8 weeks

The rules say that the social work department need not do a full financial assessment. They may fix their own rates for temporary residents[5]. They can decide what is a reasonable charge to make.

However social work departments are entitled to charge the full cost from the first day you go

---

Arranging respite care

The carer of a disabled person in England arranged a holiday and then asked the social work department to help with the arrangements under the Chronically Sick and Disabled Persons Act. The social services department were not interested because they had not suggested the idea. The court said they were wrong. If the client needed a holiday, the social services department should support them[4].

---

into respite care. If so the rules set out below apply. Age Concern Scotland carried out a survey. The survey showed that five out of the twelve social work departments in Scotland were, in fact charging the full rate[6].

This may appear very unfair. A person in Dumfries might pay £43.45 for a week's respite care, while someone in Strathclyde would be paying £280 for almost identical care. You cannot appeal against the decision of the social work department to charge the full rate. (But if you cannot afford the rate that the social work department has fixed, you can ask them to reconsider the charge they have made. See page 30). The law says social work departments are free to decide how to charge. If you are unhappy, you would have to campaign to get them to change their practice.

People in respite care for over 8 weeks

If you are in respite care for any one period of over 8 weeks, the social work department must charge you the full rate. If you cannot afford this, they will do a financial assessment to see what you should pay. We have seen above that they may decide to do this even if you are only in respite care for a short time.

This does not mean that you can only receive 8 weeks' respite care in total before you have to pay the full amount or be means tested. The department can charge you at the lower rate for each period of less than 8 weeks. It is only if a particular period of respite care is longer than 8 weeks that they must charge the full rate or do a means test. But remember that it is up to them to decide. You cannot force them to charge you the lower rate.

Generally if the full financial assessment is done, the rules about charges are the same as for permanent residents in residential care (see Chapters 7 to 13).

However there are certain differences for people who go into respite care:

- The value of your house is not taken into consideration as an asset[7]. This is because you are intending to return there and obviously it could not be sold to pay fees.

- The cost of maintaining your home, paying your rent or mortgage and other reasonable

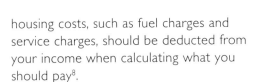
housing costs, such as fuel charges and service charges, should be deducted from your income when calculating what you should pay[8].

- Any Housing Benefit you receive will not be counted, nor will the amount of any Income Support you receive in respect of your housing costs[9].

- If you receive Attendance Allowance or Disability Living Allowance care component, these should not be treated as part of your income if you go into respite care[10]. However you may lose these if you are in respite care for over 4 weeks. (See under *Benefits*, below.)

BENEFITS AND RESPITE CARE

Special rules apply to people going into respite care. (For benefits and residential care generally, see Chapter 13.) You may need welfare benefits advice.

Residential care

If you go into residential respite care, you can continue to receive Housing Benefit and Income Support on your own house[11]. You can also get Income Support to cover the costs of respite care for up to eight weeks[12].

After 28 days in respite care, you will lose your Attendance Allowance or care component of Disability Living Allowance. If you go into respite care for separate periods of less than 28 days and these are not separated by more than 4 weeks, the periods will be added together and when they reach 28 days, these benefits will be stopped.

People in hospital

If you go into hospital for your respite care, your care will be free, but you may start losing some of your benefits after a few weeks. After four weeks you stop receiving Attendance Allowance and Disability Living Allowance care component. The linking rules for periods of less than 28 days apply here, too[13]. After six weeks you get only £14.70 personal allowance (1995/96 rate), plus your housing costs[14]. If you are in hospital for longer than 8 weeks, your carer will lose Invalid Care Allowance and their carer's premium[15].

Conclusion

- Your benefits will be seriously affected if you go into respite care for more than 28 days at a time or more regularly than every four weeks.

- If you go in for more than 8 weeks at a time, you will almost certainly have to pay the full cost of respite care or what you can afford towards this.

- You may have to pay the full amount even if you go in for a short time.

- You may need advice to help you get through the respite care jungle. See pages 160-162 for people who may be able to give advice.

NOTES

1   See Social Work Services Inspectorate for Scotland *The patchwork quilt: a study of respite care services in Scotland*.

2   Disabled Persons (Services, Consultation and Representation) Act 1986, s8.

3   "When sharing the care means also sharing the cost" *Guardian* 25/3/92.

4   *R v Ealing London Borough Council ex parte Leapman* Times Law Report 10/2/84.

5   s22(5A) of the National Assistance Act 1948 (as amended by s20(1)(a) of the Health and Social Services and Social Security Adjudications Act 1983 and by s44(6) of the NHS & Community Care Act 1990).

6   See Mary Thomas *Charging older people for care*.

7   National Assistance (Assessment of Resources) Regulations 1992, Sched 4, para 1.

8   National Assistance (Assessment of Resources) Regulations 1992, Sched 3, para 27.

9   National Assistance (Assessment of Resources) Regulations 1992, Sched 4, paras 3 and 26.

10 National Assistance (Assessment of Resources) Regulations 1992, Sched 3, para 6.

11 Income Support (General) Regulations 1987, SI 1967, Sched 4, para 1(c).

12 Social Security (Claims And Payments) Regulations 1986, SI 1968, Sched 7, paras 6(2), 7(2) and 3(c).

13 Income Support (General) Regulations, Sched 2, para 13.

14 Income Support (General) Regulations, Sched 7, para 1(a).

15 Social Security Contributions and Benefits Act 1992, s70(2), and Income Support Regulations, Sched 2, para 14ZA.

Residential care: introduction

BACKGROUND TO THE NEW SYSTEM

Although the Government hopes that in future more people will be helped to stay at home instead of moved to institutions, there will still be many elderly and disabled people who will need more intensive support than is available to them at home. Fewer people will go into hospital for this care. It will mostly be provided in hostels, residential care homes and nursing homes.

As we saw in Chapter 1, one of the main reasons for the community care reforms was the huge rise in the 1980s and early 1990s of the cost to the Government of keeping people in residential care homes and nursing homes. People in such homes who could not pay for themselves were entitled to much higher levels of Income Support than people who were living in their own homes or being looked after by relatives.

With the increasing number of elderly people, the costs were set to continue to rise. Because the money was paid as a benefit entitlement, it could not be restricted by budgets and there was no assessment of whether the person actually needed to be in the home. The Government felt that many people could be looked after more cheaply at home and that many people would prefer to stay at home if they could.

The Government's solution was to try to put residential care on a similar basis to other types of care. The intention was that people would get roughly the same DSS benefits wherever they lived. The social work department would be responsible for any extra care costs, whether it was for residential care or any other type of care. Care of whatever kind would be based on an assessment of need.

Of course, changing such a complex system threw up many problems. Although people in residential care used to be entitled to higher benefits they were often still not enough to meet the actual cost of care. This became known as the "care gap". This means that the money which has been transferred to social work departments to cover their new responsibilities may not be enough.

There are particular worries about people who need a lot of care, who will become very expensive for social work departments under the new system.

Both the old and the new system involve **means-testing**. People who can contribute to their care costs are expected to do so. The new system involves means-tests by both the Department of Social Security (DSS) and the social work department.

Although in theory members of the family do not have to pay for a relative's care, various aspects of the new rules are likely to increase pressure on them to do so. The increasing reluctance of the NHS to fund long stay care (eg in geriatric wards) will bring more people into the means tested system.

For the foreseeable future, there will be two different systems of funding – one covering people who were in a care home before April 1 1993 (see Chapter 12), and one for people who came into a care home on or after that date (see Chapters 8 – 10). There are also different rules for people in homes run by local authorities. We deal with these in Chapter 11.

WHAT IS RESIDENTIAL CARE?

There are basically 4 types of residential care:

- nursing homes
- residential care homes
- local authority homes
- hostels

Nursing homes and residential care homes have to be registered with either the health board or the social work department.

Nursing homes

Nursing homes typically offer a fairly intensive degree of care, including care by qualified nurses. They are run by private individuals, companies, or charities. Social work departments do not run their own nursing homes. All nursing homes have to be registered with the local health board[1]. A registered medical doctor or a qualified nurse must be in charge of the home.

Registration will specify the maximum number of residents and can also lay down conditions as to the age, sex and type of residents. The health board can refuse to register the home if they believe that the home is unsuitable or that the manager or any of the staff is not fit to be involved in a nursing home. The board can also cancel the registration for the same reasons. If registration is refused or cancelled, the home can appeal to the board and then to the Sheriff Court.

Health board staff have a right to inspect nursing homes at all reasonable times.

Residential care homes

Private or charitable care homes which are not registered as nursing homes will normally fall into the category of residential care homes. These homes must register with the local social work department[2] whether or not the residents are receiving any financial support from the

---

Finding out about inspections

In the past, inspection reports on homes were not available to the public. Now some councils are allowing the public access to inspection reports, or publishing guides to local residential care with extracts from them.

---

local authority. There is no minimum size of home and even a home with two or three elderly people might have to be registered.

Whether a home is legally classed as a residential care home and must therefore register is sometimes difficult to judge. The law requires it if a home provides "*such personal care and support... as may be required for the purposes of*" the Social Work (Scotland) Act. A home may have to be registered even if it does not provide board.

If the residents fall into one of the various community care categories and receive personal care or a programme of counselling or other support, the home will probably be classed as a residential care home. If the care is provided by arrangement with the social work department, the home will almost certainly have to be registered.

The social work department can refuse to register a home or cancel registration if the home is unsuitable or if the manager or any of the staff is not fit for their post. If they propose to do this, the home has to be given a chance to make its case and if that does not succeed, it can appeal to a special appeal tribunal.

As well as registering the homes, local authorities have a duty to visit residential care homes to check on the wellbeing of the residents[3].

Does registration work?

Unfortunately, registration of nursing homes and care homes has not prevented a number of scandals where people received appalling care for a considerable period. Very few homes are ever de-registered. In England, several attempts to de-register homes have been overturned by the appeal tribunal[4]. Cancelling registration is obviously a last resort since it involves moving vulnerable people from their homes.

Recently there have been press reports in Scotland of cases where homes have caused concern for long periods of time before registration was removed. However, many social work departments have strengthened their inspection and registration procedures in the last few years.

If you have a concern about how a home is operating which the home will not sort out, or which is extremely serious, it is a good idea to report it to the body which registers the home. Details will be on the Certificate of Registration which the home must display.

Local authorities also have inspection advisory committees. These include lay members and they oversee the work of inspection teams. They should provide an independent check on how inspections of residential care homes are carried out. Details of the committee will be available from the social work department[5].

The law and your rights to community care

Local authority homes

Local authorities also run their own residential care homes. (They are legally barred from running their own nursing homes)[6]. These do not have to be registered, but like private residential care homes, they are inspected by the social work department's inspection staff. These staff will normally prepare detailed reports on the individual homes for the local authority.

Hostels

Hostels may be run by district councils, social work departments, private individuals or charities. By "hostel", we mean an establishment which is more institutional or has more support provided than an ordinary flat, but has less supervision than a residential care home.

In fact, hostels do not really fall into a separate legal category for most purposes. Those which provide a substantial amount of support or care would normally have to be registered as residential care homes. Others mainly provide accommodation and are effectively shared flats.

In an unregistered hostel, the residents can claim Housing Benefit to cover their rent. (It is not normally possible to include the cost of personal care in a Housing Benefit claim, although some district councils have tried to be flexible)[7].

Because the Housing Benefit levels may be higher than the residential allowance for registered care homes, there is sometimes a temptation for hostels not to register. This is only likely to be legally possible if the residents receive relatively little care or the care is provided by some agency which is completely separate from the body running the home.

WHO PAYS FOR RESIDENTIAL CARE?

Residential and nursing care is expensive. There are four main sources of funding.

Local authority (social work department)

This is now the public body with the main responsibility for funding residential care. They can pay for places in residential care homes or nursing homes. Except in emergencies, this will be done after a community care assessment (see Chapter 2). This looks at the person's care needs. There will also be a financial assessment to decide how much a person can contribute to the cost of their care. The following chapters look at this in detail.

The Department of Social Security (DSS)

The DSS will continue to be the main source of funding for people who went into residential care before April 1 1993 (see Chapter 12). For new residents, welfare benefits will not normally be enough to cover residential care costs except in some unregistered hostels (see above). In a few cases, people have been able to get enough welfare benefits to afford places in relatively cheap residential care homes, without help from the social work department[8].

Benefits are discussed in Chapter 13.

The resident and their family

People who can afford it can, of course, pay for their own place in a private home. The social work department does not need to be involved (although homes run by charities will often only accept referrals from social work departments or health boards).

Even if a person is being financially supported by the social work department, the resident will be expected to contribute towards the cost of care if they can afford to do so.

If you have savings or a reasonable income, it may be difficult to decide whether to arrange residential care privately or through the social work department. If you pay for your care privately, you may be eligible to keep Disability Living Allowance (care component) or Attendance Allowance. Also, you will not need to disclose any financial details to the local authority.

On the other hand, if your money is likely to be used up eventually, it might be a good idea to involve the social work department from the start. This reduces any possibility that you might have to move once your money ran out because the social work department were not prepared to take over the responsibility of paying for your care later on.

The health board

The health board will normally only support people in residential care if they are being discharged after a significant period in hospital. This can happen in various ways.

Health boards may hand over money to social work departments to help pay for the care of former hospital patients. This is called "resource transfer" (see page 77). This is usually through an overall agreement covering a large number of patients. So far as the resident is concerned, all the financial and care responsibility will be on the social work department, not the NHS.

Sometimes health boards will contract with a nursing home to provide care for patients who remain legally the responsibility of the NHS. This means that the patient does not have to pay for care and continues to receive limited social security benefits.

In other cases, the board will financially support a residential care home or nursing home run by a charity which has accepted discharged patients. The patients are no longer treated as "in-patients" of the NHS. They may then be liable to a charge by the home but will also be eligible for increased welfare benefits.

It is not easy to say when people stop being NHS in-patients for benefit purposes.

In the case of *White v Chief Adjudication Officer*[9], the Court of Appeal ruled that patients with long term mental health problems who had been placed in a nursing home and claimed Income Support to pay their fees were in fact still "in-patients" and not eligible for the benefit because they were still getting nursing and medical care in a home under a contract to the NHS. Whether this applies in other cases depends very much on individual circumstances and the type of care people receive.

Insurance for long term care

If you are planning for the future, it is now possible to buy insurance policies to cover the cost of long-term care. These are relatively new. They can be expensive, especially for older people. It is very important to take expert professional advice before buying a policy.

The kind of things you need to consider are:

- How much will it cost?

- How much will it pay out and when?

- For how long are the levels of premium and benefit guaranteed? (Some policies guarantee the premium will not change for 5 or 10 years, while others may be increased at only a month's notice.)

- How will the insurers decide that you need care and so qualify for the benefits?

- What kind of care will the policy allow you to obtain?

- What care could you get if you did not buy the policy?

NOTES

1   Nursing Homes Registration (Scotland) Act 1938.

2   s61 of the Social Work (Scotland) Act 1968, amended by Registered Establishments (Scotland) Act 1987.

3   Social Work (Scotland) Act 1968, s68.

4   See Harriet Harman MP and Sarah Harman *No place like home*, a report of cases before the Registered Homes Tribunal.

5   See Scottish Office Circular SW9/1990: *Community care: inspection of establishments: organisation and role of inspection units.*

6   s13A of the Social Work (Scotland) Act 1968 (inserted by s56 of the NHS & Community Care Act 1990).

7   Housing Benefit (General) Regulations 1987, SI 1971, Sched 1, para 1. Although the cost of nursing and personal care is not eligible for housing benefit, it is possible to include the cost of *"counselling and support services"* if they are necessary for the provision of adequate accommodation or are provided personally by a landlord or a warden or caretaker whose main duty is to provide other services which qualify for housing benefit. (There have been some press reports that the Government might try to tighten up the rules for housing benefit.)

8   "Loopholes" – Gerald Wistow and Melanie Henwood, *Community Care* 17/2/94. The calculation is that an elderly person with high care needs could still claim £204.40 (at 1995/96 rates) if they can keep their Attendance Allowance and Severe Disability Premium in care. This argument appears to have been accepted by the DSS in a number of cases, although the rules are complex and of course may change. See page 67, for further discussion.

9   *White v Chief Adjudication Officer*, Times Law Report 2/8/93. The DSS interpretation of the rules is in Adjudication Officers' Guidance paras 28304 – 28334 (May 1994 Issue).

8

Getting residential care through the social work department

HOW THE PROCEDURE WORKS

If you think you might need to go into residential care and might need help with the fees (now or in the future), you should ask the social work department to do an assessment (see Chapter 2). If the social work department do a community care assessment and decide that you need residential or nursing care, they will then try to find something which suits your needs. They will also carry out a financial assessment. If the place you go to is one which is not run by the social work department, they will place a contract with that home.

The Government originally envisaged that local authorities would pay the homes the full cost of care. This left it up to the local authority to recover the resident's financial contribution.

In fact many social work departments have adopted a system where the resident pays their share directly to the home and the local authority pays the balance. This can only be done if the resident, the home, and the local authority all agree. **You cannot be made to pay the home directly if you do not want to and you should seek advice if you are concerned about this**[1].

HOW MUCH WILL THE SOCIAL WORK DEPARTMENT PAY?

The law does not fix charges for residential care homes. It is a matter for negotiation. It is legally possible for the social work department to decide that you need residential care, but that they cannot afford to pay for it. However, the basis of any decision not to meet charges for care could be important. For example, it has been suggested that some local authorities will not pay more than the maximum which the DSS paid under the old system. This may be legally permissible as a general guide, but it could be unlawful if it was rigidly applied by the local authority. This is because the local authority would be taking into account something which is not legally relevant (see Chapter 26).

If you cannot get the social work department to pay for the kind of residential care you want, it might be a good idea to specify the home you would like. The following section explains how this strengthens the social work department's duties.

YOUR RIGHT TO CHOOSE A HOME

Under the old system, people who received Income Support towards the cost of residential or nursing care could use it to pay the fees of whatever home they chose (if the home would take them). Even if their Income Support was less than the fee, they could still choose a more expensive home if someone else (eg a relative) paid the difference. Because many homes charged more than the maximum allowed for under Income Support, it became fairly common for relatives to have to contribute towards the cost of care.

Under the new system, a person who needs help from public funds to pay for care normally has to go to the social work department. It is the department who contract with the care home. The Government were anxious that people should not have less individual choice than under the old system. To try to avoid this, they issued binding directions to local authorities[2]. The guidance issued with the directions emphasises that local authorities should give *"full, fair and balanced"* information about the quality of different homes. They should also tell people about their right of choice[3].

Choice of home

The basic idea is that people are entitled to choose any residential or nursing home, provided it is available, suitable, and affordable. Even if it costs more than the local authority will pay, the resident can go there if someone else can make up the difference. A resident who is already in care has the same right to seek to move somewhere else[4].

Availability

Obviously a local authority cannot place you in a home if there is no place available. The home has to be willing to accept you. However, if the home is full but is willing to put you on a waiting list, the authority should be prepared to consider making a temporary placement elsewhere and moving you to the home you prefer when a place comes up[5].

The home has to be prepared to accept the local authority's conditions (eg about insurance, record keeping, etc.) However, a local authority would be in breach of the guidance and possibly of the law if it tried to impose strict conditions which could not be justified. Contract conditions will normally be standard, but there might be reasons why they are not appropriate in a particular case. The local authority should be prepared to be flexible. There are also legal restrictions on the types of conditions which can be imposed by local authorities (eg they cannot insist that staff belong to a Trade Union)[6].

Suitability

A home may be unsuitable if the local authority do not feel it can meet your care needs. It is up to the local authority to decide what these needs are as part of its assessment. However, they should not refuse to consider a home as suitable just because it is not exactly in line with their normal specifications, or because it has a different philosophy from the local authority. For example, you may prefer a home where rooms are shared or which is for people with particular religious beliefs. An authority which denied that choice without good reason would be breaching the guidance and possibly also the law[7].

You may wish to choose a home which is not in the local authority area. You are entitled to do so, if it is otherwise suitable, available and affordable. It will still be the local authority where you come from who will have to contract with the home, not the local authority where the home is based.

There are some technical problems, where a person who is ordinarily resident in Scotland wants a nursing home place in England or Wales.

To get round this, the Government has asked English and Welsh councils to co-operate in arranging the places[8].

Affordability

Councils should not be expected to pay an unreasonable amount. Unfortunately the test for deciding what is a reasonable cost to care for an individual person is not straightforward.

The directions say the cost of the resident's choice of accommodation should not be more than the authority would "usually expect to pay", bearing in mind the assessment of that person's needs[9].

According to the guidance, this does not mean that the social work department should always compare the charges with the actual cost of placing the resident somewhere else. Just because one home in an area is providing very cheap accommodation does not necessarily mean that the local authority should refuse to pay any more for anyone else. On the other hand, a temporary shortage of a particular type of accommodation need not mean that homes will be able to force prices up at the local authority's expense.

The authority must tell you how much it would normally pay and what accommodation is available at that price. The local authority cannot impose a particular level of charges unless there is a reasonable prospect of finding suitable accommodation at that price.

There may be particular problems with people with expensive or unusual care needs. The local authority must take account of the individual assessment and not set a rigid maximum level for a particular group (eg, people with learning disabilities).

In deciding what is affordable and suitable, difficult decisions may have to be made about how much account has to be taken of factors such as cultural and personal preferences. For example, if you have a medical need for a particular diet then that would be part of the assessment of need. It is not so clear whether you could insist on more expensive accommodation if you needed this to meet a personal or religious preference over diet.

The case of Mr. Hazell[10] (discussed in more detail at page 46) is important. He successfully argued that he should go to more expensive accommodation than the council wanted to pay, and that his own wishes should be taken into account.

It is also not clear how the local authority should decide on affordability if you want a place in a private or voluntary home and the only other places are in the authority's own homes, or vice versa. Because the funding is still different for council-run homes, it could be difficult to say whether the "cost" to the local authority was greater or less. However, it is one of the stated aims of the current Government to encourage a move away from local authorities managing their own homes. Any attempt to deny people the choice of a private home could well be stopped by a further binding direction in future.

PAYING EXTRA FOR CARE

Where a third party contributes

If you choose a home which costs more than the authority will pay, but there is a third party (ie, not you or your spouse) willing and able to make up the difference, the local authority must agree to place you in that home[11].

The home must be available and suitable (see above). The third party could be a relative, friend, charity or trust fund.

It will still be up to the local authority to make a contract with the home for the whole cost of the place. They will then have to make arrangements to recover the extra money from the third party. They are entitled to expect that the person will be able to afford the extra charge for as long as you are at the home.

Many local authorities are likely to ask the third party to sign some sort of contract to cover their contribution. This might include provisions for:

- how payments will be made

- what happens if charges go up

- what happens if the third party cannot continue to contribute at the agreed level

- what to do if there is a dispute

- whether interest is chargeable if payment is late

A third party should not sign any agreement without taking proper advice. The local authority should be prepared to negotiate, within reason. If they insisted on the precise wording of a standard contract without proper justification, they could be in breach of the Government's binding direction on choice.

If you think a relative might have to go into residential care, you might want to make arrangements in advance to contribute to the cost. It is important to be careful about how this is done. For example, if you buy an annuity to provide income for a relative, the income might be assessed as part of the resident's income.

That might reduce their welfare benefits or the amount the social work department will contribute to their care. The money has to clearly come from a "third party", not the resident's own money. A **discretionary trust** might be one option, but you should take professional advice.

Where the resident or spouse pays extra

The direction about third party payment does not apply where the resident wishes to buy more expensive care from their own resources. Those resources will all be taken into account in deciding how much the resident can contribute towards the cost of accommodation within the normal price range of the local authority.

The direction does not cover payments by a resident's husband or wife either. This is because the spouse is expected to contribute towards the ordinary care costs rather than pay for better care (see page 48: *Couples*).

If the resident or the spouse has money left over after paying for their normal contribution, and they want to spend this on more expensive care, the local authority can agree to fund a more expensive place with an increased contribution from the resident or relative. However, if a person has that amount of money, they may be better off making their own arrangements with the home and not approaching the local authority at all. See page 40: *The resident and their family*.

A two-tier system?

Some people are worried that relatives will be pressurised into contributing to residential care and only people who can pay will get good care. It is very important to realise that the local authority cannot set an arbitrary limit and expect relatives to pay anything over that. The limit which they will pay must be realistic in terms of the needs of the individual resident.

WHERE NO CHOICE EXISTS

Unfortunately for many people there is no real choice since there is often a shortage of suitable places. The directions only require the local authority to try to respect the resident's choice if there is a choice available. They do not create an obligation to ensure that there are particular types of care which comply with people's particular preferences. Nevertheless, people should always make sure that their assessment sets out what they would really like, even if it is not currently available. This means that better services can be planned for the future.

CHOICE BETWEEN RESIDENTIAL CARE AND STAYING AT HOME

The direction on choice only covers the situation where everyone accepts residential care is appropriate. In some situations, you might want residential care but the local authority do not think it is necessary. It would not seem to be possible for the authority to fund part of the cost of residential care in that situation and expect you or a third party to pay the extra over the amount which care at home would have costed. In that situation, the best course of action is probably to challenge the basis of the assessment that residential care is not necessary.

If, on the other hand, you want to stay at home but the authority wants you to go into care, a check should be made to see if you might qualify for help from the Independent Living Funds (see page 31). As well as this, you should challenge the assessment or ask for it to be reviewed.

IF YOU ARE UNHAPPY WITH THE LOCAL AUTHORITY

You may be unhappy because the local authority:

- will not pay the fees for the home you want

- will not accept that the home you want is suitable

- cannot agree a contract with the home you want

- expects someone else to pay more than you think is reasonable

- cannot come to a reasonable agreement about a third party contribution

In all these situations, you would be entitled to use the statutory complaints procedure (see page 126). However, you may also have a legal case (see Chapter 26). If the complaints procedure does not resolve your problem, or if it is an emergency, you should seek legal advice.

NOTES

1   National Assistance Act 1948, s26(3A) inserted by s42(4) of the NHS & Community Care Act 1990.

2   Social Work (Scotland) Act 1968 (Choice of Accommodation) Directions 1993 in Social Work Services Group Circular SW05/93 (The circular contains both the guidance and the Directions). Hereafter referred to as *Choice of accommodation*.

3   *Choice of accommodation*, para 17.

4   *Choice of accommodation*, para 12.

5   *Choice of accommodation*, para 7.9.

6   *Choice of accommodation*, paras 7.10 – 7.12.

7   *Choice of accommodation*, paras 7 – 7.3.

8   The problem is that s13A of the Social Work (Scotland) Act 1968 only allows Scottish social work departments to contract with nursing homes covered by Scottish legislation. There is no similar problem with residential care homes. Social Work Services Group Circular *Choice of accommodation: cross-border placements* (SW6/1994) encourages councils to co-operate to allow maximum choice to residents. Eventually the problem should be sorted out by regulations.

9   *Choice of accommodation*, Direction 3 (b), paras 7.4 – 7.8.

10 *R v Avon County Council ex parte M* [1994] 2 Family Court Reports 259.

11 *Choice of accommodation*, Direction 4, paras 8 – 12.

Moving into residential care: the financial assessment

INTRODUCTION

In Chapter 7, we explained that most people moving into residential care after April 1 1993 will need financial support from the social work department of the local authority, but that people who can contribute towards the cost are expected to do so.

This chapter explains how the contribution is worked out. There are special rules for people in homes run by social work departments, which are explained in Chapter 11. People who go into care who own a house or have other significant savings should also read Chapter 10.

THE "DOUBLE ASSESSMENT"

To calculate how much you will have to contribute, the social work department must carry out a financial assessment (except for periods of care lasting less than 8 weeks – see Chapter 6)[1]. This assessment will cover your income from welfare benefits and other resources such as savings or occupational pensions.

If you have little or no income or savings, you are entitled to claim Income Support to contribute towards the cost of your care. The claim for Income Support will be the subject of a separate financial assessment by the Department of Social Security (DSS).

The fact that most people have to have two financial assessments makes things particularly complicated. The rules are similar but not identical. Where they differ, problems can arise. This chapter focuses on the local authority assessment. Chapters 10 and 13 highlight the main differences in the Income Support rules.

Before April 1 1993, local authorities had wide discretion about how they carried out financial assessments, but there are now detailed rules they must follow[2]. They must also take account of official guidance from the Scottish Office[3].

WHAT IS THE MAXIMUM PAYABLE?

There is no fixed maximum. You can be required to contribute up to the full cost of the residential place. There is no minimum charge either, although most people will have to pay something because they have either an income or assets, or receive DSS benefits.

HOW MUCH CAN YOU KEEP?

The personal allowance

The charges for your care should not take all your income. From your assessed income (including benefits and any savings you have), you must be left with a personal allowance (£13.35 as at April 1995[4]).

Increasing the personal allowance

It may be possible for the personal allowance to be increased. Although the local authority will normally allow people to keep the standard personal allowance, they have the power to allow a resident to keep more *"in special circumstances"*[5].

This means that the charge they impose on the person will be less.

The law does not say exactly what special circumstances would be relevant. You can always argue that there are special circumstances in a particular case. The local authority would then be required to consider whether it was appropriate to allow someone to keep a greater personal allowance. Examples might include:

- a resident with outstanding debts

- a resident who is developing skills in handling money or buying food who would benefit from more independence

- a resident with dependent relatives (see page 48 for the situation of couples)

- at least one authority allows for the cost of maintaining the resident's pet

How income is calculated

The basic idea is that, apart from your personal allowance, any other money you have coming in should go to pay for your care. However, there are various types of income which are "disregarded".

This means that they are not counted in calculating how much you have to pay for your care, and you can keep them.

Some items are completely disregarded[6]. Others are partially disregarded. The full list is set out in the guidance. It is similar to the list of income which is disregarded for Income Support. Important disregards include:

- **People who are working can keep at least £5 a week of their wages.** If you receive Disability Living Allowance or Disability Working Allowance or various other disability benefits, you can keep £15 a week from your wages.

- **Disability Living Allowance (mobility component) is completely disregarded.** You get this on top of your personal allowance. Disability Living Allowance (care component) is only disregarded for temporary residents (see page 37).

- **Income in kind is completely disregarded.** This means any food, clothing or other items received by a resident should be ignored.

- **Charitable and voluntary payments may be partly or completely disregarded.** This includes payments from relatives (if there is no legal obligation to make them). It could also include payments from a **discretionary trust**. If a payment is specifically to buy something which is not covered by the home's fees (eg, a personal phone or television, or a regular outing), it will be completely disregarded. Otherwise, up to £10 a week will be disregarded. If the payments are not regular, they will be treated as capital, not income – see page 48.

(NOTE: there are special rules about payments by husbands and wives – see *Financial support by partners*, page 49)

"Less dependent residents"

There is also the possibility of special treatment for "*less dependent residents*"[7]. This means people who are in private or voluntary sector accommodation which is not registered as a residential care home, and people who are in local authority homes but who do not receive board.

The local authority does not have to use the normal rules for assessing income and savings if a person counts as a less dependent resident and the authority consider it reasonable in the circumstances. This means that the local authority might choose to ignore more of the resident's income or savings in deciding what charge to make.

The idea appears to be to encourage independence by allowing the resident to spend more of their own money. It may also be a method of encouraging a resident to take on employment by allowing him or her to keep more of their wages.

Even if the authority has no general scheme for less dependent residents, it is always open to such a resident to ask for special treatment. The authority would have to consider whether to do so.

NOTE: The definition in the regulations of "*less dependent resident*" does not appear to exclude people in registered nursing homes, although they are excluded in the guidance. This may be an oversight. If you are in a nursing home, it might be worth testing this by asking to be treated as a less dependent resident. The regulations have greater legal force than the guidance.

How are savings treated?

The rules are similar to Income Support (savings are called "capital" in the rules). **If you have more than £8,000, you will have to pay the entire cost of your care** (until your savings drop below that level)[8]. If you have over £3,000, the rules treat you as if you had income from these savings. The assumed income is £1 a week for every extra £250 up to £8,000. Every £1 of assumed income will increase your weekly charge by £1[9]. You can keep savings below £3,000.

The capital rules do not just cover savings in the bank. They cover any assets you have (eg, homes, land, shares, etc.). Their value will be counted unless the rules say it should be disregarded[10]. Chapter 10 looks at the particular rules about homes belonging to people in care and the rules about giving property away. It also explains what happens where capital is owned jointly.

Other important items which are disregarded include:

- personal possessions such as clothes, paintings or jewellery. These will be disregarded unless they were deliberately bought to dispose of capital (see page 55, *Buying personal items*)

- payments of arrears of welfare benefits. These will be disregarded for 52 weeks from the date of payment

- the surrender value of life insurance policies and annuities is disregarded completely

- payments in kind (ie, not in cash) from a charity are disregarded completely

- trusts are disregarded if there is no "absolute entitlement" to capital, and capital is not paid over[11]

This is not a complete list.

COUPLES

INTRODUCTION

There are special rules covering what happens when one member of a couple moves into care. Unfortunately they are very complicated.

This section explains:

- how the assessment is done

- when a husband or wife might be asked to contribute towards the cost of their spouse's care

- how payments by a partner to a person in care are treated

- what happens to the partner when the breadwinner goes into care

THE FINANCIAL ASSESSMENT

The local authority only has the power to assess the resources of the person in care[12]. If they are married, the authority must separate out what income or savings belong to that person. If the couple have a joint bank account, the rule is that half the money belongs to each person. Page 52 explains what happens with other joint property.

Although the full assessment can only be done on the person in care, the local authority may still expect the partner to contribute towards the cost of care as a "liable relative".

This is because a man is legally liable to maintain his wife, and a woman her husband[13]. This particular rule only applies to married couples and not to divorced couples or unmarried couples who lived together.

There is a similar rule for Income Support. However, whereas the DSS rarely use this rule, it seems that local authorities will often expect a liable relative to make a contribution.

The local authority will normally act in the following order:

- Assess the resources of the resident to see whether he or she can meet all the costs of his or her care.

- If the resident cannot meet all the costs, establish whether there is a husband or wife who is a "liable relative".

- If the resident is getting Income Support, the local authority may not pursue the matter. This is because any money the spouse contributes would reduce the resident's Income Support entitlement, leaving the local authority no better off. Scottish Office guidance advises local authorities that pursuing maintenance is not worthwhile in this situation[14].

- If the liable relative obviously cannot pay a contribution (eg, because they get Income Support), no further action will be taken.

- If it seems that the liable relative could make a contribution, the official guidance advises the local authority to decide an 'appropriate' contribution after discussion with the spouse. The local authority must take all the circumstances of the relative into account, including his or her normal standard of living, and not ask for more than the relative can reasonably afford. **The Scottish Office guidance states that it is not appropriate to expect the spouse's resources to be reduced to Income Support levels to pay maintenance[15].**

Exactly how this will work is left vague in the guidance. It is clearly stated that the local authority cannot carry out a full financial assessment on the relative in the way that they would for a resident[16]. It is left up to the local authority to decide what is a reasonable contribution. A relative does not seem to be under any obligation to provide the local authority with information about their assets.

The guidance does not tell the local authority what to do if the relative will not give information or make a reasonable contribution. Ultimately, the authority can go to court for an order requiring the liable relative to maintain their spouse. The court will look at all the circumstances. They may well disagree with the social work department about what is a 'reasonable' contribution.

Until such a court order, the local authority does not have the right to take account of a contribution which it believes the relative should make but which is not in fact made.

Remember:

- It is only spouses who can be made to pay for a relative's care

- The full means test can only be done on the resident, not the spouse

- The resident is entitled to a service, whether or not the spouse has agreed to pay

- The local authority rules for assessing the spouse's contribution are not legally binding. If agreement is not reached, it is up to the court to decide what is a fair contribution.

FINANCIAL SUPPORT BY PARTNERS

Supporting the person in care

There are special rules for how any money paid by a partner to a resident is treated. Although it is only a husband or wife that can be forced to make a contribution to fees, the rules covering financial support by partners also cover divorced spouses. These payments are called "liable relative payments".

"Liable relative payments" will normally be counted as income of the resident, whether they are made voluntarily or under an arrangement with the local authority[17]. This means they will be included in calculating how much a resident can contribute to their care.

In other words, there may be little point making such payments, unless you are required to. (As we explained above, the local authority can *ask* you to make payments to support your husband or wife, but it is only a court that can *make* you pay.) However, there are some ways for a partner to financially support a resident which will result in a real benefit. The following are two of the most important ones[18].

Gifts of up to £250

A liable relative can give up to £250 to their partner in any 52 week period. This will be treated as capital, not income. So long as the resident's total capital does not go above £3,000, it will be ignored by the DSS and the local authority (see page 47 for capital over £3000).

The gift of up to £250 does not have to be made at once. There can be a number of payments, but it would be safer not to make more than 2 or 3 in any year. If the payments are too frequent or regular, they may be treated as "periodical payments" of income, which will result in an increase in charges by the social work department.

Payments to third parties

A payment made to someone else on behalf of the resident (eg settling a bill) will normally be counted as the income of the resident. This means it will increase the charge for care. However, the local authority do not have to count it as a "liable relative payment" if it would be *unreasonable* to do so. They will look at the purpose and terms of the payment and the amount. Presumably this means that they will ignore small payments. The guidance to local authorities suggests that it might be unreasonable to count payments to a TV rental company; or for mail order clothing; or of a telephone bill as liable relative payments.

Even if the local authority decide not to count something as a liable relative payment, that does not necessarily mean it will be completely ignored. It will be treated as if it was a payment made by someone else. The rules set out on page 47: *How income is calculated – charitable and voluntary payments* would apply.

Supporting the person at home

We have explained that the income and savings of a husband and wife are assessed separately when one partner goes into care. Sometimes the couple will have relied on the income of the person who is now in care. A common example is where the husband has an occupational pension. If the husband goes into care, it is possible that the whole pension will go towards paying for that care, leaving the wife with nothing. She would have to claim Income Support.

This could lead to some very harsh situations. The way round it is for the local authority to allow the resident to keep a higher personal allowance (see page 46) in order to continue to support the partner at home. The Government guidance encourages social work departments to consider this. It says:

> *"The use of this discretion should be considered and negotiated in the light of the individual circumstances of each case, but it would be reasonable for the local authority to take into account factors such as the usual standard of living of the spouse at home, and if the spouse has higher outgoings for whatever reason."*[19]

However, it is left very much up to the social work department to decide what is fair.

Another option (although obviously not a pleasant one) would be for the spouse to sue the resident for maintenance. Although guidance

The law and your rights to community care

does not mention this explicitly, it is hard to see how a local authority could object to a resident keeping a higher sum than the normal personal allowance, if it is needed to meet a court order for maintenance.

CHALLENGING THE FINANCIAL ASSESSMENT

What if you do not accept the social work department's assessment? Can you appeal?

The surprising answer is no. There is no formal appeals procedure like that for social security benefits. We believe this is a major flaw in the system, because social work departments are having to apply very complex rules and make very difficult judgements about people's financial and personal situation.

What you should do depends on what the disagreement is about.

If you think the department has applied the rules wrongly (for example, it has counted savings which should be disregarded), you should tell them. If they ignore you, seek advice. You may have a legal case.

Sometimes the department has a **discretion** (eg, it can decide whether to increase a resident's personal allowance). If you think the way it exercised that discretion was unreasonable, the first step would probably be a formal complaint (see page 126). Chapter 25 explains what other steps you might consider and Chapter 26 explains when you may be able legally to challenge the way a discretion has been exercised.

If you are a spouse who is being asked to make a contribution (see page 48), it is not really up to you to appeal. It would be up to the social work department to go to court if they weren't happy with the contribution you were prepared to pay.

Remember, the social work department should not refuse to provide care because of a disagreement about money (see page 30). If they threaten to do this, seek advice.

SUMMARY – KEY POINTS

- If you go into residential or nursing care arranged by the social work department, they must do a financial assessment to decide how much you can contribute towards the cost of your care.

- If you have a low income and little savings, you will probably be entitled to Income Support. If you claim this, there is a separate financial assessment by the DSS.

- You must be left with at least £13.35 a week to live on. Sometimes you may be able to keep more.

- Apart from this money, any income you have is used to pay for your care, unless the rules say it can be disregarded.

- If you have savings of over £8000, you are expected to pay the whole cost of your care.

- If you have savings between £3000 and £8000, you will have to pay something towards your care costs.

- All your savings and assets (including property) are counted unless the rules say they can be disregarded.

- When you go into residential care, you are assessed separately from your partner.

- Husbands and wives can be asked to contribute towards the cost of their partner's care.

- There are no rules about how much a husband or wife should pay. If a partner does not agree with what the local authority wants as a contribution, it would be for a court to set a fair amount.

- If partners do make payments, there are special rules about how these are treated.

- When the partner at home needs financial support from the person in care, the local authority can allow this.

- There is no straightforward appeal process. You can complain. In some cases, legal action might be appropriate. If you are worried, seek advice.

NOTES

1   National Assistance Act 1948, s22.

2   National Assistance (Assessment of Resources) Regulations 1992 SI 2977 as amended by 1993 SI 964 and 1993 SI 2230, 1994 SI 825 and 1994 SI 2386. Note that many of the regulations make little sense unless read alongside the Income Support (General) Regulations 1987 SI 1967, as amended.

3   This has been updated several times. The guidance (issued by the Social Work Services Group) was reprinted completely in *Community Care: National Assistance (Assessment of Resources) (Amendment No 2) Regulations 1993: Regulations and Guidance* issued on 21/1/94 (hereafter referred to as Guidance Circular 21/1/94). Parts have been amended by further guidance issued on 9/5/94 and 30/11/94.

4   The amount is laid down every year in the National Assistance (Sums for Personal Expenses) Regulations.

5   National Assistance Act 1948, s22 (4) and see para 5.005 of Guidance Circular 21/1/94.

6   National Assistance (Assessment of Resources) Regulations 1992 SI 2977, Scheds 2 and 3.

7   National Assistance (Assessment of Resources) Regulations 1992 SI 2977, reg 5.

    Section 2 of Guidance Circular 21/1/94.

8   National Assistance (Assessment of Resources) Regulations 1992 SI 2977, reg 20.

9   National Assistance (Assessment of Resources) Regulations 1992 SI 2977, reg 28.

10 National Assistance (Assessment of Resources) Regulations 1992 SI 2977, Sched 4.

    Guidance Circular 21/1/94, s6.

11 Guidance Circular 21/1/94, Section 10 covers trusts in detail.

12 Guidance Circular 30/11/94, para 4.001:

13 National Assistance Act 1948, s42.

    Social Work (Scotland) Act 1968, s87.

    Guidance Circular 21/1/94, s11.

14 Guidance Circular 21/1/94, para 11.003.

15 Guidance Circular 21/1/94, para 11.006.

16 Guidance Circular 21/1/94, para 11.005.

17 National Assistance (Assessment of Resources) Regulations 1992 SI 2977, reg 30.

18 National Assistance (Assessment of Resources) Regulations 1992 SI 2977, regs 29 – 34.

    Guidance Circular 21/1/94, paras 11.008 – 11.014. There are also special rules for separation and maintenance payments.

19 Guidance Circular 30/11/94, para 4.003.

Paying for residential care: how the family home and other property is treated

INTRODUCTION

This section explains how the home a person lived in before care is treated in the financial assessment by the local authority. Many of the rules also apply to other major items of property.

At page 46, we explained that people who claim Income Support are also financially assessed by the Department of Social Security (DSS). The DSS rules are similar to the rules for the social work department, but in this chapter we point out some significant differences.

ASSESSING THE HOME

If you own your house and move into residential or nursing care, the basic rule is that the house should be sold to help pay for the costs of your care. It is treated as a capital asset, both for Income Support and for assessing how much you pay the social work department towards your care costs. Chapter 9 explains the general rules about the financial assessment by the local authority.

HOW IS IT VALUED?

The valuation starts by looking at the current market value. Any outstanding debts owed on a mortgage will be deducted. 10% of the total value is also deducted to take account of the cost of selling the property (whatever the actual cost)[1].

WHERE THE RESIDENT OWNS A PART SHARE IN PROPERTY

Many people own their home or other property jointly with their partner or members of their family.

Such a share will still be counted as part of your capital (but see below for the rules where a relative is still living in the home).

However, it is unlikely that you will have to sell your home. This is because of the way the value of the share is worked out.

The local authority will look at how much the resident's share would receive if sold *on its own* to a willing buyer. It then deducts 10% to cover the cost of the sale[2]. The market for a part share in a home is likely to be very limited and the value might be virtually nil. If there is any legal reason why the share could not be sold on its own, the value would be nil.

The DSS operate on a similar principle. There is a small difference in that the DSS assume that everyone owning a share in joint property has an equal share[3] (with land and houses, the local authority looks at the share the person actually owns)[4]. Where the shares are not equal (eg, one person owns 50% and two people own 25%), the DSS calculation may work out differently from the local authority assessment.

In any case, the key point to remember is that it is *not* a proportion of the value of the whole house which is assessed. It is the value of the resident's share on its own, which will normally be far less.

Where the resident disputes the value with the local authority, the authority will normally ask for an independent professional valuation. The DSS will use the District Valuer.

WHEN IS THE HOME NOT COUNTED?

There are a number of special cases where the value of your house is not counted.

Where the resident intends to return home

If your stay in care is temporary and you intend to return home, the value of your house is ignored by the local authority[5]. The guidance states that the value should be ignored even if your stay in care was initially meant to be permanent but turned out to be temporary. Presumably this means that if your stay in care does not work out, you might be able to get a refund of charges or have them cancelled[6].

The DSS seem to apply the same principle, although the rules are extremely complex[7]. Therefore, you should be able to go into residential care on a temporary basis for up to a year, without having to sell your home.

Where someone else still lives in the home

Even if a house is solely owned by someone who is in care, there are special rules to help where someone else is living in the house who should not be expected to move.

The value of the house will be ignored if there is anyone from the following categories staying in the house. It does not matter whether or not they lived there before the person went into care[8].

• The resident's spouse or partner

"Partner" means someone who was living with the resident in a heterosexual relationship. This concession does not apply if the couple are divorced or estranged (although they might still qualify under one of the categories below).

• A relative aged 60 or over

The rules specify that a "relative" means:

(a) parents (including parents-in-law and step-parents)

(b) children (and children-in-law and step-children)

(c) brothers and sisters

(d) grandparents

(e) grandchildren

(f) uncles and aunts

(g) nephews and nieces

(h) spouses or partners of the people listed at (a) – (c)

• An incapacitated relative

The meaning of "relative" is the same as the above list. There is no definition of "incapacitated" in the DSS or local authority regulations.

According to the guidance for local authorities, people should qualify if they get a disability benefit (eg, Incapacity Benefit, Severe Disablement Allowance, Disability Living Allowance, or Attendance Allowance).

Even if they do not get one of these benefits, they should still qualify if they have a disability or need for care which is severe enough to meet the tests for at least one benefit. The relative may be asked to produce medical evidence to back this up.

• A child under 16

This must be a child whom the resident is "liable to maintain"[9]. This normally means a natural child of the resident.

This concession is in the local authority regulations but not the DSS regulations. This is only likely to be significant in a few cases. Most of the time the child is likely to be looked after by the partner, and so the house would be disregarded by the DSS anyway (under the above rules about the resident's spouse or partner).

There might be a problem if the child is living with, for example, a divorced spouse. Even then, it might be possible to argue that the child should be treated as an "incapacitated relative". (Even if the child is not disabled, they may need an equivalent degree of support as a disabled adult.) If this argument failed, the box *What happens if the DSS do count the home?* explains what would happen.

What happens if the DSS do count the home?

There are a few situations where the local authority may ignore the value of the home but the DSS count it. That would mean a loss of Income Support. Provided you qualify for some other benefit (eg, Old Age Pension, Severe Disablement Allowance), the effect would not be great. The charge imposed by the social work department would be reduced to take account of any loss in Income Support.

However, if you do not qualify for other benefits and have no other income, there could be a problem. Without Income Support, you will not even have the standard personal allowance of £13.35 a week. You may have to put the house on the market, which would, at least, allow the DSS to disregard its value for 26 weeks.

• Other deserving cases

Even if a person living in the home does not fall within these categories, the local authority can still disregard the value of the home if they consider it would be reasonable to do so[10].

The guidance suggests that it might be reasonable to disregard the home if it was occupied by someone who had left their own home to care for the person, or by an elderly companion. These are just examples. It is up to the local authority to decide what is reasonable in any particular case. (See Chapter 26 for an explanation of how a local authority's discretion should operate.)

The DSS does not have a similar discretion to disregard a property on the grounds that it would be 'reasonable'. Unless the person living in the house falls within the first three categories above, they will take the property into account. This could mean a person loses Income Support even though the social work department do not expect them to sell the house. See the box *What happens if the DSS do count the home?* for what this means.

DISPOSING OF PROPERTY

INTRODUCTION

If you have to sell your house to pay for your care, this will take time. During that time, you will have no money from the property to pay for care. There are rules to cover this.

There are also special rules to deal with situations where people give away property (eg, to relatives) or do not sell it. These may allow the local authority to ignore a transfer, or to charge the people who received the property, or impose a mortgage on the property.

Many people who go into care do so because their ability to manage their own affairs is affected. This may cause legal problems in disposing of property (see Chapter 20).

SELLING THE HOUSE

Under the DSS rules, the value of a house which is being sold will be disregarded for up to 26 weeks. This period can be extended indefinitely if the DSS accept that it is reasonable to do so[11].

There is no specific disregard in the local authority rules to cover the period when a house is being sold (except for temporary residents – see note 6). They will set their charge as if the money from the sale of the house was available. This means that either:

- the fees will need to be paid out of other income

- someone else pays the fees meantime

- the fees are not increased because there is some other reason to disregard the house or

- the charges will build up as a debt owed by the resident.

The charge will not go down until the house is sold.

This could have a particularly harsh effect. Until the house is sold, its value will stay the same and so the charges will presumably stay high. If the resident actually had cash in hand, it would be used up to pay the fees, and so future fees would go down. The rules say that a debt can only be "set off" against capital assets if there is a security (ie, a mortgage).

One way round this, if you are having problems selling the house, would be for the local authority to take out a mortgage on the home (see page 56). The charges will then be treated as a debt secured on the house and they will be deducted from the net value[12]. This means that future charges will go down.

It may even be better for the person to give the property away (see below), but you should seek advice.

Another option is described in Chapter 13 (*Using the benefits system to pay for your care*, page 67).

GIVING PROPERTY AWAY

There has been a lot of publicity about people having to sell their home and use up their savings to pay for care (although this is not actually a new part of the system). Some people resent having to use up savings in this way. Family members feel they have lost their inheritance.

An obvious way to try to avoid this is to give the property away, often to the children. **It is vital that this is not done without professional advice**, because there are rules designed to catch people who do this. (There is also the problem of whether someone who may have dementia, for example, is legally capable of giving away their property.)

Where a person gives property away, or sells it for less than its market value, either to reduce the charge for residential accommodation, or to increase entitlement to Income Support, the local authority or the DSS can treat the person as if they still owned the asset. This is called "intentional deprivation" and the assets are treated as

"notional capital"[13]. In other words, the fees for care will be exactly the same as if the property had not been given away.

This rule applies to the family home and to other property, such as money in the bank.

The level of notional capital will be reduced each week by the amount in extra charges which is payable[14]. This is called the "diminishing notional capital" rule. Eventually this would mean that the charges would go down, when the total of actual capital and notional capital fell below £8000.

The reason for giving away the property is crucial. The property can only be treated as notional capital if the resident *intended* to reduce charges or increase benefit. If the purpose was completely different, it should not be treated as notional capital.

On the other hand, the intention to reduce charges or increase benefit does not have to be the only or even the main reason for giving the property away. If it was a *significant* reason in the mind of the resident, the notional capital rule will apply[15].

Since the DSS or local authority are expected to decide what is in the mind of the resident when they gave the property away, there is obviously a huge potential for disputes.

How the DSS decide

DSS guidance to its officers sets out a number of points to consider when deciding whether there has been intentional deprivation for the purpose of increasing Income Support[16]:

- Each case must be decided on its own merits. It is up to the DSS to prove that there was an intention to increase entitlement.

- The officer should consider whether the claimant had any real choice. For example, if a debt was repayable at that time, the claimant had no choice in the matter, so should not be penalised.

- The officer should ask the claimant why they disposed of the capital. However, the DSS can also draw conclusions from the surrounding circumstances.

- A person cannot be guilty of intentional deprivation if he or she did not know that giving property away would affect benefit entitlement. Therefore, the officer should ask the claimant if they knew about the capital limits and judge whether the person had some idea that capital limits existed. The

officer should consider the claimant's level of education and understanding, and any evidence that they have been told of the capital limits. They may ask the claimant what he or she intended to live on.

The timing of the disposal may be a clue as to the claimant's purpose (eg, giving property away just before going into care).

How the local authority decides

The regulations do not say how a local authority is meant to guess why someone gave property away. The Government guidance gives more help[17].

Important factors include the *timing*. It would be unreasonable to assume that someone intended to avoid paying for care if they gave property away long before, or when they were fit and well.

In practice, some authorities seem to ignore property given away more than 6 months before the person went into care. This may be because they cannot transfer the fees to the person who received the property if it was given away more than 6 months before the admission to care (see page 56 – *Charging the person who is given property*).

The guidance gives three examples where the Government thinks local authorities should *not* treat someone as having notional capital. These are:

- money given to a spouse from the sale of the family home to buy a smaller home

- a person paying off a bank loan for home improvements

- a person who bought a car shortly before going into care who did not anticipate going into care and who gave the car to his son

These are merely rules of thumb. It is always possible to challenge the decision on the basis of your own circumstances. If you can reasonably argue that you would have done exactly the same thing if you were not going into care, this will help your case. For example, you might have transferred some of your property to your children for tax purposes, or because the children needed somewhere to live.

BUYING PERSONAL ITEMS

The same rules about intentional deprivation can apply if you deliberately spend your savings on personal possessions in order to reduce your savings. There is a risk that you will be treated as if you still had the money you spent. However, it would be reasonable to spend money where, for example, you need new things because of the move into care.

Appeal rights

If you disagree with the DSS about whether there has been intentional deprivation, there is a right of appeal to a social security appeal tribunal and then to a social security commissioner. Unfortunately, there is no proper appeal procedure against the local authority assessment. The best option is probably to use the statutory complaints procedure (see Chapter 25). If that failed, you could take legal advice on whether the local authority had exercised its discretion properly (see Chapter 26).

CHARGING THE PERSON WHO IS GIVEN PROPERTY

Even before April 1993, it was not uncommon for local authorities to try to increase the charges for a place in a local authority home where the resident had given away their home or other assets to their family. However, this was often ineffective because the resident had no money left to pay the increased charge.

Now, if a person receives an asset for less than its real value from someone who goes into care, the local authority has the power to make that person contribute to the care costs of the original owner[18].

For this to apply, the person disposing of the asset must have done so knowingly, and with the intention of avoiding care charges (see above – *How the local authority decides*). Also, the transfer must have take place while the person was in care, or no more than 6 months before they went into care. The property must have been given away or sold for less than its real value.

As we explained above, the resident is treated as still owning the property (notional capital). The value of the asset will be the market value. The value of any outstanding mortgage will be deducted, as well as a "reasonable" amount to cover the cost of a genuine sale. The reasonable amount should include things like estate agents' and legal fees.

The amount the person who received the property has to pay is the difference between the payments actually made by the resident and the charges due to the local authority when the notional capital is included.

The recipient cannot be required to pay more than they actually received as a benefit.

The motives of the person who received the property are not relevant. The local authority only looks at why the person who had the property gave it away.

Again, there is no proper right of appeal. Anyone being charged for someone else's care under this rule should seek advice about a complaint (Chapter 25) or possible legal action (Chapter 26).

MORTGAGING THE HOME BY THE LOCAL AUTHORITY

Even if your home is being assessed as an asset, the local authority has no power to force you to sell the home to pay the fees. What they can do if fees are not paid is impose a type of mortgage (called a Charging Order) on the home[19].

This will ensure that their fees are paid when the home is sold. Unlike an ordinary mortgage, the charging order can be taken out without the consent of the home owner.

The local authority draw up the Charging Order in the form laid down by the regulations and register it in the relevant public register (the Register of Sasines or the Land Register). Once

---

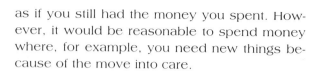

The notional capital rule: case study

A man goes into care with an income of £80 a week and a house worth £30,000. His care costs £200 a week. He gives the house to his son for nothing. The local authority decide this was done to avoid charges.

Because the resident has notional capital of over £8,000, he will be required to pay the full cost of care (£200). He will contribute £66.65 a week from his income (keeping a personal allowance of £13.35 at 1995/96 rates). The son will be charged £133.35 a week.

Under the "diminishing notional capital" rule, the value of the house will be deemed to reduce by £133.35 a week. It will therefore take roughly 3 years before the notional capital falls below £8,000, when the charges would be substantially reduced.

it has been recorded, they must notify the owner of the property of the Order and its effect.

This power can only be used where the property still belongs to the resident. It cannot be used to place a mortgage over property which has been disposed of by the resident.

The Charging Order can only be placed where the person is in arrears of payment of charges for residential care. The arrears can be any amount, however small. Once the Order is in place, it will also cover any future arrears[20].

Because there is a debt secured over the property, the net value of the house will go down as unpaid charges rise. This means that eventually the weekly charge may go down because the value of the house has been used up. Sometimes, nothing will happen under the Charging Order until the resident dies. At that point, the people winding up the estate (the executors) will have to pay off the fees before the house can be disposed of.

The authority can only take action during the resident's lifetime if:

- the resident is insolvent (ie unable to pay their debts and liable to be made bankrupt) *or*

- the resident attempts to sell or give away the property *or*

- action is taken by someone else with a mortgage over the property

If a mortgage is taken out by the local authority, they can also charge interest on the arrears of charges from the date of death of the resident. No interest is chargeable before death. The rate of interest is up to the local authority, although it must be "reasonable"[21].

What to do if a resident may receive property

The financial assessment means that a person in residential care who comes into money may get relatively little benefit. Most of the money may be used to pay for care.

Where possible, it may be a good idea to try to make arrangements to avoid money being assessed as belonging to the resident. One way of doing this might be to put the money into a **discretionary trust,** since these are relatively favourably treated under the DSS and local authority assessments[22].

This has been successfully done for:

- money left in wills or gifted by relatives

- payments of Criminal Injuries Compensation and personal injury awards[23]

- savings being administered by a hospital, which were placed in trust when the patient was discharged into the community

Expert advice is needed, since there are pitfalls:

- money which a claimant has an 'absolute entitlement' to claim is normally treated as belonging to the claimant

- a claimant putting his or her own money into trust may be guilty of 'intentional deprivation' (see above)

- the rules may change in future[24]

SUMMARY – KEY POINTS

- Your home is normally counted as an asset in calculating how much you can pay for your care. Any outstanding mortgage will be deducted, as well as 10% of the value, to cover sale costs.

- A part share is only counted for the value it has in its own right.

- There are cases where the home is not counted. These include:

  - temporary residents who will return home

  - some cases where relatives or other people still live in the home.

- The local authority may count a home as an asset even while it is being sold.

- A resident who gives away his or her home may still have to pay charges as if they owned property, if they gave it away deliberately to reduce their fees.

- A person who receives property for less than its real value may have to pay some of the care fees of the person who gave it away.

- The social work department can impose a mortgage on a resident's home if there are arrears of residential care fees.

- If a person in residential care is likely to come into money, it is worth seeing if this could be done through a trust.

NOTES

1   National Assistance (Assessment of Resources) Regulations 1992 SI 2977, reg 23 (1).

    Income Support (General) Regulations, reg 49 (1).

    Social Work Services Group Guidance Circular *National Assistance (Assessment of Resources) (Amendment No 2) Regulations 1993: Regulations and Guidance* issued January 21 1994 (hereafter referred to as Guidance Circular 21/1/94), paras 6.010 – 6.016.

2   Guidance Circular 21/1/94, paras 7.012 – 7.014.

    National Assistance (Assessment of Resources) Regulations 1992 SI 2977, reg 27 (2).

    Chief Adjudication Officer v Palfrey and others Court of Appeal 8/2/95. Times Law Report 17/2/95.

3   Income Support (General) Regulations, reg 52.

4   National Assistance (Assessment of Resources) Regulations, reg 27.

5   *"Temporary resident"* means a resident whose stay is unlikely to exceed 52 weeks, or, in exceptional circumstances, unlikely substantially to exceed 52 weeks – National Assistance (Assessment of Resources) Regulations, reg 2 (1).

6   National Assistance (Assessment of Resources) Regulations, Sched 4, para 1 as amended by 1994 SI 825. For temporary residents, the value of the home will also be ignored by the local authority if the resident is taking reasonable steps to sell it in order to buy another property to live in.

    Guidance Circular 9/5/94, para 7.002.

7   The Income Support (General) Regulations, Sched 10, para 1 state that a dwelling is only disregarded if it is occupied as the tenant's home. Schedule 3, para 4 states that, for the purpose of qualifying for help with mortgage costs, a person is treated as occupying a dwelling as his home for a temporary absence of up to 52 weeks if he intends to return and the property has not been rented out. We assume that the DSS would use the same definition of 'occupying' a home when deciding whether the value should be disregarded.

8   Income Support (General) Regulations, Sched 10, para 4.

    National Assistance (Assessment of Resources) Regulations, Sched 4, para 2 as amended by 1993 SI 964.

    Guidance Circular 21/1/94, paras 7.003 – 5.

9   Under the National Assistance Act 1948, s42.

10 National Assistance (Assessment of Resources) Regulations, Sched 4, para 18.

    Guidance Circular 21/1/94, para 7.007.

11 Income Support (General) Regulations, Sched 10, para 26.

12 National Assistance (Assessment of Resources) Regulations, reg 23 (1) (b).

    Guidance Circular 21/1/94, para 6.010.

13 National Assistance (Assessment of Resources) Regulations, reg 25(1).

    Guidance Circular 21/1/94, paras 6.056 – 6.067.

    Income Support (General) Regulations, reg 51.

14 National Assistance (Assessment of Resources) Regulations, reg 26.

    Income Support (General) Regulations, reg 51A.

15 Commissioner's Decision R(SB)38/85.

16 Adjudication Officers' Guidance 30308 – 30342 (May 1994 Issue).

17 Guidance Circular 21/1/94, paras 6.061 – 6.063.

18 Health and Social Services and Social Security Adjudications Act 1983 (hereafter HASSASSA), s21.

    Social Work Services Group Circular SW15/93.

19 HASSASSA, s23.

    Charging Orders (Residential Accommodation) (Scotland) Order 1993, SI 1516.

    Social Work Services Group Circular SW15/93.

20 Sometimes there will already be a mortgage over the property. Broadly speaking, any security recorded before the Charging Order would have first preference on the sale proceeds. Any security recorded later would rank behind the Charging Order. s13 of the Conveyancing and Feudal Reform Act 1979 applies to Charging Orders, subject to variations set out in 1993 SI 1516.

21 HASSASSA, s24.

22 Income Support (General) Regulations, regs 42 and 51.

    Guidance Circular 21/1/94, s10.

23 Trusts arising from personal injury awards have specific concessions in the regulations.

    Income Support (General) Regulations, Sched 10, para 12.

    National Assistance (Assessment of Resources) Regulations, Sched 4, para 10.

24 *Making a will*, a free leaflet from ENABLE, gives more details.

Local authority residential care

INTRODUCTION

Before April 1993, there were basically two categories of care (although there was some overlap). People in private and voluntary sector homes who could not pay their fees were mainly supported by the Department of Social Security (DSS). People in homes run by local authorities got very limited support from the DSS. The cost of their care was largely met by the local authority.

In April 1993, the costs of caring for new residents in the private and voluntary sector were largely transferred to the local authority. DSS benefits were intended to be made roughly equal, whether or not the claimant was at home or in care. However, local authority homes were kept on a different system and people in these homes still get less support from the DSS than people in private homes.

Before April 1993, residents in local authority homes even got a lower personal allowance than people in private homes. This anomaly has now been corrected. The resident is no worse off in a local authority home. It is the local authority that loses out, by getting less money from the DSS than private homes get.

The reason for keeping local authority homes on a different basis from private homes appears to be to encourage local authorities to move away from running their own homes and to make the maximum use of the independent sector.

People in local authority homes before April 1993 were subject to a financial assessment by the local authority to see how much they had to pay towards the cost of their care. This was on a different basis from the assessment for Income Support.

The assessment is now done on the same basis as for other types of residential care (see Chapters 9 and 10). Some people will lose out as a result of the change and there are transitional measures to protect people in that situation.

INCOME SUPPORT ENTITLEMENT

As we explain in Chapter 13, how much you get in Income Support is based on comparing:

- what the rules say your *resources* are, with
- what the rules say your *needs* are.

The assessment of the resources of a person in a local authority home claiming Income Support is exactly the same as for anyone else.

The difference is in the assessment of their needs. The rules say that a person living permanently in a local authority care home "needs" a fixed amount. This amount is set at the same level as the standard old age pension. A single claimant will receive £58.85 a week (as at April 1995)[1]. They will not receive a "residential allowance" or any of the normal premiums.

The resident will keep a personal allowance (£13.35 a week at 1995/96 rates) and will have to pay the rest to the local authority. (See page 46 for the local authority's discretion to allow a larger personal allowance to be retained. For respite care, see Chapter 6. For "less dependent" residents, see page 47).

LOCAL AUTHORITY ASSESSMENT OF CHARGES

Fixing the charges

Before April 1993, there was a standard maximum charge which people in local authority care could be asked to pay. People who were assessed as being unable to pay this were charged less. There was also a minimum rate. This was linked to Income Support levels. Under the new rules, there is no minimum charge. The maximum is not a standard rate but the actual cost of care for the individual person.

Assessing ability to pay

The old rules for deciding how much the resident could afford to pay were set out in Schedule 1 Part III of the Supplementary Benefits Act 1976. Some significant differences from the new rules were:

- People's savings began to be assessed at £1,200 (instead of £3,000)

- The assumed income from savings was £1 a week for every £200 (instead of £1 per £250)

- There was no maximum limit of savings after which the resident had to pay the full charge (the new rules say people with over £8000 pay the whole cost of their care)

- The rules about what income should be disregarded were different

- In general, the old rules were less detailed and gave the local authority more discretion

After April 1993, the local authority has to do the same assessment of ability to pay for people in local authority homes as it does for people being supported in private care (see Chapters 9 and 10).

Transitional protection

People who were already in care who are better off under the new rules should have received the benefit of this immediately the system changed in April 1993.

Some people will be worse off. (In particular, this is likely to apply to people with more than £8,000 in savings.) They will be entitled to **transitional protection** if they were already in local authority care before April 12 1993[2].

If a person who was in local authority care as at April 12 1993, *either* has more than £8,000 in savings *or* was more than £1 a week better off under the old income rules, the increase in their contribution is phased in over 3 years. Their contribution did not increase until April 1994. From April 1994 to April 1995, the resident pays one-third of the increase they would normally have to pay. From April 1995 to April 1996, they will pay two-thirds of the normal increase. All protection ceases in April 1996.

Changes in circumstances

There are complex rules to cover situations where a person who is getting transitional protection becomes better or worse off.

If someone loses income or capital so that they would pay less in charges than they are paying under the transitional protection, they will stop paying the protected rate. Instead they will pay on the basis of their actual income or savings[3].

If someone receives capital which would take them over the £8000 limit, they lose their protection and start paying the full rate for their care[4].

Otherwise, increased income or capital does not affect the protected amount[5].

NOTES

1   Income Support (General) Regulations, reg 21 and Sched 7, para 13.

2   National Assistance (Assessment of Resources) Regulations 1992 SI 2977, (as amended by 1994 SI 825), reg 8 and Sched 1. Guidance is in Social Work Services Group Circular SW4/1994, section 13.

3   National Assistance (Assessment of Resources) Regulations (as amended), Sched 1, para 9. The protection is also lost if the rate on the basis of the resident's actual income is less than £1 a week over the protected rate.

4   National Assistance (Assessment of Resources) Regulations (as amended), Sched 1, para 8 (8).

5   National Assistance (Assessment of Resources) Regulations (as amended), Sched 1, para 8. There is one exception. If the increase is because a third party is contributing towards the fees (see page 44), the charges under the old and new systems are recalculated and a new protected amount is set. However, this is unlikely to happen often. Relatives would normally only be contributing to a more expensive private home, not one run by a local authority.

People in residential care before April 1993

INTRODUCTION

We explained in Chapter 7 that, before the system changed in April 1993, people in residential care homes run by charities or private businesses could claim higher levels of Income Support. These were intended to meet most or even all of the home's fees. When the system changed, the idea was that the old rules would still apply for people who were already in care. This chapter explains:

- who can still claim higher levels of Income Support

- when people who are covered by the old system can get help from the social work department

INCOME SUPPORT ENTITLEMENT (PRESERVED RIGHTS)

Broadly speaking, most people who were living in a residential care home or nursing home on March 31 1993 will continue under the old arrangements. If they qualify financially for Income Support, they will have a **preserved right** to the old higher rates (sometimes called "board and lodgings allowances"). These allowances will continue to be uprated to meet inflation every year[1].

Who qualifies?

You are entitled to a preserved right if you were living in a home registered with the social work department as a residential care home or with the health board as a nursing home or private hospital as at March 31 1993. (Abbeyfield homes, or homes, run by housing associations, which provide care equivalent to residential care, will also qualify.)

You qualify even if you were paying your own fees at that date and only later need to claim Income Support.

You can still qualify if you had been living in one of these homes but were away on March 31 1993, provided your absence did not exceed a total period of up to 13 weeks (if you were a permanent resident), or 4 weeks (if you were a temporary resident).

If you were absent because you were in hospital, you can still qualify so long as your total period in hospital was not greater than 52 weeks[2].

You will keep the preserved right while you are in residential or nursing care provided any future, single period of absence is no greater than 4 weeks (for temporary residents), 13 weeks (permanent residents), or 52 weeks (for people who go into hospital).

What if I move?

You can keep your preserved rights if you move from one care home to another. Again there can be a gap of 4, 13, or 52 weeks between the two placements, depending on whether you were originally a temporary or permanent resident or spent time in a hospital.

Special cases

There are some situations where people who were living in a care home before April 1993 will not have preserved rights.

- *Small homes.* Originally, a resident who was living in a home which cared for less than 4 residents and who was paying his or her own fees before April 1993 did not have preserved rights. This is still the case in England and Wales, but in Scotland they were given preserved rights as from October 1994[3].

- *Homes run by close relatives.* If you have lived since before April 1993 in a home which counts as a care home, but is run by a close relative, you cannot claim the higher "board and lodging" allowance of Income Support. However, if you move to a home which is not run by a close relative (or if the ownership of the home changes), you will have a preserved right[4].

If you have preserved rights but you move (or the home changes) so that you are being looked after by a close relative, you will lose your preserved rights. You may need to approach the social work department for help (see Chapter 8)[5].

NOTE: The rules covering people in homes run by close relatives are very complicated and we have not had space to give all the details (for example, there may be a possibility of claiming Housing Benefit). If you are in this situation, you should consider getting expert benefit advice.

How much Income Support can I get?

The way Income Support is calculated is explained in Chapter 13.

If you have preserved rights, you can claim the fee charged by the home, up to a maximum limit. The limit depends on the degree of care being provided[6]. In addition, you are entitled to a personal allowance (£13.35 as at April 1995). The personal allowance is meant to be the resident's own money for their day-to-day expenses.

The appropriate maximum fee does not depend on the category you fall into, but the type of care being provided. For example, a person in a nursing home for people who are terminally ill may be entitled to payment at that rate if she receives that degree of care, even if she is not herself terminally ill[7].

WHAT IF THE FEES ARE TOO HIGH?

It is quite common for homes' charges to be more than the maximum which the Department of Social Security (DSS) will pay.

If the board and lodging payments are not enough to meet the actual fees, you may have to be supported by relatives or friends[8]. Another possibility is that the home may ask you to pay over some or all of your personal allowance. This is not illegal but many people feel it is a bad practice because it leaves you with no money of your own. If it happens, it may be worth taking the issue up with the body which registers and inspects the home (see page 39).

The social work department may be able to give financial help but the Government has strictly limited the circumstances where they can do this if you have preserved rights.

The basic rule[9] is that local authorities have no power to pay for accommodation for people who were already in residential or nursing care as at March 31 1993.

The intention seems to be to avoid money which has been transferred to local authorities to deal with new cases being used up on people who are already receiving higher levels of state benefits. However, it is clear that this could put the places of many people with preserved rights at risk if their benefits are not enough to meet their fees. Therefore the Government has issued regulations and guidance saying when people can have preserved rights and still be "topped-up" by the social work department[10].

Unfortunately, some people have still lost out. The BBC TV programme *Watchdog* reported on the case of a woman in a nursing home where the charges were higher than the DSS maximum. The social services department were willing to help her when her money ran out, but could only do so legally if she moved to another home.

Who can be financially supported by the social work department?

- Anyone who was already being financially supported by the social work department on March 31 1993 (in other words, their fees were being "topped up"). This would normally apply to people under pensionable age who have expensive care needs.

- Anyone who does not have preserved rights. This includes the special cases listed above. If they later gain preserved rights because their situation changes, the social work department will no longer be able to support them under this power.

- Anyone who loses their preserved rights. For example, people who have been absent from residential care for longer than the prescribed periods, then go back into care.

- Anyone under pensionable age (65 for a man and 60 for a woman).

- Anyone over pensionable age who had been financially supported by the local authority before reaching pensionable age.

NOTE: There is a restriction to the last two categories if the resident has been evicted or threatened with eviction from their care home or nursing home. In that situation the social work department can only support the person if they go to live in a home which is not owned or managed by the person who ran the home they were being evicted from (unless they had to move because the home was closing down). This is to prevent homes from "holding local authorities to ransom" by threatening to evict residents if they do not get money from the local authority on top of Income Support.

- People over pensionable age who are threatened with eviction from a residential care home. If a residential care home is about to close or a resident will lose their place in it, the local authority can support them in a new place. They cannot place the person in a home run by the person who ran the resident's previous home unless the whole home has closed down. Again, this is to avoid undue pressure being placed on local authorities by private homes.

NOTE: This last category does not normally apply to people who were in a nursing home (rather than a residential care home), or who are assessed by a local authority as needing a nursing home place. The only situation where the local authority can fund a nursing home place under this power is where a person lost their place in a residential care home and was then supported by the local authority. If they later move to a nursing home and are again threatened with eviction, the local authority can continue to give financial support. The justifications for treating nursing homes differently are presumably that local authorities had no powers to arrange nursing home places prior to April 1 1993 and such homes also get higher levels of DSS support than residential care homes.

In all cases where a local authority decides to help a person with preserved rights, it must be done after a community care assessment (except in an emergency). (See Chapter 2.) The payment arrangements will be the same as for people going into care after April 1 1993 even though the amount of Income Support may be higher because of the preserved rights.

SUMMARY – KEY POINTS

- Most people who were living in residential or nursing care on April 1 1993 and were getting Income Support to pay the fees will have preserved rights, and the DSS will continue to pay the fees.

- You will also have preserved rights if you were living in residential care on that date and only later claim Income Support.

- If you leave residential care for certain periods you may lose your preserved rights.

- If the DSS benefits are not enough to pay the fees, there are rules limiting the power of the social work department to help.

- These rules should not be a problem if you are under pensionable age. The social work department can also help if you might lose your place in the home, but you might have to move.

NOTES

1 Income Support (General) Regulations 1987 SI 1967 (especially regs 19 and 21) as amended by Social Security Benefits (Amendments Consequential Upon The Introduction Of Community Care) Regulations 1992 SI 3147.

2 Income Support (General) Regulations, reg 19 (1ZB). A person is defined as a *"permanent resident"* if the home is *"his principal place of abode"*. Otherwise, they will be treated as a *"temporary resident"* – reg 19 (17 H).

3 Income Support (General) Regulations, regs 19 (1ZE) and 19 (1ZEA).

4 Income Support (General) Regulations, reg 19 (1ZC).

5 Income Support (General) Regulations, reg 19 (1ZG).

6 Income Support (General) Regulations, Sched 4. As at April 1995, the weekly maximum charges are:

	Residential care home	Nursing home
Old age	£197	£295
Mental illness	£207	£296
Drug/alcohol dependency	£207	£296
Mental handicap	£237	£301
Physical disability	£267	£331
Terminal illness	£197	£295
Old age and blind/ high care needs	£227	£295
Others	£197	£295

Note – there are different rates for London.

7 Adjudication Officer's Guidance 28120 – 28123 (March 1994 Issue).

Income Support (General) Regulations, Sched 4, para 10.

Another example would be a home for people with severe learning disabilities, some of whom are also physically disabled. If everyone got the same degree of care that the physically disabled residents got, they might all be able to claim the physical disability rate.

8 These payments will be ignored in calculating the income of the resident for Income Support – Income Support (General) Regulations, Sched 9, para 15 (2). However, 'liable relative payments' will not be disregarded (see page 49) .

9 NHS & Community Care Act 1990, s57 – introducing new s86A to Social Work (Scotland) Act 1968.

10 Residential Accommodation (Relevant Premises, Ordinary Residence and Exemptions) Regulations 1993 SI 477.

Social Work Services Group Circular SW11/93 – *Local authorities' powers to make arrangements for people in independent sector residential care and nursing homes on March 31 1993.*

Residential services – benefits in care

INTRODUCTION

Before you make a decision about moving into a care home, you will want to know how this affects you financially. The previous chapters explained the very complex rules about paying for care, but you may also need to work out how going into care might affect your and your family's Social Security benefits. There is only room here to mention some of the main differences. Benefit rules change very frequently. It is a good idea to seek advice from a welfare rights expert about your own situation[1].

Remember, most of these benefits will be counted towards your income in deciding how much you can pay for your care, if you are being cared for through an arrangement with the social work department. The main exception is Disability Living Allowance (mobility component).

COUPLES AND FAMILIES

If you are a member of a couple, moving into care may affect benefit for you and your partner. Married couples who live together are treated as a single "unit" for many welfare benefits. The same applies to unmarried couples who live together as if they were married (but not to same sex couples)[2].

Once you move into permanent care, you and your partner will be treated as separate individuals. You might get more benefits or less, depending on your circumstances.

INCOME SUPPORT

Summary – key points

Income Support is an extremely important benefit and its rules are very complex. It is the basic benefit intended to ensure that everyone has enough to live on.

The basic idea of the community care rules is that people get roughly the same Income Support whether they live at home or in care. However, it is not as simple as that. These are the main differences:

- Couples are treated separately if one or both of them are permanently in residential care[3]. Each person's entitlement will depend on their own needs and other income and savings.

- People in residential care receive a residential allowance (£51 a week at 1995/96 rates) to help with their care costs. This is instead of Housing Benefit.

- People in residential/nursing care may lose the Severe Disability Premium.

- Carers who receive Carers Premium will lose it after 8 weeks if the person they care for goes into care.

People in care before April 1 1993 are covered by special rules. These are explained in Chapter 12. People in homes run by local authorities are covered by special rules which are explained in Chapter 11.

DETAILS

In deciding your entitlement to Income Support, the DSS look at your *needs* and your *resources*, according to their rules[4].

The rules for working out resources are similar to the rules the social work department use in deciding how much you have to pay for care (see Chapters 9 and 10, which also explain the main differences).

Calculating needs

In working out how much you need, the DSS looks at three elements: a personal allowance, special premiums and housing costs.

The law and your rights to community care

The Personal Allowance

This is a standard amount to cover basic living costs. It is the same whether you are in or out of residential care. In April 1995 the amount for a single person aged 25 or over was £46.50.

NOTE – If you are in residential care, this personal allowance paid by Income Support is not the same as the personal allowance you are allowed to keep after paying your share of the costs of the care – see page 46.

Premiums

These are additions to cover people in particular groups, eg pensioners, people with disabilities and lone parents. With one exception, claimants have the same entitlement whether or not they are living in residential or nursing care or at home.

The exception is Severe Disability Premium. This is additional Income Support payable to severely disabled people. It is only payable while the claimant receives Attendance Allowance or Disability Living Allowance (care component). These benefits often cease when a person is in residential care (see below). If that happens, at that stage the Severe Disability Premium will stop.

In some cases, the rules have the opposite effect. If a person is in a couple, he or she may not get Severe Disability Premium while they live with their partner. If they go into care, they will be treated separately from their partner. This means they might qualify for Severe Disability Premium, at least for as long as they still get Attendance Allowance or Disability Living Allowance (care component).

There is also a premium for carers. If you are a carer claiming Income Support, who would be entitled to Invalid Care Allowance (see below) you are entitled to a Carers Premium (£12.60 at April 1995). If the person you care for moves into residential care so that you are no longer entitled to Invalid Care Allowance, you will lose the Carers Premium. However, there is an 8-week extension. This means you still get the benefit for 8 weeks after you stop caring[5].

Housing costs

These do not normally include rent since this is covered by Housing Benefit. However, some people can get additional Income Support to pay mortgage interest.

People living permanently in residential or nursing care can claim a "residential allowance" as part of their Income Support entitlement. This is a standard sum (£51 a week as at April 1995) to cover their accommodation needs. They will not receive any of the other elements of Income Support which cover housing costs and they will not receive Housing Benefit. (For respite care, see Chapter 6.)

People can continue to receive the residential allowance during a temporary absence from the care home of up to 3 weeks (or 6 weeks if they are absent because they are in hospital)[6].

INVALID CARE ALLOWANCE

You may be entitled to this if you care for a person who qualifies for disability benefits. You have to be providing care for more than 35 hours a week. If the person you care for moves permanently into full time residential care, you are less likely to be providing that level of care. You may lose the benefit. However, if the person is at home some of the time so that the 35 hours a week test is passed, the benefit could still be claimed. If you are not sure, seek advice.

DISABILITY LIVING ALLOWANCE AND ATTENDANCE ALLOWANCE

There are special rules for Disability Living Allowance (DLA) and Attendance Allowance. DLA has two elements – mobility component (replacing the old Mobility Allowance) and care component (which partially replaced Attendance Allowance). These are treated completely differently.

Disability Living Allowance (mobility component)

You can continue to claim DLA (mobility) in residential or nursing care. This is not counted in the local authority assessment. In other words you can keep this benefit and it should not be used to meet your care costs[7].

Disability Living Allowance (care component) and Attendance Allowance

DLA (care component) and Attendance Allowance are benefits meant to help disabled people pay for care. The Government argues that if you are getting public money to pay for care from somewhere else (like the social work department), you shouldn't get DLA (care component) or Attendance Allowance. However, it is not as simple as that.

You *can* still get DLA (care component) or Attendance Allowance when you are in a care home in the following situations:

- for the first 28 days you are in care (If you are using respite care regularly – Chapter 6 explains how this applies – you should take advice to see if you can arrange your respite to keep as much benefit as possible.)

- if you are terminally ill and in a hospice[8]

- if you are paying for your own care in a private or voluntary home without getting financial help from the social work department[9]

NOTE: there has been some confusion over whether it is only possible to keep Attendance Allowance if you arranged the place yourself, without going through the social work department. However, we understand that some people have succeeded in keeping Attendance Allowance or DLA (care component) after being placed in residential care by the social work department, so long as the resident is paying all the costs from his or her own income and savings.

Using the benefits system to pay for your care[10]

The Government seems to have assumed that no one would get enough money from Social Security benefits alone to pay for a place in a care home. However, some people have managed to obtain a package of benefits which is enough to fund a cheap place. For example, a pensioner who is entitled to the higher rate of Attendance Allowance might receive the following benefits (at 1994/95 rates).

INCOME SUPPORT	
Personal Allowance	46.50
Higher Pensioner Premium	25.15
Residential Accommodation Allowance	51.00
Severe Disability Premium	35.05
ATTENDANCE ALLOWANCE	46.70
Total	£204.40

There has been considerable confusion over two questions:

Do the rules allow this?

The DLA and Attendance Allowance rules seem to suggest that a person who gets Income Support while in care cannot get DLA (care component) or Attendance Allowance as well. However, at the moment, people have succeeded in claiming the benefits shown above, provided they are getting no financial help from the social work department.

What happens if the social work department are involved?

There is no doubt that the above package of benefits is not available to anyone whose care fees are being partly met by the social work department. What is less clear is whether you will lose Attendance Allowance or DLA (care), and Severe Disability Premium, if your place is arranged by the social work department after a community care assessment, without them making a financial contribution.

The DLA and Attendance Allowance rules disqualify people whose costs *are, or may be,* partly met under social work legislation. What this actually means is not clear. Most people who have written about paying for care through benefits have said that it must be done without the social work department being involved.

What are the pros and cons of paying for care through benefits?

Pros

- If you don't want the social work department involved, you can avoid it.

- If you are selling your house, it may be financially beneficial. This is because the DSS ignore the value of the house while it is being sold (normally for up to 26 weeks). The social work department do not and would claw back charges once the house is eventually sold. (Of course, if you live in the care home long enough after the house is sold, the difference will cancel out. The proceeds of the sale will go towards fees until your savings are down to £8000 under both systems.)

Cons

- If there is no community care assessment, you may not be getting the most appropriate help. The social work department might have been able to arrange a package of care for you which met your needs better.

- There is no guarantee that you will be able to keep a weekly amount for your own personal expenses.

- If you did it to save money while your home was being sold, the social work department may not be prepared to continue the place once the money runs out.

SOCIAL FUND (COMMUNITY CARE GRANTS)

Community Care Grants can be made by the DSS to help people remain in the community or move into it from institutional care. They are not normally paid to people living in residential or nursing care, because the DSS regards this as being in institutional care. This applies even if the person may have moved there from an institution such as a hospital. Some people have tried to argue that some kinds of residential homes should not be counted as institutional care, but this usually has not succeeded. Anyone trying to argue this would need advice from a benefits expert[11].

INDEPENDENT LIVING FUNDS

There are now two funds – the Independent Living (Extension) Fund and the Independent Living (1993) Fund to help with personal care for people with severe disabilities. Neither is payable to people in residential/nursing care[12].

HOUSING BENEFIT

You cannot get Housing Benefit to pay for residential or nursing care. You may be entitled to Housing Benefit if you are living in an unregistered home or hostel (see page 40). If you are temporarily in a care home, you may still get Housing Benefit to pay for the rent of your own home (see page 37).

NOTES

1   For information on benefits, see CPAG – *National welfare benefits handbook* and *Guide to non means tested benefits*. Also the *Disability rights handbook,* published by the Disability Alliance.

2   Social Security (Contributions & Benefits) Act 1992, ss136 and 137.

3   Income Support (General) Regulations 1987, reg 16(3).

4   The regulations are the Income Support (General) Regulations 1987 SI 1967 (as amended). More details are in Income Support leaflet IS 50 – *Help if you live in a residential care home or nursing home,* published by the Benefits Agency.

5   Income Support (General) Regulations, Sched 2, para 14ZA.

6   Income Support (General) Regulations, Sched 2, para 2A(4A).

7   Income Support (General) Regulations, Sched 9, para 6.

8   Social Security (Disability Living Allowance) Regulations 1991 SI 2890, reg 10(6).

    Social Security (Attendance Allowance) Regulations 1991 SI 2740, reg 8(4).

9   Disability Living Allowance Regulations 9 and 10(8).

    Attendance Allowance Regulations 7 and 8.

10 This option was highlighted in "Loopholes" by Gerald Wistow and Melanie Henwood in *Community Care* 17/2/94. It has also been promoted in a magazine for care home owners *This caring business.*

11 See *R v Social Fund inspector ex parte Ibrahim* High Court 9/11/93 (discussed in the Social Fund Annual Report for 1993/94). In that case, a Social Fund application was refused for someone coming out of a hostel for single women, because the Social Fund inspector decided this was not institutional care. Therefore, leaving it did not count as moving into the community. The inspector's decision, which was upheld by the Court, said:

    "Institutional or residential care is not defined in the directions. In my opinion, it means a place which assumes responsibility for the well-being of people who have been unable to cope in the community. The Social Fund guide suggests [para 5141] that it means a place where the residents receive a significant amount of care or supervision, such as a hospital, nursing home, or residential care home."

    The main rules are set out in binding directions issued by the Secretary of State, particularly directions 4 and 25 – 27. They are reproduced in the *Disability rights handbook.*

12 Under the Disability (Grants) Act 1993, the Independent Living (Extension) Fund inherited cases from the original Independent Living Fund, which was wound up in 1993. It will not accept new applications. The Independent Living (1993) Fund was set up by the Government but is run by trustees under a deed of trust. It can pay for help to support a disabled person living at home, provided they are already getting services worth £200 from the social work department. For further details, see the *Disability rights handbook* or contact the Fund at PO Box 183, Nottingham NG8 3RD (and see page 31).

Housing and community care

This chapter looks at your legal rights to get help with your housing and tries to explain the duties of the different organisations involved.

INTRODUCTION

Community care aims to support people in their own homes wherever possible. People need to live in houses which suit their needs, and they may need extra help at home to help them stay there. Housing departments, social work departments and health boards will need to work together to make sure that this happens[1].

This chapter is in six sections:

- The role of housing agencies

- Help for people at home. (This looks at getting more help in the home, getting home adaptations, and getting help when a carer dies.)

- Moving to a new home. (This looks at getting help from the social work department and housing department, moving to a different area and help for homeless people.)

- Your legal rights in residential care or supported accommodation. (This looks at tenancy agreements and your rights as a tenant, and the right to buy local authority housing.)

- Carers' rights (This looks at carers' rights to take over tenancies if the tenant dies.)

- The final section looks at where to go for advice and help on housing matters.

THE ROLE OF HOUSING AGENCIES

There are a number of bodies providing public sector housing in Scotland. They include:

- district councils

- Scottish Homes (this funds housing associations and also owns its own houses)

- housing associations and co-operatives

- voluntary bodies and charities

- New Town Development Corporations (these will be wound up by December 1996)

District councils have the main strategic role of considering overall housing need in their area. When doing this, they must consider the special needs of people who are chronically sick and disabled[2]. They should then make plans to meet these needs.

The Government believes that in the past community care has not been properly considered in looking at housing (and vice versa[3]). It wants housing plans to set clear targets for providing housing for community care groups[4]. It also encourages councils to set up housing forums and to prepare assessments of the need for housing for community care users[5].

HELP FOR PEOPLE AT HOME

Getting extra help in the home

You may want to stay in your home if you can get extra help. You might need help with domestic tasks such as cleaning and cooking or help with personal care, such as help getting dressed or with baths. You can, of course, arrange this yourself, and you would not need to see a social worker.

But if you cannot make the arrangements yourself or if you may need help towards the cost of care, you should ask the social work department for an assessment of your needs (see Chapter 2). The person from the social work department will help you work out what you need.

Remember that if you are chronically sick or disabled you may have a legal right to help. You might be able to stay at home if you had better recreational or leisure facilities or if you had help with transport to get to a lunch club or day centre. If the social work department decides that this is what you need, it must be arranged. You may also have a legal right to a home help or domiciliary services (see Chapter 3).

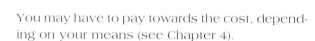

You may have to pay towards the cost, depending on your means (see Chapter 4).

Home adaptations

If you have become disabled or sick, your house may need adaptations or equipment to make it more safe or convenient. You should contact the social work department to ask for an assessment of your needs. Grants may be available to help with the cost. For more details see page 22.

When a carer dies

If you were living with a relative and they die, you may inherit their district council tenancy. (See page 73 for the rules.)

If the person who died was caring for you, you might think that you will not be able to stay in the house without them. But you might be able to stay if you can get some extra support. **You should not give up the tenancy until you have spoken to the social work department.** They might be able to arrange for you to have some help at home.

MOVING TO A NEW HOME

Getting help from the social work department

If you want to move to a house or residential home which can give you more support, you can arrange this yourself and you do not need to contact the social work department. But you might want to ask them for advice about what is available. They should have a list of residential facilities in your area. Many of the organisations listed at the back of this book will be able to give you advice, too.

If you need help to work out what would be best, or help with the cost, you should contact the social work department for an assessment of your needs (see Chapter 2). They will consult the district council about your housing needs. You might want to go into an ordinary house nearer family or friends, into sheltered housing or into residential care or a nursing home. We look at residential care in more detail in Chapters 7 to 13.

If you are going into ordinary housing with support arranged by the social work department, your social worker will have to work out with you and your new landlord who is responsible for what. If you need help in paying rent, claiming benefits or in running the home, you will need to know who will help you. It could be a person from the social work department or the housing department or a support worker from a voluntary organisation or housing association.

Getting on the council waiting list

If you want housing from the district council, you will normally have to go on a waiting list. Many councils have "points" systems, and you can get extra points if you have medical or other special needs.

Extra points mean that you may get a house more quickly or get offered a better house. Remember you will have to tell the council of anything which might give you more priority. The housing department can give you details of the system in your area.

What if you want to move nearer to relatives or carers to get extra help? Will you be able to put your name on the waiting list? Often you need to live in the area already or work there before you can go on the list.

However, if you are 60 or over and you want to move somewhere to be near a younger relative, the council must put your name on the waiting list.

If you are under 60 and there are special social or medical reasons why you want to live in a particular area, you can go onto the list, too[6].

For instance, you might want to live near friends or relatives who could help you, or you might go to a day centre or hospital and want to live near to it. In both these cases you should be able to apply for district council housing in that area.

The Government has advised district councils that they should have housing policies which are sufficiently flexible to take account of the needs of all community care groups[7].

Obtaining housing as a homeless person

If you have community care needs and you are homeless, and qualify on other grounds, the housing department may have a legal duty to offer you permanent housing[8]. This could be the case if you are vulnerable because of:

- old age
- mental health problems
- a learning disability
- a physical disability or
- some other special reason[9] (This could be sickness or youth; or liability to exploitation, or any other circumstances which make you vulnerable. If the housing department think you might be vulnerable, they should ask the social work department for advice[10].)

If you are homeless you can apply to either the housing department or the social work department for help[11].

The law and your rights to community care

Homelessness: overcrowded and unsuitable homes

You may have somewhere to live which is unsuitable for your needs. You may still qualify as a homeless person. The law says that if your house is overcrowded and damaging to your health you have the same rights as a homeless person[12]. **If the place you live is somewhere where it is not reasonable for you to live, you can ask for rehousing[13].**

If you are disabled, for instance, you might be able to argue that it is not reasonable for you to live in a tower block with a lift which keeps breaking.

If you are ill and your house is very damp and damaging your health, you could ask the housing department to consider you as a homeless person.

If you have mental health problems you might say that living in bed and breakfast accommodation is adding to your stress and not helping your recovery.

The law is very complicated, and if you think you should be treated as homeless even if you have somewhere to live, you should seek advice. See pages 160-162.

The housing department may ask the social work department for help in working out your needs. The social work department must give the housing department whatever help is reasonable in the circumstances[14]. If you go to the social work department as a homeless person with community care needs, they must tell the housing department and ask them what help they will offer you[15].

A carer may also have priority for homeless person's housing. If you live with someone who is vulnerable, you qualify for help. You also qualify if you could reasonably be expected to live with the person but are not now doing so. It would be reasonable to expect that a member of the person's family or a carer might live with them.

You should be given immediate temporary housing while the housing department makes enquiries into your case. If the housing department decides that you qualify for permanent housing, it must supply this.

If you are coming out of hospital, you should not be discharged into homeless persons' accommodation[16]. Proper housing should be arranged for you before you are discharged. If this does not happen, you should complain (see Chapter 25).

LEGAL RIGHTS OF TENANTS AND PEOPLE IN RESIDENTIAL CARE

Types of housing agreement

Your legal rights as a resident of community care housing depend on what kind of housing you have.

Tenancy agreements

If you live in housing owned by a local authority or a public body, such as Scottish Homes or a new town development corporation, and you have a tenancy agreement, you will be a "*secure tenant*". The same applies if your landlord is a registered housing association and your tenancy began before 1989.

If your landlord is a voluntary organisation, or a private individual or company, you will probably be what the law calls an "*assured tenant*". You will also be an assured tenant if your landlord is a housing association, and the tenancy was created after 1988.

Secure and assured tenants have certain rights. The most important right is called "security of tenure". This means that you can only be asked to leave in certain circumstances, laid down by law[17].

Occupancy agreements

If you are in housing which provides support or personal care, you may not have a tenancy agreement. Your agreement may be called an "occupancy agreement" or a "residents' agreement", or it may have some other name.

The agreement will spell out the circumstances in which you might be asked to leave. If you do not break the agreement, you can only be asked to leave at the end of the period of the agreement. Even then you cannot be forced to go until the landlord has got a court order.

The law about whether a person is a secure tenant or just an occupant is very complex. It does not just depend on what the agreement says. If you are being evicted, you may want to seek legal advice.

The law and your rights to community care

Hostel residents

You may not have a written agreement, but you should be given some written information explaining your rights and responsibilities while you are in the hostel. You should be told how long you can stay for and what kinds of things might mean you have to leave sooner. If you are asked to leave a hostel, your rights will depend on whether you are a tenant or simply an occupant. You would need to get legal advice.

Signing residents' agreements

When you move into any new accommodation, you should get a written agreement from the provider of the housing spelling out your rights and the rules of the house. You may also get a tenants' handbook with rules about pets, cleaning, visitors etc.

(See Chapter 23 for more information about signing contracts. Chapter 20 explains what happens if the new resident is not able to understand a contract.)

Keeping to the agreement

If you do not do what your residents' agreement says, you could lose your house. If you do not pay your rent or other charges when they are due or if you do not keep the property in good condition, the landlord may be able to end the agreement. You should try to discuss any difficulties before this happens. You could tell either your landlord or the social work department.

Remember that the landlord must also do the things the agreement says they will do. If this does not happen, you should ask why not. If you are not satisfied, you may want to complain or take legal advice. See Chapters 25 and 26.

Protection against eviction

If you have a tenancy and the landlord wants you to leave, you must be given a "Notice to Quit" by the landlord. This is in a special form and must spell out your rights.

If you are not a tenant but you have some other kind of agreement, the agreement will generally tell you about how you can be asked to leave. It will probably say that notice should be given in writing. The agreement may give you the right to appeal against the decision to ask you to leave. You may want to complain if you think the decision to ask you to leave is unfair. See Chapter 25.

> ## Before you sign
>
> You should read the residents' agreement before you sign it. You should make sure you understand everything it says. If anything is not clear, you should ask questions. If you disagree with something, you should ask if it can be changed. If you need help to do this, ask the social work department.

If you live in a hostel, you may be asked to leave a hostel without any written notice, unless the hostel has said it will give you written notice.

Everyone (tenants, residents of care homes and most hostel dwellers) has protection against being physically evicted from a house. **It is a criminal offence to try to evict someone by force or to harass them into leaving**[18]. If you refuse to go, the landlord will have to go to court to get an order to remove you.

The right to buy

Many council tenants and tenants of housing association properties have the right to buy their houses. However certain groups of tenants receiving community care do not have the right to buy.

You do not have the right to buy if you live in sheltered housing which has a warden and a call system and is designed for pensioners or disabled people[19].

You do not have the right to buy if your house is owned by a housing association and is in a group of up to 14 houses and normally at least 50% of the houses are let to people with mental health problems, a learning disability, a physical handicap or addiction to alcohol or drugs[20].

If you live in a house which is not sheltered housing but which is designed or adapted for use by elderly people, you may be able to buy the house, but the landlord may insist on being given the right of "pre-emption". This means that if you want to sell, the landlord has the right to buy it back from you.

If your landlord does not want to sell "amenity" housing, he or she can apply to the Secretary of State for Scotland for an order saying that the house should not be sold[21].

If you want to buy your house, you should seek advice. Remember, if you buy your house and later move into residential care, the house may have to be sold to meet the fees. See Chapter 10.

CARERS' RIGHTS

If you have been looking after a relative who was the tenant of a district council house and they die, you might have the right to take over the tenancy.

Succeeding to a tenancy

You have the right to take over a district council tenancy if the tenant dies and you were living with them before they died[22]. You have this right if you are:

- the husband or wife of the tenant or

- someone who was living with the tenant as husband or wife or

- a member of the tenant's family and you have been living in the house as your main home during the 12 months before the tenant died

Tenants of other public landlords have a similar right. This includes regional councils, new town development corporations, Scottish Homes, and fire or police authorities. It also includes housing associations, if your tenancy started in 1988 or before[23].

If the landlord is a private individual or company, a voluntary organisation or a housing association[24], you can also sometimes take over the tenancy. You can if you are the husband or wife of the tenant and were living with them when they died. Relatives can also take over tenancies if they were living with the person for at least two years before they died[25].

Some tenancy agreements give rights to other carers to take over when the person dies; you should check.

When you take over a new tenancy you gain all the rights of the old tenant. The most important of these is security of tenure: you cannot be asked to leave. However, if the property is specially adapted or sheltered accommodation the landlord may ask you to move to another property if you do not need the special accommodation[26]. The landlord would have to offer you a suitable alternative.

GETTING HELP OR ADVICE

Many of these matters are very complicated, and you may need further advice. Any of the following could give advice:

- a Shelter Housing Aid Centre

- a housing advice centre run by your district council

- a Citizens Advice Bureau

- a Law Centre or Legal Services Agency advocacy project (see pages 160-162).

NOTES

1 The Scottish Office has given advice about how this should be done in *Community care: the housing dimension* (Circular SW7/1994). (This circular gives a lot of policy guidance which will be of interest to campaigning groups and advisers.)

2 Housing (Scotland) Act 1981, s1.

3 *Community care: the housing dimension*, para 1.3.

4 *Community care: the housing dimension*, para1.8.

5 *Community care: the housing dimension*, paras 3.7 and 3.17.

6 Housing (Scotland) Act 1987, s19(2).

7 *Community care: the housing dimension*, para 5.2.

8 Under the Housing (Scotland) Act 1987.

9 Housing (Scotland) Act 1987, s25(1)(c).

10 See the case of *Kelly v Monklands District Council* 1986 Scots Law Times, page 169.

11 If you are too ill to understand the nature of the application, because of a mental illness, a learning disability or dementia, for example, the housing department may not accept your application. This is because of a recent English House of Lords case, which said that a person had to be able to understand the application for it to be valid. *R v London Borough of Tower Hamlets ex parte Begum* [1993] 25 Housing Law Reports, 319, House of Lords.

12 Housing (Scotland) Act 1987, s32(5).

13 Housing (Scotland) Act 1987, s24(2A). This new provision was inserted by the Law Reform (Miscellaneous Provisions) Act 1990.

14 Housing (Scotland) Act 1987, s38.

15 Social Work (Scotland) Act 1968, s12A(3). (See Chapter 2.)

16 *Community care: the housing dimension*, para 3.24.1.

17 For further details about tenants' rights, see C M G Himsworth *Housing law in Scotland*. It is a reasonably non-technical guide to a very complicated subject. There is a free leaflet on assured tenancies: *Assured tenancies in Scotland: a guide for private landlords and tenants* is available from Citizens Advice Bureaux and Housing Advice Centres.

18 Rent (Scotland) Act 1984, s22 and Housing (Scotland) Act 1988, s36 and s37. This protection is not given to people living in hostels run by local authorities, Scottish Homes or registered housing associations. Housing (Scotland) Act 1988, s40.

19 Housing (Scotland) Act 1987, s61(4)(a).

20 Housing (Scotland) Act 1987, s61 (4)(f). For further details on the right to buy, see Himsworth, mentioned at footnote 17 above.

21 Housing (Scotland) Act 1987, s69. See Himsworth, para 8.7.

22 See Housing (Scotland) Act 1987, s52.

23 For further details see Himsworth, paras 5.6 and 5.8.

24 Provided the tenancy began after 1989.

25 Housing (Scotland) Act 1988, s46.

26 For public sector tenants, see Himsworth (above) page 76, paras 11 – 13 and page 103, footnote 6 for "group homes". Housing (Scotland) Act 1988, Sched 5, Part II, Ground 9 for assured tenancies.

Health services: how the NHS is organised

INTRODUCTION

The National Health Service (NHS) has, since it was founded, played a major part in providing care for people who are elderly or disabled. It has never been easy to draw a line between the type of services which the NHS provides and those provided by social work departments. This is one of the reasons why Sir Roy Griffiths' report[1] felt that community care services were poorly organised. Without clear responsibilities, it is easy for services to duplicate each other or, more seriously, not be provided at all.

This is one reason why there has been a move towards defining more strictly what the NHS should do compared with what local authorities should do. Local authorities are now supposed to be the main providers of community care or "social care". The NHS is to provide "health care" (see page 84 for an explanation of the difference).

There are other pressures which have added to this need to clarify who does what. When money gets tight, organisations become anxious to avoid spending scarce resources on things which they could argue are other people's responsibility.

The fact that the NHS is free, but people who use social work services may be means tested, has created anomalies where two people might be getting a similar service but only one has to pay for it. We look at this on pages 83-85.

The other major change, which was happening long before the recent community care reforms, is the move away from large institutions. Psychiatric, mental, and geriatric hospitals have been closing down for more than 20 years. It has been increasingly recognised that they provided a poor quality of life for many people who did not need that kind of service.

Over the next few years, there will be a move away from health services funded by the NHS to services arranged by local authorities. However, there is still a lot of money tied up in NHS budgets and properties and it will take a long time before that is transferred to community care services.

What this all means for service users is that they may find their care arrangements being transferred from one body to another (Chapter 16 discusses this). Even worse, they may find they do not get a proper service at all because of arguments about who should pay for it. This chapter sets out the legal responsibilities of the NHS and how it should work with local authorities to deliver community care.

THE STRUCTURE AND ROLE OF THE NATIONAL HEALTH SERVICE

It is the job of the Secretary of State for Scotland to ensure a *"comprehensive and integrated health service in Scotland"*[2]. This is the National Health Service, which works through various different bodies.

Health boards and NHS Trusts

There are 15 health boards which cover the whole of Scotland. It is the job of each board to make arrangements to provide health services for its area on behalf of the Secretary of State[3]. These services include general practitioners (GPs) and hospital services.

The Secretary of State also has a responsibility to make arrangements *"for the prevention of illness, the care of persons suffering from illness or the after care of such persons"*. This includes the care of people with mental health problems, learning disabilities, dementia or brain damage, as well as any other disability which requires medical treatment or nursing[4].

Under these responsibilities, the NHS provides psychiatrists, psychologists, occupational therapists, physiotherapists, community nursing and other specialist services. The Secretary of State has a power to provide invalid carriages and other vehicles for physically disabled people[5].

Unless there is a specific legal power to charge, all NHS services have to be provided free[6]. These services are for everyone, including people who are in residential care.

The members of health boards are appointed by the Secretary of State. It is up to the boards to arrange services locally, but they are not independent of the Secretary of State in the way that local authorities are. They are expected to follow guidance from the Secretary of State and are obliged to follow his directions[7].

Because health boards and other NHS bodies act on behalf of the Secretary of State, it used to be held that they were part of the Crown. This meant that various pieces of legislation (eg health and safety, and food hygiene) did not apply to them and there were restrictions on suing health boards. Most of these special privileges ("Crown immunities") have now been abolished[8].

Before the recent NHS reforms[9], the Government gave a fixed amount of money to each health board and the board used it to provide health services. The reforms introduced a distinction between *purchasers* and *providers* of NHS care. The board has become the purchaser of health services. Separate parts of the NHS have become providers (eg an individual hospital) and sell their services to the board. The hope is that the units which provide services will have more room for flexibility and initiative, and the board will have a greater choice for the services it wants since it is free to ask different providers to compete.

(In some ways, this is similar to the idea that social work departments should arrange community care services, rather than provide them directly. The social work department is increasingly the purchaser of care, with the private and voluntary sectors being the providers.)

NHS Trusts are an extension of this idea. They are *providers* who set themselves up as bodies which are legally separate from the health board (but still part of the NHS). They have even more freedom to choose how to deliver services (eg what staff they employ and how much to pay them). However, they cannot provide any service at all unless a purchaser (normally the local health board) will pay for it. Most of the parts of the NHS which provide health services have become NHS Trusts. This includes providers of community care and related services[10].

Although the health board may no longer be the provider, it is still their legal responsibility to make sure that an effective health service is delivered to patients. It is up to them to plan, to set standards and to buy the necessary services. Health boards also have the power to fund local authorities and voluntary sector bodies to provide community care services.

GP SERVICES

Health boards have a duty to provide general practitioner services for anyone in the area who wants to use them[11]. This means that anyone living in the community or in residential or nursing care is entitled to register with a GP. This will enable the person to get access to the ordinary health care that everybody uses. In some areas, the GP also acts as the link to certain specialised services.

Some people are worried that people who need community care may find it difficult to get a GP, either because they need expensive treatment, or because they may behave in a way which GPs find hard to deal with.

If a person has problems finding a GP, they can ask the health board to place them on a GP's list. That GP must offer treatment although, if there are problems, he or she can remove the patient from the list. If no other GP is willing to take the person on, the whole process has to be gone through again.

If you are unhappy with your GP, it is now very easy to change (if you can find a doctor who is willing to take you). You fill in a form applying to be a patient of the new doctor. That doctor gets in touch with your old doctor to get your records.

Some GPs have become **fundholders** (although still a minority in Scotland).

GP fundholders are not providers but purchasers. They are given direct responsibility for a sum of money to manage for their patients. They use this to buy specialist services from providers such as hospitals.

HEALTH BOARD PLANS

Health boards do not have the same legal duty as social work departments to produce community care plans, but they are required to do so by the Secretary of State as part of their overall planning[12]. They have to prepare local health strategies which look at the needs of the population over the next ten years, including the need for community care[13]. There is no consultation procedure laid down by law, but boards are expected to consult social work departments and voluntary sector bodies in drawing up their plans. Many of the recommendations of good practice for consulting by local authorities (see page 21) would also be relevant for health boards[14].

Nevertheless, health boards are generally less open to the public than local authorities. If you want to influence the health board's community care plans, the best place to start is probably your local health council. It should be able to tell you how to get hold of the current plans and what arrangements are in hand for new plans. Local health councils should be part of the consultation process and also would be able to tell you if there are any special arrangements for meeting representative organisations to discuss community care issues. Most local health councils would welcome any input or comments from users of the NHS.

CO-OPERATION BETWEEN THE NHS AND LOCAL AUTHORITIES

Because health boards and social work departments provide services which may be similar, and people may need to use both, co-operation between boards and local authorities is very important. All health boards and local authorities in Scotland (including regional and district councils) have a legal duty to co-operate with one another *"in order to secure and advance the health of the people of Scotland"*[15]. Unfortunately, this duty is so vague that it is very difficult to enforce.

The legislation was amended in 1986 to strengthen co-operation in services for disabled people and people aged over 65[16]. The duty to co-operate now specifically includes joint planning of services for such people and consultation with relevant voluntary organisations.

In 1986, the legislation also made provision for joint plans to be published by local authorities and health boards and for *"joint liaison committees"* to advise health boards and local authorities. The requirements for joint plans and joint liaison committees were abolished by the NHS & Community Care Act 1990[17].

However, the Government is still keen to see joint planning. The new arrangements are described in Chapter 24 *(Planning agreements and joint plans)*.

NHS FUNDING COMMUNITY CARE

Health boards have the power to transfer money to social work departments, local authority housing departments, housing associations and Scottish Homes[18]. This power allows money to follow patients out of long stay NHS care into the community.

These payments should be part of agreements usually between health boards and local authorities. Although the exact arrangements are different across the country, the Government's aim is that the amount of money which the NHS saves by not having to care for a person in hospital will be transferred to develop services for that person in the community[19].

Health boards can also directly fund independent voluntary non-profit making organisations who provide housing or social care[20].

The law and your rights to community care

NOTES

1 *Community care: agenda for action*, para 4.14.

2 National Health Service (Scotland) Act 1978, s1.

3 National Health Service (Scotland) Act 1978, s2. The boards are Argyll & Clyde, Ayrshire & Arran, Borders, Dumfries & Galloway, Fife, Forth Valley, Grampian, Greater Glasgow, Highland, Lanarkshire, Lothian, Orkney, Shetland, Tayside, Western Isles.

4 National Health Service (Scotland) Act 1978, ss37 and 108.

5 National Health Service (Scotland) Act 1978, s46.

6 National Health Service (Scotland) Act 1978, s1(2).

7 National Health Service (Scotland) Act 1978, s2(5). See also s77 (Default powers).

8 NHS & Community Care Act 1990, s60.

9 NHS & Community Care Act 1990, ss27 – 41, and *Working for patients*.

10 The legislation is not clear about whether NHS Trusts can sell services to social work departments. The NHS Management Executive issued guidance (NHS MEL (1994) 38 12/4/94) that this can be done in exceptional circumstances.

11 National Health Service (Scotland) Act 1978, s19.

12 *Community care planning* (Circular SW1/91).

13 *Community care planning* (Circular SW 1/91), para 3.3.

14 Social Work Services Group Circular 4/1993, *Community care plans: directions on consultation*, para 17.

15 National Health Service (Scotland) Act 1978, s13.

16 National Health Service (Scotland) Act 1978, s13A – inserted by NHS (Amendment) Act 1986, s5.

17 Sched 10 of the NHS & Community Care Act 1990 repeated s13A(1)(c) and s13B of the NHS (Scotland) Act 1978.

18 s16A of the National Health Service (Scotland) Act 1978 (inserted by Health and Social Services and Social Security Adjudication Act 1983).

19 Scottish Office Circular 15/9/92 *Community care: joint purchasing, resource transfers and contracting: arrangements for inter-agency working*, para 13.

20 National Health Service (Scotland) Act 1978, s16A.

The National Health Service and community care

INTRODUCTION

In this chapter we look at:

- hospital closures

- discharge from hospital

- who pays: health and social care

- your legal rights to medical treatment

- getting help through local health councils

One of the Government's aims in promoting community care is to reduce the number of people who are living in hospital on a long term basis. Some people with mental health problems and learning disabilities have lived in hospital for many years. Some elderly people spend the last years of their lives in hospital.

The Government believes that hospital is not the right place for most people to live and that most people could live more happy and fulfilling lives in smaller, more homely surroundings in the community. The Government has committed itself to reducing 600 long stay hospital beds a year over the next ten years to help this process[1].

Some hospitals will close altogether. The money should be used to improve health and social services in the community.

This process has already started. We are seeing people move out of psychiatric hospitals and hospitals for people with learning disabilities. Young disabled people are moving out of hospital into supported accommodation in the community. But the same is not true for elderly people. The Government has said that it is not the intention that frail elderly people living in NHS long stay facilities should be discharged into the community[2]. What will happen instead is that there will be a reduction in the numbers of new people being admitted to long stay facilities.

As hospitals are run down, and new projects set up, there will be a transfer of money from health boards to social work departments. This will enable social work to take responsibility for organising new types of services.

The precise amount which will be transferred will be negotiated between individual health boards and social work departments. It should be based on the amount a health board saves in running costs by making the closures[3].

Whilst most people broadly welcome community care, two main concerns have been expressed:

- Will the facilities and services provided in the community be adequate to meet the needs of people being discharged from hospital? Or will some people be discharged without proper support? As pressure on bed spaces grows, will some people be discharged while they are still ill and needing a place in hospital?

- Will people who were told that they were entitled to a free National Health Service "from the cradle to the grave" now, at the end of their lives, find that they have to pay for the nursing and medical support they need?

A great deal has been written about what the future is likely to be for the NHS and for community care under the new regime. Many people are very concerned[4]. We will not repeat those arguments here. Instead we have tried to look at what rights the individual user of NHS and social work services might have when they face some of these issues.

CLOSURE OF HOSPITALS

You may have heard that hospitals or other NHS facilities in your area are to be run down or even closed. How do you find out what is planned for your area? How can you judge whether what will be put in its place will be as good? How can you have your say? What do you do if things go wrong?

The first place to look is your local community care plan. There may also be a public consultation exercise. You could also get in touch with your local health council or the health board itself.

Community care plans

The Government has said that health boards, social work departments, housing agencies and other interested agencies, such as education departments, should work together to produce plans which show how services in their area should develop. The social work departments, who have the lead responsibility for community care plans, are required to consult a wide range of bodies, including representatives of users and carers, on the plan (see Chapter 24).

When services are being planned, or when it is planned to reduce or withdraw a service (such as a hospital) this should not be done by one agency on its own, but in consultation with the other agencies involved, so that all can be satisfied that alternative provision exists which will be able to cope with the proposed changes[5].

If you want to find out what is going on in your area, you should consult the most up-to-date community care plan (see Chapter 24 for community care plans). If you are a member of a voluntary or users' group, you may well have been consulted about the plan (see page 120).

Chapter 24 explains that the Government has recently changed its requirements for the format and content of plans. The new style plans should look at the needs of the area and should set out the levels of service being planned to meet those needs. The Government has stressed the importance of health boards and social work departments preparing joint plans. The Scottish Office Guidance says that it can be helpful if plans go on to specify on a district by district basis exactly what services there are in the area and what is planned for the future (but the Government does not say the plans *have* to provide this information)[6].

So you may find some information both on hospital closures and on changes of a smaller nature, such as ward closures, from joint community care plans. The health board may also have published its own plans (see page 122).

Consultation with the public

In the past, if a health board proposed to close down any NHS facilities or to change the use of any NHS premises, it had to carry out a full consultation with all the relevant organisations, including local health councils, representatives

of the public, social work departments, Universities, GPs' organisations and MPs[7].

The final decision on whether a service should be closed or changed rested with the Secretary of State.

However it is now the new **NHS Trusts** who own most of the hospitals in Scotland. They have the power to close them down and change the facilities they offer if they think this is the right thing to do[8]. The Secretary of State has the power to issue directions to NHS Trusts requiring them to seek his consent before they change the facilities they provide[9], but as yet, he has issued no such directions.

The Scottish Office is consulting on how hospital closures should be debated in future. It has said that the health boards should consult about their plans to buy services from the NHS Trusts[10]. This is what will affect whether hospitals stay open. However some people feel this will make it more difficult for the public to monitor the provision of local services.

Local health councils and closures

You can also ask your local health council about what is planned for the future. They will have been involved in the plans and should have a good idea what is going on. (See below for local health councils.)

Opposing hospital closures

If your local community is faced with a hospital closure and you do not believe you have been given sufficient advice or information, you might want to take further action. You might want to take political action. You might want to make a complaint, and you might want to join with other people who are affected to consider legal action. A local health council might want to do this, too. You might want to get in touch with the Secretary of State. See Chapters 25 and 26 for other things you could do.

If you are living in a hospital which is faced with closure, you should expect to be consulted, and so should your relatives and carers. In England nursing home residents successfully took a local authority to court when they closed the home without consulting them (see page 147). While this was an English case, the law might well be the same in Scotland.

DISCHARGE FROM HOSPITAL

If someone is being discharged from hospital into community care, what can they expect? What help should they be given before they are discharged? In this section we look at the legal duties of hospitals and social work departments and also at the guidance given them by the Scottish Office.

There are different concerns according to whether the person is elderly, has mental health problems or has a learning disability and we look at the position of each group separately.

The legal position

Duties of the hospital

There is no law saying that a hospital should not discharge you until you are completely better and you have proper support in the community.

The nearest we came to this was a rule that if someone with a *"mental disorder"*[11] had been in hospital for 6 months or more, the health board and social work department should assess their needs before discharging them. This requirement was in the Disabled Persons (Services, Consultation and Representation) Act 1986[12]. It has never been brought into effect, and now the Government has said that it does not intend to bring it into effect.

On the other hand the law would not look kindly on hospitals which discharge ill patients from their care. While you have no legal right to insist on medical treatment[13], the law might say that a doctor who has taken over a patient's care should not discharge that duty irresponsibly.

In Chapter 26 we look at the "duty of care". A doctor treating a patient owes the patient a duty of care. If the doctor discharges the patient when they are still so ill that they or other people could be at risk, the courts might say that the doctor was "negligent" and liable for any suffering caused.

So far as people with a *"mental disorder"* are concerned, the doctor's duty to take care is emphasised by the fact that if someone's health or safety is at risk or other people could need protection, the doctor can keep them in hospital even if they do not want to stay, by sectioning them under the Mental Health (Scotland) Act. (A mental disorder would include a mental health problem, a learning disability and dementia. This could also include a person with brain damage or a stroke victim, if his or her mental facilities were impaired.)

Of course it is not much use saying that a doctor or hospital might have to pay you damages if they discharge you wrongly. What you want to do is to stop them discharging you. You would have to go to court to try to get what is called an "interdict". (A court order to stop someone doing something).

We are not aware of any cases where this has been done, but if you were urgently concerned, and this seemed the only solution, you could take legal advice. Even if you do not intend to go to court, a lawyer might be able to help you negotiate with the hospital.

Before you get to that stage, however, you should try to talk to the hospital and the doctors to try to persuade them to keep you in. You may want to use an advocate or patient's supporter (see Chapter 19).

Duties of social work department

Many people being discharged from hospital will have community care needs. If so, they should be given a **community care assessment**. (See Chapter 2.) Once the social work department has been told of the person's needs, the law says it must do an assessment. Since this should be done before the person gets a community care service (except in emergencies), it should be done before the person leaves the care of the NHS.

There is an additional legal protection for people who have a *"mental disorder"*. The law says that nobody with a *"mental disorder"* should be discharged from hospital without at least some contact with the social work department. The social work department must provide them with after-care[14].

You would, therefore, be entitled to some support from the social work department, although as we have said (page 25), the law is not clear about how much or for how long this should be given.

It is very important to remember that the duty to provide after-care applies no matter how long you have been in hospital; even a person who has been in hospital for a few weeks is entitled to after-care; not just someone who has been there for many years.

Co-operation between health boards, NHS trusts and social work departments

One of the problems about arranging proper after-care for someone leaving hospital is that it relies on co-operation between the hospital and the social work department. Many health boards and local authorities are working out ways of building this co-operation into the system. But what if your hospital and social work department do not co-operate to work out a proper care plan for you?

Health boards, NHS Trusts and local authorities have a legal duty to co-operate with one another to secure and advance the health of the people of Scotland[15]. They also have to co-operate with the education authorities (see Chapter 17). If this does not happen and you are affected, you could complain (see Chapter 25). You might also want to take this to the local government ombudsman or health services ombudsman. Finally, you could even find out whether legal action for breach of statutory duty would be possible (see page 150).

Government guidelines

As well having legal duties, health boards and social work departments have received guidance on discharge procedures from the Government. The guidance imposes clear duties on them not to discharge people until they are ready.

You might be able to take further action if Government guidelines are not complied with (see page 145). You might be able to take legal action, but equally, you might want to use one of the complaints procedures outlined in Chapter 25.

Unfortunately the guidance is not in just one place, but in at least five. This cannot make it any easier for providers of services to work out what they are supposed to do. The guidance is contained in four Scottish Office circulars and in the Mental Health (Scotland) Act *Code of Practice*. It might be helpful if separate guidance were issued on the discharge of patients from hospital.

There are some general principles which apply to discharges from all types of hospitals. We will consider these first and then look at the different considerations for different groups of people.

The guidance says that there are certain basic requirements before any patient is discharged from hospital:

- **People should not leave hospital until the essential services have been arranged for them.** There must be close collaboration between local authorities and health boards to ensure this.

  The Scottish Office says "All the agencies involved with a particular individual need to consider from an early date the services that he or she will require...to ensure that patients do not leave hospital until at least the essential community based services that they will need on discharge have been agreed with them, their carers and all the agencies concerned."[16]

- **Before a person is discharged, there should be a clinical assessment by the doctor in charge of the patient's care to confirm that the person does not need to be cared for in the hospital[17].**

There is additional guidance to deal with the discharge of people with mental health problems and dementia.

Discharge from psychiatric hospitals

There is a very real fear that, because of pressure on beds, some people are being discharged from psychiatric hospitals too early, before proper support services are available for them in the community[18]. If this happens to you, you might want to complain or even, perhaps, take legal action. (See Chapters 25 and 26.)

The Government has issued additional guidance about the care of people with a long term mental health problem being discharged from psychiatric hospitals[19]. It sets out standards which should apply *in addition* to those set out above. It says that:

- **Nobody should be discharged until the health board has formally notified the social work department and they have had an opportunity to arrange for an assessment of the person's needs[20].** (See Chapter 2 for assessment of needs.)

- **People with a long term psychiatric illness who are being discharged from hospital should have their own care programme.** This should include details of how their social and medical needs will be met. They should be consulted about this, as should their carer[21].

- **If a person's health and social needs cannot be met in the community, they should not be discharged from hospital[22].** Nor should they be discharged without suitable accommodation[23]. A person should never be discharged into homeless persons' accommodation[24].

- **Once a person leaves hospital, there should be regular monitoring and review of their progress.** Every effort should be made to keep contact with them[25].

The Scottish Office is emphatic, therefore, that people should not be discharged from a psychiatric hospital without adequate support and proper housing. This applies to both long term and acute patients[26]. If things are not happening like this in your area, you might want to tell the Scottish Office, as well as complaining to the hospital or health board (see Chapter 25).

Discharge protocols

A lot of health boards and hospitals have done a considerable amount of work on "discharge protocols", looking at how patients will be discharged from psychiatric hospitals.

If you are concerned about discharges in your area, you could ask the health board or hospital if it has a discharge protocol you could see. The discharge protocol should try to put the Scottish Office guidance into effect in your area. If it does not seem to do this, you might want to complain. (See Chapter 25.)

The discharge protocol sets standards for the discharge of patients. If a hospital does not comply with the standards it has set, you have the right to complain. You may also have grounds for legal action under the principle of **legitimate expectation**.

Discharge from learning disability hospitals

In Scotland, up till now at least, there has probably been less concern about people with learning disabilities being discharged from hospital without having proper services to go to. (In fact, a lot of people are concerned that people are not moving out quickly enough.) Most people with learning disabilities who move out of hospital move into some kind of residential care or group home, although there are sometimes disagreements about whether this is right for the individual person.

Perhaps because there have been fewer problems, there is less Government guidance for learning disability than for mental health. There is no specific circular similar to the guidance for people with a mental illness and dementia, discussed above. However the general duties for all patients being discharged apply.

- A doctor must confirm that the person does not need to be cared for in hospital.

- The person will be entitled to a community care assessment. They will be entitled to after-care from the social work department.

- In addition, a person with learning disabilities who has come out of hospital has the same right to *"suitable training and occupation"* from the social work department as other people with learning disabilities in the community (see page 25). There can be problems if the person's needs for day services are not sorted out before he or she leaves hospital, so this should be looked at as part of the community care assessment.

Elderly people being discharged from hospital

Elderly people may be in hospital for a number of reasons. They may have dementia requiring long term care. They may have an illness which can be treated, but also be frail and find it increasingly difficult to cope. They may have been in hospital for a long time or for a short course of treatment.

People with dementia are covered by the same rules and guidance as people with a mental illness. Therefore the section above on *Discharge from psychiatric hospitals* would apply (even if the person was not actually in a psychiatric hospital).

Not all long stay patients in geriatric wards have dementia. If a patient does not have dementia, the duty of after-care in the Mental Health (Scotland) Act does not apply and of course the patient could not be detained unwillingly under that Act. However, the law would still require:

- a clinical assessment before discharge *and*

- a community care assessment

The Government's guidance on assessment also applies! (See learning disability section above, and Chapter 2.) Community care services should be planned well in advance and in place before discharge.

Where an elderly person goes into hospital for a short spell of treatment (for example, after a fall), there will not automatically be a community care assessment. However, the person may need extra help when they are convalescing or they may be finding it generally harder to manage in their home.

The NHS is now less likely to keep this kind of patient in hospital indefinitely. However, they should not discharge an elderly person who needs continuing medical care – see the ombudsman case on page 85. It will be the social work department's job to do a community care assessment. If the hospital don't tell the social work department, then anyone else (including the elderly person, their carer or a friend) can ask the department to do an assessment (see Chapter 2).

A community care assessment should not automatically mean that the elderly person goes from hospital to a nursing home. It should start by looking at the person's needs, and see if they could be met in the person's own home[27].

WHO PAYS? HEALTH AND SOCIAL CARE

Another of the aims of the community care system is to break down the barriers between the different agencies all providing different kinds of care. A person living in the community may have different kinds of needs. They will need

The law and your rights to community care

somewhere to live, social supports and perhaps some medical care. All the agencies should work together to help provide a package of care to meet the person's needs. They should work out between themselves who provides what. They may even pool their resources to provide a "kitty" to pay for certain parts of community care.

It all sounds very reasonable. But for people who have been brought up under the old model of the National Health Service, the new one has thrown up problems which, we believe, were not properly discussed when the laws were brought in.

One of the major problems is who pays for care. Care under the NHS is free. But we saw in Chapter 4 that the social work department can charge for the services it provides. This includes not only charging for residential care (for which it *must* charge: see Chapters 7 to 12) but also charging for services such as home helps, home adaptations and other support services.

So if you move out of hospital into a nursing home, you may move from free care into care which you will pay for, according to a means test. If you have been receiving respite care, you may find that where once you were charged a nominal sum, you will now be charged the full cost. However, if you still receive respite care in a hospital it will continue to be supplied free of charge.

And this is where who provides what becomes important. It is important to the recipient of services to know who provides them. Whilst community based services will in many cases be preferable to services in a hospital, services in a hospital or provided by the NHS will be free, whereas services provided or arranged by the social work department could be expensive. So the recipient of services will always need to know: is it health or social care?

There are all sorts of areas where this question could become important: if you need long term medical or nursing care; if you need respite care and if you need services in the home. In all of these areas if the help is provided by the NHS it is free. If social work department arranges it they can or must charge for it.

So far most of the discussion about the implications has arisen over hospital care.

People needing continuing care

We have seen above how the government is running down long term beds in the NHS. This applies to beds for elderly people, beds for people with psychiatric illnesses and learning disabilities and beds for people who are chronically sick who require continuing care. While many of these people may need medical care, they do not necessarily need to be in hospital to receive it. The Government believes that in most cases people are better off in the community and in smaller, more homely accommodation.

So for many people the "cradle to the grave" care promised by the National Health Service will no longer exist. They cannot assume that, as they become older and frailer, perhaps with nobody to look after them, they will be able to go to hospital, and stay there for the rest of their days.

The alternatives may well be better, a nursing home, residential care or sheltered housing. Or perhaps the person will be able to stay at home, given some help. But they may have to pay for this help or at least pay a proportion of the cost, depending on their means. This has come as a great shock to a great many people.

How do the Health Service and the social work department decide who should take responsibility for a particular person? Who pays?

The basic rule is that the NHS should be responsible for health needs and the social work department for social needs. The Scottish Office has said that:

> *"people who require continuing specialist medical and nursing supervision are clearly the responsibility of the NHS*[28].
>
> *The guiding principle should be whether or not a person .... has needs which in the [health] board's assessment can be met only by medically-led health care staff. If they do, the needs ...should be regarded as health care needs. The needs met by many other staff, including unqualified staff currently working within the NHS, can be regarded as social care needs."*[29]

In other words, a person who needs treatment by a doctor or who needs their care supervising by a doctor has health care needs. (Some people have interpreted this as meaning that the person needs to be under the care of a consultant. The guidance says that your consultant is the person to decide whether you need *"specialist medical and nursing supervision"*. It is a question for the *"clinical judgement"* of the doctor.)

If a person needs specialist nursing the NHS should provide this. But a person who perhaps needs help with washing, lifting or dressing has social needs because unqualified people could do this and they do not need to be supervised by a doctor.

The distinction is not always easy to make, however. The example often given is of bathing.

Does a person need a bath for health reasons, because of some illness, or for social reasons? We now have a situation where some people have free baths provided by the NHS, while others have them arranged by the social work department, for which they can be asked to pay.

What about a person with emotional or support needs or someone with very profound care needs? How will the consultant decide whether their needs can best be met by qualified or medically unqualified people? Does a doctor need to supervise their care? These can be very difficult questions to answer.

What can you do if you think you have medical needs rather than social needs? You would have to try to discuss this with the consultant at the hospital or with the health board[30]. You might want to put in a formal complaint. You would probably want to get some advice (see pages 160-162). You might want to go to the health services ombudsman. We examine below whether there is any legal action you could take.

The Scottish Office has said that it will introduce a new appeals procedure for people who are told that their needs for care will no longer be met by the NHS. This should make it easier for you to get your case reconsidered.

The answer you get may depend on where you live. The guidance says that it is for the individual health boards and social work departments to negotiate between them how the responsibilities will devolve. Many people are beginning to believe that this is an unsatisfactory solution, because it will mean that there is no uniform standard of care throughout Scotland. What care you get and who provides it will depend on where you live.

THE RIGHT TO MEDICAL SERVICES

If you are told that you have social needs rather than medical needs, what rights do you have? You cannot appeal against this decision. Can you take legal action to ensure you get medical treatment? Does the law say that the Government must maintain the NHS at its present levels?

In this section we look at your legal rights to insist on medical treatment.

The National Health Service (Scotland) Act says that the Secretary of State for Scotland has a duty to provide hospital accommodation throughout Scotland. He has to provide enough accommodation to meet what he considers are all reasonable requirements for beds[32].

Continuing care: The duties of the health board

Once a doctor has accepted responsibility for you, it may be difficult for them to discharge you and say that you should no longer be cared for by the NHS.

In 1994 the health services ombudsman criticised the Leeds Health Authority who discharged a man with long term brain damage into a nursing home, where his wife had to pay the fees. The doctors accepted that the man needed long term medical and nursing care, but said that the health board did not have the facilities to arrange this. It had run down its long-stay beds.

His wife complained to the health authority. She was unsatisfied with their reply and complained to the health services ombudsman.

The ombudsman said that the health authority should continue to provide the nursing care the man needed, free of charge under the NHS. He told them to compensate his wife for the fees she had already paid. From now on the health board should pay the nursing home fees[31].

The ombudsman also criticised the doctors for failing to carry out the discharge in accordance with procedures laid down by Department of Health guidance (which the doctors said they had not seen).

This case could have very far reaching effects. It means that a health board cannot simply stop taking responsibility for someone because it does not have the facilities to care for them. While this case related to health care in England, it could have very important implications for Scotland too. We need someone to take up the same point here, perhaps with the health services ombudsman in Scotland, to see if he would take the same line on the right to medical treatment in Scotland.

This is not a clear cut duty. It is up to him to decide what is reasonably necessary. His decision would be influenced by what resources were available to him. But that decision would have to bear some relation to the facts. If evidence was coming in to the Secretary of State that pressure on bed spaces was becoming intolerable, if people were not getting beds when they needed them, someone who could not get into hospital might possibly be able to challenge the Secretary of State by means of judicial review (see Chapter 26).

The Secretary of State also has a duty to provide medical, nursing and other services, and arrangements for the care and after-care of people who are ill . Again the test is what he thinks is necessary to meet all reasonable needs[33]. He does this through the health boards for the different areas, although he remains liable for seeing that it gets done[34].

The National Health Service (Scotland) Act says that the Secretary of State must consider what the needs of the population are and provide what he thinks is necessary. If you need long term nursing or medical care, and you feel that he has not met his legal obligations so far as your area is concerned, you might have a case for judicial review. (See page 144.)

But it is generally accepted that, under the law, people do not have the right to compel the Secretary of State to give them the treatment they may need. The courts realise that the Government does not have unlimited budgets and must set their own priorities. The cases in the box below are English, but the Scottish courts would probably take the same line.

It would all depend on the particular facts of your case, but so far the courts in England have been unwilling to give patients the right to force hospitals to provide them with medical treatment if the resources are not available.

The courts said that they would not interfere with the discretion of ministers and health boards in allocating resources. The only circumstances when they would do so would be if a minister (or health board) acted in a way in which no reasonable minister or health board would have acted.

GETTING HELP: LOCAL HEALTH COUNCILS

Local health councils are independent bodies which try to protect the interests of users of health services. They help with individual complaints and they also take up matters of general concern, such as hospital closures and the running down of facilities. They might be able to help if you have concerns about any of the matters raised in this chapter.

See under health council in the phone book.

What can health councils do?

Lothian Health Council is considering taking court action against Lothian Health Board. This follows an announcement that the board is to stop admitting elderly people to long stay beds over the next few years.

The health council criticised the lack of consultation over the planned strategy and is considering applying to the court for an interdict, or court order, to stop the changes taking place[37].

Patients needing medical care: Their right to treatment

Case one: In 1979 a group of patients urgently requiring hip-replacements took the English Minister of Health to court to get an order compelling him to make facilities available so that they could have their operations and to pay them compensation for the pain and suffering they had been caused. Their claim did not succeed. The court said that the Minister could fix priorities for the health service and that his duty to provide facilities was limited by the resources available[35].

Case two: In 1987, the parents of a baby needing surgery for a heart defect tried to get a court order compelling the health authority to carry out the operation. Again the court said that if the resources were not available, they would not make the order. The family could not demand immediate treatment[36].

SUMMARY – KEY POINTS

- Over the next few years, the majority of long stay patients will be discharged from hospital.

- Before a hospital is closed, there should be consultation with patients and their families.

- Before a long stay patient is discharged, there should be:

  - a clinical assessment by the doctor, *and*

  - a community care assessment by the social work department (which should involve the patient and any carers).

- Patients will be likely to be discharged if their needs are for "social care", not "health care". However, this distinction is not totally clear. Also, Government guidance clearly states that long stay patients should not be discharged until alternative services are available for them in the community.

- Social work departments have a duty to provide "after-care" for patients with mental illness, learning disability, brain damage or dementia.

- People who are only in hospital for a short period will not automatically get a community care assessment but are entitled to one if they need help when they leave.

- Once a person is not being cared for by the NHS, they may have to pay for their care, depending on their means.

- If the hospital has followed the correct procedures, legal action to prevent a person from being discharged would be difficult. However, the NHS ombudsman is concerned about people being made to pay when they still need a high degree of care.

- If you believe a patient being moved out of hospital would receive worse care, check this chapter and Chapter 25 and 26 carefully. If you are concerned about the patient paying for care, see also section 2.

NOTES

1 Appendix B of *Accountability reviews, priorities and planning: guidance for 1994/5.* Scottish Office Circular MEL (1993) 155.

2 Letter from Social Work Services Group to Directors of Social Work and General Managers of Health Boards 11/3/94.

3 (Not the cost of setting up new services.) This topic is covered in more detail in a Scottish Office Circular of 15/9/92: *Community care: joint purchasing, resource transfers and contracting: arrangements for inter-agency working*, Scottish Office Circular MEL (1992) 55, paras 11 to 15.

4 See, for example the 1993 Annual Report of the Mental Welfare Commission. (Available free from the Commission.)

5 See Scottish Office Circular: *Joint purchasing, resource transfer and contracting* NHS MEL (1992) 55.

6 See *Community care planning* (Circular No SW14/1994), Annex A, para 8.

7 See Scottish Office Circular NHS Circular No 1975 (GEN) 46.

8 National Health Service (Scotland) Act 1978, Sched 7A, para 16(a) (inserted by NHS & Community Care Act 1990 (Sched 6)). Their powers must be exercised in accordance with their functions. The functions of each Trust are set out in the Statutory Instrument which creates it.

9 National Health Service (Scotland) Act 1978, Sched 7A, paras 6(2)(d) and (e). The Secretary of State can stop NHS Trusts disposing of assets. He can also order them to comply with any guidance or directions which he gives or has given to health boards.

10 See draft guidance: *Consultation on purchasing plans and service changes.*

11 Defined as *"mental illness"* or *"mental handicap".*

12 s7.

13 See page 85.

14 Under the Mental Health (Scotland) Act 1984, s8 (see page 24).

15 s13 of the National Health Service (Scotland) Act 1978 (amended by NHS & Community Care Act 1990, Sched 9, para19(4)).

16 *Assessment and care management* (Circular No SW11/1991), para 15.

17 *Community care: joint purchasing, resource transfers and contracting: arrangements for inter-agency working*, para 8.

18 See pages 5 and 19 of the 1993 Annual Report of the Mental Welfare Commission.

19 *Guidance on care programmes for people with a mental illness including dementia* (Circular No 1992/1).

20 *Guidance on care programmes for people with a mental illness including dementia*, para 1.4. (This applies mainly to people with a "long-term" psychiatric illness.)

21 *Guidance on care programmes for people with a mental illness including dementia*, paras 2, 5 and 6.

22 *Guidance on care programmes for people with a mental illness including dementia*, para 3.1.

23 Mental Health (Scotland) Act 1984 *Code of Practice*, para 3.3. Published by HMSO.

24 *Community care: the housing dimension*, (Circular SW7/1994) para 3.24.1.

25 *Guidance on care programmes for people with a mental illness including dementia*, para 7.

26 *Community care: the housing dimension*, para 3.24.1.

27 *Assessment and care management*, para 6.2.

28 *Community care: joint purchasing, resource transfers and contracting: arrangements for inter-agency working*, para 7.

29 *Community care: joint purchasing, resource transfers and contracting: arrangements for inter-agency working*, para 9.

30 However even they may not always get it right. On page 41 we looked at the case of *White v Chief Adjudication Officer*, where the court said that, although a hospital thought it had discharged patients into "the community", so far as social security benefits were concerned, they remained hospital patients.

31 See Report of the Health Service Commissioner: 1993-94 *Failure to provide long-term NHS care for a brain-damaged patient*, HMSO.

32 National Health Service (Scotland) Act 1978, s36(1).

33 National Health Service (Scotland) Act 1978, s36 (1)(c) and s37.

34 National Health Service (Scotland) Act 1978, ss2(5) and 2(8) and Functions of Health Boards (Scotland) Order SI 1991 No 570 paras 4(c) and 4(d).

35 *R v Secretary of State for Social Services ex parte Hinks*. See J D Finch *Health services law* , pp38-39.

36 *R v Central Birmingham Health Authority ex parte Walker*, Reported in the Times 26/11/88. *R v Central Birmingham Health Authority ex parte Collier*, Reported in the Times 6/1/88.

37 "Legal threat over care of elderly" *Scotsman* 17/11/94.

Education

INTRODUCTION

You may want to improve your skills, such as literacy or office skills. You may want to train for a job. Or you may just want to study something because it interests you.

GETTING HELP FROM THE SOCIAL WORK DEPARTMENT

If you are not quite sure what you need you could ask the social work department to help. When you have your **community care assessment** you could say that you think you would like to take an educational course.

Social workers should have a good idea of what courses might be available in your area. Colleges must let social work departments know about the services they provide for people with special needs. The colleges can also help assess your needs[1]. If your social worker does not know what is available, you could ask them to arrange a meeting for you with the special needs officer for your local careers office.

Duties of the social work department

- The Government has told social work departments that they should consider people's educational needs when they carry out community care assessments. If they think you need access to education, they should tell the education department[2].

- If you are chronically sick or disabled and the social work department thinks you need help in using educational facilities, it has a legal duty to help arrange this. This also applies if you have a learning disability or a mental health problem (see Chapter 3).

- If you have a learning disability, the law says the social work department must arrange suitable training and occupation for you. This could well include access to an appropriate college course (see page 25).

WHO PROVIDES EDUCATION?

Education can be basically split into four categories: school education, further education, community education and higher education.

School education

This is provided by regional councils (and, of course, by private schools). We do not discuss it in detail here because this book is mainly concerned with adults[3]. Chapter 2 talks about future needs assessments because that is the start of the transition from school to community care for young people with special needs.

Further education

This is provided by further education colleges. They used to be part of regional councils but since 1992 they have been run by independent boards appointed by the Secretary of State.

Their main purpose is to provide vocational education for people who have left school. In other words, education which trains people for a particular job or for the world of work.

However, they are also responsible for some other types of education, including extra instruction for people with learning difficulties who are in further education and preparation for students for more advanced or higher education (eg "access" courses[4]).

Further education colleges have a legal duty to consider the needs of people with disabilities and other special needs, which we explain below.

Community education

This is also run by regional councils. Basically, it covers everything that was left when further education colleges became independent. In other words, it is broadly non-vocational adult education. This includes evening classes and education for groups such as retired people etc[5].

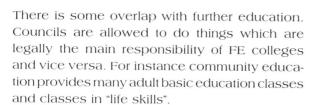

The law and your rights to community care

There is some overlap with further education. Councils are allowed to do things which are legally the main responsibility of FE colleges and vice versa. For instance community education provides many adult basic education classes and classes in "life skills".

Although this kind of education is obviously important for many people with disabilities or special needs, there is no law which says that councils must make special provision in community education for you if you have special needs. Many of them do, but you have no clear legal remedy if they do not.

Higher education

This is academic education, often at degree level. It is provided at universities and some colleges, which are all independently managed. Many universities do make provision for students with disabilities or other special needs, but there is no legal duty on them to do so. So if you are a student with a disability and now want to go to university, there would be no legal duty on the university to consider whether it could meet your special needs.

Many universities are becoming aware of the need to make provision for students with disabilities and other special needs, and several of them now have disabled students' advisory officers[6]. A new, free guide has recently been published to help students.

Access to success gives advice to students with disabilities, including physical disabilities, learning disabilities and students with medical conditions[7]. It does not, unfortunately, give advice to students who have a mental health problem or who develop these problems while they are in higher education.

Every university should be able to tell you about the facilities it has for people with disabilities or learning difficulties and what support it can provide. They should also tell you about any extra funding for which you might be eligible[8].

FURTHER EDUCATION COLLEGES AND STUDENTS WITH SPECIAL NEEDS

Will a college be able to cope with your special needs? Will they be able to make proper provision for you? In many cases, they will. A great deal of work has been done to improve education for students with special needs.

Further education colleges now have a legal duty to consider the needs of people with *"learning difficulties"* who are over school age[9]. The Scottish Office, which funds further education colleges, also has to make sure that the colleges consider people's special needs[10]. It does this by offering the colleges help and guidance and by checking that they have proper plans in place to help meet people's needs. The Scottish Office also gives extra money to colleges which provide help to students with special needs.

When we talk of people with "learning difficulties", most of us mean people with a learning disability or a "mental handicap". But the learning difficulties referred to in the Further and Higher Education (Scotland) Act go far wider than this. The Act says that a person has a learning difficulty if:

- he or she has significantly greater difficulty in learning than the majority of persons over school age *or*

- he or she suffers from a disability which either stops him or her from making use of further education facilities or makes it more difficult for him or her to use the facilities of the college[11].

So if, for example, you could not get into the college because of lack of ramps, the law would say you had a learning difficulty. You would find it difficult to learn if you could not get into the lecture theatre! Or if you suffered from a mental health problem which meant that you could not attend lectures which were too early in the morning or you did not like being in small enclosed rooms, that would be a learning difficulty. The college would have to try to see whether it could help.

There are other kinds of people whose needs should be considered too. You might have a specific learning problem, such as dyslexia. You might have a sensory disability such as deafness or blindness. You might have communication problems, or behavioural problems. You might need special equipment or extra help in the class room.

In all these cases, the colleges are supposed to see whether they can help.

Further education colleges are also required to help with the future needs assessments of young people leaving school[12] (see Chapter 2).

Education

Finding out what is available

Most colleges will have a booklet explaining the courses they run and giving general information about the college. The booklet should give you the name of someone to get in touch with if you have special needs.

Different people need different kinds of support:

- you might need *learning support:* extra help to help you with course work or with personal care while you are at college

- you might want to go on a *special course* for people with special needs

- you might need *special equipment* to help you communicate or hear what is going on, or help moving round the college

- you might need help with *transport* to college or an *escort* while you are in college. You should get some help with transport costs from the local authority, as part of your bursary (see below). The college can also help pay for transport. The social work department can help with arranging transport, too. In fact, it may even have a legal duty to do so if it thinks you "need" this. But you may have to pay for this help. (See Chapters 2 and 4.)

  The college will try to work out with you what your needs are, and they will probably write this up, in a formal assessment. You may have what is called a "personal learning and support plan" which will spell things out in some detail.

Grants

If you qualify for a place at a further education college, you should get a bursary from the local authority. If you need extra equipment to help you with college, the regional council may make an extra grant available so that you can buy this. The college should be able to help you arrange this.

If you are taking an advanced further education course, you may get a grant from the Scottish Office Education Department. You might also be eligible for a Disabled Students' Allowance. You should be able to get help in arranging this from the college. Unfortunately, the allowance is not available to part-time students.

Complaints

What if you think a further education college does not make adequate provision for students with special needs? The place to find out about the college's policy is its "development plan". Ask to see a copy of this. Write to the board of management and point out where you think the plan goes wrong. If you are still dissatisfied, write to the Secretary of State for Scotland (see page 131).

Or perhaps the policy is fine, but it doesn't seem to work out like that in practice. Write to the board of management to complain.

If you have a complaint about community education you should write to the Director of Education at the regional council. If you are still unhappy, you may be able to complain to the local government ombudsman (see Chapter 25).

Every university will have a formal complaints system. New students will be given details.

The *Further and Higher Education Charter* (see footnote 8) gives details of other ways you can complain.

DISCRIMINATION AND EDUCATION

Many people feel that what we need is anti-discrimination laws, which would make it illegal for bodies to discriminate against disabled people in the services which they provide. Universities are not allowed to discriminate against students on the grounds of race or sex. An anti-discrimination law would say that a university which did not take a student simply because they were deaf or blind or had a physical disability would be unlawfully discriminating against them. The Government is now looking into some forms of anti-discrimination laws, but has said that there is no need for laws against discrimination in education.

NOTES

1   Scottish Office Circular FE 3/93: *Further education for students with learning difficulties*.

2   *Assessment and care management* (Circular SW11/1991), para12.3. *Community care planning* (Scottish Office Circular SW14/94), para 2 stresses how important education can be in community care.

3   See instead *The law of the school* and *In special need*, both written by the Scottish Consumer Council. (HMSO).

4   Further and Higher Education (Scotland) Act 1992, s6.

5   Education (Scotland) Act 1980, s1.

6   Universities are funded by the Scottish Higher Education Funding Council. When the SHEFC was set up in 1992, it was told that one of its functions should be to consider how to help students with special needs gain access to higher education. It has now appointed a national co-ordinator for students with disabilities, based at Dundee University.

7   Published by the Scottish Higher Education Funding Council, Donaldson House, 97 Haymarket Terrace, Edinburgh EH12 5HD (Tel: 0131.313 6500).

8   See the *Further and higher education charter for Scotland*. Available free from the Scottish Office Education Department, New St Andrews House, Edinburgh EH1 3TG. The Charter also contains helpful directories about provision in colleges and universities for people with special needs.

9   Further and Higher Education (Scotland) Act 1992, s12.

10 Further and Higher Education (Scotland) Act 1992, s1.

11 Further and Higher Education (Scotland) Act 1992, s1(4).

12 Further and Higher Education (Scotland) Act 1992, s23.

Employment

INTRODUCTION

Too often, employment is seen as something which is nothing to do with community care. In fact, for many people with disabilities or mental health problems, gaining employment or good quality training can be the key to independent living. Therefore a person's employment and training needs will often be a vital component of a care plan.

The law does not specifically require social work departments to look at employment and training needs or to consult with the Employment Service when doing a community care assessment. However, Scottish Office guidance does list employment as one of the issues which may come up when doing a community care assessment and encourages the social work department to liaise with all the relevant agencies[1].

You are unlikely to get a community care assessment if all you need is a job, but if you are having an assessment and think you need help with finding employment or training or would prefer this to a day care place, you should ask the social work department to think about this in your assessment and contact the relevant agencies.

For people with learning disabilities, there is a duty on the social work department to provide *"suitable training and occupation"* (see page 25).

WHERE DO I START?

There are many different organisations working in employment. To make things worse, many of them seem to change their name every few months. This is a basic guide of who you might wish to contact if you use community care services and want help with employment or training.

Job Centres

For most people, this will be the best place to start. They are run by the Employment Service, which is a Government agency. They provide information about job vacancies and training opportunities. Most Job Centres will have a Dis-ability Employment Adviser who gives special help to people with disabilities (this includes people with physical and learning disabilities and people with mental health problems). If you wish to be registered as disabled (see page 94), this is done through the Disability Employment Adviser.

The Disability Employment Advisers are part of PACTs (Placing, Assessment and Counselling Teams). These are run by the Employment Service and work on a regional basis. They provide advice to disabled people and employers and can arrange for services to meet individuals' needs.

Careers Service

This service is particularly relevant for young people when leaving school. They can advise on training and employment options and should have specialists to help young people with special needs. Where a young person has a **Record of Special Educational Needs**, the Careers Service may participate in the future needs assessment (see page 17).

You should be able to get details of your local Careers Service from the education department of the regional council or from a local library. Although they may not automatically visit some special schools, they are available to all school leavers.

Local Enterprise Companies

These are bodies which fund most of the Government's training schemes, including Training For Work. They are part of a national organisation, Scottish Enterprise. They ought to be able to give you information about training schemes locally which might be suitable.

Charities and voluntary organisations

Many of the best training and employment schemes for disabled people are run by charities and they also often have helpful information. You could speak to a charity which works in the area that concerns you (eg cerebral palsy, mental health, etc.) or contact Disability Scotland for information[2].

Local authorities

Regional councils have a legal power to make special arrangements for the employment of disabled people[3], as well as a duty to provide training and occupation for people with learning disabilities (see page 25). Some councils have used this power to fund sheltered workshops or supported placements (see below). Some councils are now starting to link employment more to community care and are funding more flexible employment schemes run by charities. This can be both cheaper than paying for a social work day place and more in line with what the disabled person wants.

Some regional and district councils also seek to have policies to promote the employment of people with disabilities in their workforce and may have specialist officers who can give advice.

Libraries

Local libraries are good places to find addresses. They often also have books and leaflets on careers and sometimes lists of job vacancies.

Newspapers

As well as adverts for jobs, newspapers sometimes carry advertisements by people providing training schemes for special needs. However, before taking up something you see in the newspapers, you may wish to take proper advice to make sure that it is the best available option.

WHAT ARE THE OPTIONS?

Again, there is a huge variety of schemes which frequently change. These are some of the most important possibilities.

Training For Work

This is a training programme for unemployed people. (It used to be called Employment Training, then Adult Training). The Local Enterprise Companies fund private companies, local councils, and charities who run individual training schemes, usually for a year at a time. Some of these specialise in training for people with disabilities.

Youth Training/Skillseekers

This is similar to Training For Work, but is specifically for young people. The normal maximum age limit is 18, but this can be extended to 24 for disabled people.

Access To Work

This started in June 1994 as a unified programme to cover various services which are available for people with disabilities. The scheme can provide up to £21,000 of help for a disabled worker over a period of 5 years. It can pay for a variety of things, including special equipment or adaptations, or a person to assist with things like communication, reading, getting to work, or even practical help in doing the job. Access to Work is run by the local PACTs (see above).

Supported or sheltered employment

One version of this is the sheltered workshop. These are often run by charities and employ people with disabilities in productive work. An example are the Blindcraft factories employing visually impaired people to make beds and furniture.

However, there is a move away from segregated workplaces to schemes to help disabled people into normal working environments. One of these is the Supported Placement Scheme, run by the Department of Employment. A person with a disability is given a permanent job at the normal wage rate. The company where the person works pay part of this wage based on the productivity of the disabled person. The balance is paid by a "sponsor" (either a charity or local council) who is funded by the Employment Service.

LEGAL RIGHTS OF DISABLED WORKERS

For many people with disabilities, the biggest need is not for special schemes but a fair chance to compete for the same jobs as everyone else. Unfortunately their legal rights are currently extremely limited.

The Quota Scheme

The law states that every employer with more than 20 employees has a duty to employ workers[4] who are registered as disabled, amounting to not less than 3% of the total workforce[5]. Employers who are below quota should give preference to disabled workers in recruitment. Also they should not dismiss a disabled worker if that would take them below this quota. There is a register of disabled people (now maintained by the Employment Service)[6] in order to establish whether employers have met the quota.

However, this scheme is totally ineffective in practice. It is easy for employers to obtain permission to fail to meet the quota[7] and prosecutions are almost unheard of. The individual disabled person cannot take legal action against an employer who fails to meet the quota.

In practice, hardly any major employers meet the quota and so a large number of disabled people do not bother to register.

The Government has said it will abolish the quota when it brings in anti-discrimination legislation (see below).

Discrimination

Currently (early 1995) there is no law which prohibits discrimination against disabled people (including in employment) in the same way that discrimination on the grounds of race or sex is illegal[8].

For many years organisations of disabled people have campaigned for legislation, culminating in the Civil Rights (Disabled Persons) Bill which was introduced in 1993. The Bill was stopped by the Government but created so much controversy that in July 1994 the Government issued a consultation document on measures to tackle discrimination[9]. It states that the Government is sympathetic to a new statutory right for disabled people not to be unjustifiably discriminated against in employment.

In early 1995 the Government published the Disability Discrimination Bill containing this new right. At the time of writing, many disability organisations fear that the new rights may be difficult to enforce in practice.

There has also been action at an international level. The United Nations recently passed *Standard rules on the equalisation of opportunities for persons with disabilities*[10]. The European Commission has proposed adopting these Standard Rules[11] and has suggested various other measures to help disabled workers[12].

EMPLOYMENT AND BENEFITS

Taking up any kind of employment or training is likely to have significant consequences for welfare benefits. These are too complex to detail here but it is a good idea to get specialist advice[13].

NOTES

1 *Assessment and care management* (Circular SW11/1991), para 12.1.

2 Disability Scotland, Princes House, 5 Shandwick Place, Edinburgh EH2 4RG (Tel: 0131.229 8632).

3 Disabled Persons (Employment) Act 1958, s3.

4 Disabled Persons (Employment) Act 1944, s1 defines *"disabled person"* as a person who *"on account of injury, disease or congenital deformity is substantially handicapped in obtaining or keeping employment...of a kind which...would be suited to his [or her] age, experience or qualifications". "Disease" includes a physical or mental condition arising from imperfect development of any organ"*. Although the language used is out of date, this probably includes nearly everyone who would see themselves as disabled (eg, physical disability, learning disability, sensory impairment and most recognised mental health problems).

5 Disabled Persons (Employment) Act 1944, s9.

6 Disabled Persons (Employment) Act 1944, s6.

7 Disabled Persons (Employment) Act 1944, s11.

8 Until recently, the Government favoured a voluntary approach. In 1993, the Employment Service issued a Code of Good Practice on the employment of disabled people.

9 *Disability – on the agenda: a consultation on Government measures to tackle discrimination against disabled people.*

10 Adopted by General Assembly 1/10/93. The rules do not bind member states but there is a monitoring mechanism.

11 European Commission White Paper *European Social Policy – a way forward for the Union*, July 1994, p39.

12 eg, a proposed Directive on Transport to Work of Workers with a Reduced Mobility.

13 Sources of information include: *Workout – the benefits of employment for people with disabilities*, ENABLE and Tayside Social Work Department, *Disability rights handbook*, Disability Alliance.

Advocacy – helping people make decisions

INTRODUCTION

At its simplest, advocacy simply means speaking for somebody. It is not only done by lawyers. It has been recognised that many people who use community care services may need help in speaking for themselves or may need someone to speak for them when they are dealing with professionals and even with carers. Sometimes this is because the service user finds it difficult or even impossible to say clearly what they want. Sometimes they are able to do this, but cannot get people to listen.

Several different models of advocacy have been developed. Sometimes there are paid advocates but often advocates are simply friends or relatives. This section sets out the rights an advocate has and the limits of the role. Much of Chapter 20 would also be relevant.

LEGAL STATUS OF ADVOCATES

Normally an advocate has no formal legal status. They are not appointed by the courts. They are not legal guardians. A guardian takes decisions for a person. An advocate helps the person to make a decision, or makes sure that other people who take decisions affecting a person have considered the person's needs and wishes.

There was an attempt to give advocates for disabled people legal rights in the Disabled Persons (Services, Consultation and Representation) Act 1986 (the "Tom Clarke Act"). Sections 1 and 2 of this Act would have given disabled people the right to appoint *"representatives"*. Where a disabled person was not able to appoint a representative, the social work department would have had to appoint one for that person.

The representative would have had the right to accompany the disabled person to meetings, receive information about the disabled person (eg, their social work file), and generally to act for the person in dealing with the local authority.

Although this legislation was approved by Parliament, it was not brought into force by the Government, and they have made it clear that they do not propose to bring this legislation into force in the foreseeable future.

Although advocates do not have a general legal status, there are various procedures which give specific rights to advocates.

The NHS

The NHS in Scotland has published guidelines for *"patients' supporters"*[1]. These are people who can help a patient in dealing with the NHS over their care and treatment. It is not a formal appointment and it is up to the patient whether they want one and who they choose.

A patient can insist on having a supporter with them in meetings with NHS staff. As well as discussing the patient's treatment with doctors and nurses, the supporter can:

- give moral support
- help to explain things
- help the patient make decisions about treatment and care
- help with complaints and questions

Unfortunately, the guidance does not properly cover the needs of NHS patients who may not be able to choose a supporter (eg, people with profound learning disabilities or severe dementia). Some hospitals have set up advocacy schemes with paid staff but these are not yet universal.

The guidance does not rule out people who work in the NHS (eg, nurses) being patients' supporters. However, most people in the advocacy movement believe it is important for advocates to be independent whenever possible, so that they can truly represent the service user without any conflict of loyalties.

A carer can be a patient's supporter or can help the patient find one, perhaps through a local voluntary agency or local health council.

Social work

There is no overall scheme for advocacy within social work, but a number of social work departments have funded advocacy schemes and a few have committed themselves to the principles of the Tom Clarke Act[2].

An advocate can initiate a formal complaint and should be able to speak at any formal review (although the precise procedure for a review is up to the local authority). In the assessment process, the guidance states that representatives or advocates may be included if the user or carer wishes[3].

Where local authorities are funding other organisations to provide care, the contract will often specify that users have the right to an advocate.

The police

There is special guidance to the police when they interview people with learning disabilities or mental health problems, whether as victims of crime, witnesses, or suspects[4]. Interviews and other procedures should be conducted in the presence of an *"appropriate adult"* who should be independent from the police.

The circular emphasises that the appropriate adult's role is to assist in conducting the interview, not to be a kind of "lawyer for the defence". (This is different from England and Wales where the appropriate adult has more of a protective role)[5]. Nevertheless, an appropriate adult can be seen as a kind of advocate. Anyone who might be asked to accompany a person with a learning disability or mental health problem to a police interview should find out about the circular and what they can and cannot do[6].

Education

In the education system, parents of a child with a Record of Special Educational Needs will normally have a *"named person"* appointed[7]. This is a kind of advocate, although the rights of the named person and their role are not clearly set out in the law. They should be able to give advice and support to parents in their dealings with teachers and education staff. The official role ends when a young person leaves school and moves to community care services, but the named person can be an important source of help during the future needs assessment (see page 17) which is the first formal consideration of the child's community care needs.

WHAT CAN AN ADVOCATE DO?

See the person

Unless a person is under some form of legal detention (or possibly guardianship), they should have the right to see anyone they wish. This includes an advocate. A refusal to allow access to an advocate would justify a formal complaint (see Chapter 25). Where a person cannot express their wishes, there should still be no reason to deny access to an advocate unless there is some evidence of the advocate causing harm.

Attend meetings

Often neither an advocate nor the actual service user have any legal right to attend meetings. However, there is no reason in principle why an advocate could not attend a meeting either on behalf of or with the service user.

Obtain information

If a person has asked for information to be shared with an advocate, there is no legal reason why it cannot be done. Even if the person could not give consent, there is no general legal bar on sharing appropriate information with an advocate (see page 105). A person who cannot act for themselves is not in a position to protect their interests against the people who hold the information and may need an advocate to do this.

NOTES

1   *Patients supporters*, Scottish Office/NHS In Scotland Management Executive.

2   Grampian Regional Council are one authority who have formally committed themselves to the Act's principles.

3   *Assessment and care management* (Circular SW11/1991), para 8.

4   SHHD Circular Police (CC) 2/1990 – *Interviewing of mentally handicapped or mentally ill persons.*

5   Statutory Code of Practice under Police And Criminal Evidence Act 1984.

6   Unfortunately the procedure is still not widely known, even among police officers. The best developed procedures to date are in Fife: see *Facilitating police interviewing of people with a mental handicap – practice guidelines* – Fife Appropriate Adult Working Group. The Scottish Office is currently reviewing the Circular mentioned at footnote 4. Anyone having difficulty obtaining the Circular should contact ENABLE.

7   Education (Scotland) Act 1980, s62(2)(c). For more information see the HMSO publications *In special need* and *A special partnership.*

Incapacity – taking decisions on behalf of someone

INTRODUCTION

Many people who need care may have problems in understanding their affairs or taking decisions. For example, they may have a learning disability, a mental health problem, or be elderly and confused. This does not always mean that a person is legally incapable of acting for themselves. They may simply need support and advocacy.

However, some people cannot act for themselves. This is called "legal incapacity" or being incapax. It can be difficult for people such as friends and relatives to know what they are allowed to do on that person's behalf. This section looks at how this affects the provision of community care[1].

The law assumes that you are not incapax unless there is evidence to show that you are. Legal incapacity means that you do not have the ability to understand a decision or to give instructions. It is not the same as being unable to read or write. A person can enter a contract which they can't read, so long as they understand it. On the other hand, some people can read but would be incapax because they couldn't understand what they are reading.

GETTING AN ASSESSMENT

See Chapter 2

Anyone can ask a social work department to carry out a community care assessment on someone they think needs help. The request could come from a carer, doctor, relative, or simply a concerned neighbour. The social work department must then consider whether an assessment is needed[2]. They can even do a community care assessment when the person concerned does not want one, although they would normally be reluctant to do this unless there was a good reason (eg the person's condition meant they did not appreciate their situation).

GOING INTO RESIDENTIAL CARE

See Chapters 7 – 13

This can cause major problems, particularly because of the financial aspect.

Choosing a care home

On page 42, we explained that residents have rights to choose a care home.

In some cases, the resident might not be able to state which home they prefer because of mental disability. However, their relatives or carers may have strong views about where the person should go.

A **mental health guardian**, and in most cases a **tutor dative**, would have the right to exercise the choice on behalf of the resident. In some cases, this might also apply to a person with a **power of attorney**.

Otherwise, a relative or other interested person does not have the right to force the social work department to fund their choice of home. The social work department has to act in the way it believes is in the resident's best interests. However, the guidance clearly states that it should take account of the views of a carer or advocate[3], as well as any views which the resident has previously expressed. If they totally ignored those views, that would justify a complaint or even, in extreme cases, legal action.

Paying the charges

This is not a problem for most people if their charges are paid out of their benefits. If they are not able to handle their benefits, an **appointee** can be appointed by the Department of Social Security (DSS) who can pay the charges on their behalf.

Often the appointee is someone from the care home, but there is no requirement for this to happen. Some homes will seek to insist that they take over the appointeeship when someone goes into care. If someone else (eg, a relative) is unhappy about this, they could take the matter up with the DSS or the body which registers and inspects the home[4] (see page 39). If a person is seriously concerned about how a home administers the resident's benefits, they could also contact the **Mental Welfare Commission** (see page 134).

The situation is more difficult where a person has to pay charges out of other assets. In theory, if a person is unable to manage their own affairs, this should be done by a **curator bonis** or under an **enduring power of attorney**. In practice, many people do not have a curator or attorney. Families often have to make arrangements with banks to pay bills out of a disabled person's account. These are basically informal arrangements. They may be legally justified (under the principle of **negotiorum gestio**), but there are no rules about how they should operate.

SIGNING A "CONTRACT FOR CARE"

See Chapter 23

Chapter 23 explains that people who use community care services are often asked to sign a contract or agreement, setting out what kind of help they need or can expect. In particular, most homes expect a resident to sign some kind of contract when they go into care. This sets out what the resident can expect from the home and what the home may expect of the resident. Many are intended more as a statement of general principles than a legally binding agreement.

If the resident cannot understand the contract, the home may ask a relative or advocate to sign it. In most cases, this will not have any legal effect (unless the person is a curator or tutor or has a power of attorney). Generally, there is no harm in a relative signing such an agreement, provided they are happy with it and everyone understands what legal effect (if any) the signature will have. If in doubt, it is wise to seek legal advice. **No one should be denied a service because a relative cannot or will not sign a contract.**

PROVIDING CARE AGAINST A PERSON'S WILL

Many people do not want to go into residential care and give up their home. Normally a person could not be forced into care against their will (although there is often an element of strong persuasion). However, there are mechanisms for placing a person in residential care, particu-

larly if they are mentally disabled or living in very poor surroundings.

Guardianship

A person who has a learning disability, dementia, or a mental health problem may be placed under guardianship[5]. This allows the guardian (normally the local authority) to require the person to live in a particular place.

The procedure is normally initiated by a **mental health officer**, who is employed by the social work department. The guardian is actually appointed by the local sheriff court. Guardianship would normally only be used as a last resort where there was serious concern about a person's welfare.

Guardianship can also be used to require a person to receive occupation or training or to see specified people (eg, doctors or social workers).

National Assistance Act

There is also a separate power under the National Assistance Act which allows a person who is suffering from *'grave chronic disease'* or who is *'aged or infirm...and living in insanitary conditions'* to be committed to hospital or another suitable place on the order of the court[6]. This power is also rarely used nowadays.

There are of course also legal provisions for detention of mentally disordered people, which are not discussed in detail here[7].

PAYING FOR CARE

Even if a person has been forced into residential care against their will, they are still expected to contribute to the cost of that care out of their assets, if they have any. However, the procedures for placing someone into care do not give the social work department any extra power to recover their charges. For example, a mental health guardian has no power to deal with financial matters[8].

If the person refuses to pay, the social work department may place a **Charging Order** on any home or land (see page 56). If the person does not own a home or land, the authority would have to use normal debt recovery procedures.

If the person is not capable of handling their affairs, the social work department may have to apply for a curator bonis to allow them to recover their charges.

Selling the family home

If a person is not able to understand the effect of selling their home, they could not legally sign any deed doing so. The sale would need to be carried out by:

- someone with a power of attorney (but only if the person had sufficient understanding when they signed the deed, and it was an "enduring" power)

- a curator bonis

- a tutor dative

Even if there is no-one who has the right to sell the home, it could still be treated as a capital asset by the social work department and the DSS, and increased charges could be due if the person has moved into residential care.

The social work department could place a Charging Order on the home (see page 56) and wait till the resident dies to collect the arrears. Alternatively, they could use their power to apply for a curator bonis to be appointed[9]. It will probably be simpler for them in most cases to impose a Charging Order. However, if the curator would be better for the resident, they have a legal responsibility to apply for a curator if no-one else is doing so (the relatives could also apply to have a curator appointed).

Where a person will not need long term financial management, a tutor dative may have advantages over a curator bonis. A tutor could be appointed specifically to sell the house and make arrangements to pay the fees, and could then be discharged. However, each case must be weighed up carefully[10].

A person who has a power of attorney may be tempted to transfer the home into their own name, or sell it for less than its market value, to reduce the level of the financial assessment of the person in care (see Chapter 10). There are dangers in doing this. The DSS or social work department may still treat the property as belonging to the person in care (see pages 54-56). In extreme cases, such a transaction could even be a crime (eg, fraud or embezzlement).

SIGNING A TENANCY AGREEMENT

See Chapter 14

If the tenant would not be able to understand enough to sign a tenancy agreement, this can be done by a curator bonis or tutor dative[11]. If there is no curator or tutor, the legal position is not clear. Some local authorities have accepted a relative's signature as negotiorum gestor, but this seems legally doubtful. Historically, a tenancy was a contract and could not be entered into unless the tenant had legal capacity. However, the law has created tenants' rights for people in a particular situation. It could be possible to argue that a person whose circumstances make them a tenant will have those rights even if they could not sign a contract.

If a person does not have tenants' rights, they still have some rights as an occupant (see page 71).

GIVING UP A TENANCY

Problems have arisen where people have gone into residential care from a local authority tenancy. If the person no longer has legal capacity, they cannot legally give up the tenancy. In order to bring the tenancy to an end, some councils have taken action to evict the tenant (on the grounds of non-payment of rent) after the person has moved into care. Obviously this is not an ideal solution. The law is not particularly helpful, since getting a curator bonis or tutor dative appointed to give up the tenancy could take a long time and be expensive.

Where it is clear that the person will not be coming home, it may be possible to persuade the council to accept that the tenancy is ended without legal proceedings. In some cases, they may accept the signature of a relative or carer, acting as a negotiorum gestor, although they would be entitled to expect independent verification that the tenant has left permanently.

If they insist on legally terminating the tenancy, the best course seems to be for the council to repossess the house on the grounds of abandonment[12]. This requires notices to be served but need not involve court action and could take as little as four weeks.

HOSPITAL CLOSURES

See Chapter 16

Relatives are sometimes unhappy about decisions to discharge a person from hospital into the community. If relatives do have an involvement in a person's life, it would normally be good practice to include them in discussions about that person's future, and there may be a right to a proper consultation process (see page 80). However, they will, in general, have no legal

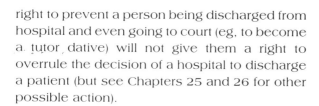

The law and your rights to community care

right to prevent a person being discharged from hospital and even going to court (eg, to become a tutor dative) will not give them a right to overrule the decision of a hospital to discharge a patient (but see Chapters 25 and 26 for other possible action).

ACCESS TO FILES

See Chapter 21

Where a person is able to ask to see their social work or health files, but might not be able to understand them, they can ask someone else (eg, a carer) to look at the files on their behalf[13].

If the person is not able to authorise someone else to look at the file, the law is not absolutely clear. A tutor dative would probably have the right to see the file and some appointments of tutors specifically mention this. The guidance for social work files suggests that access should be given to a curator bonis[14]. For health records, the Access to Health Records Act[15] says that anyone appointed by a court to manage the patient's affairs is entitled to access. This would include curators, tutors, and possibly mental health guardians.

Where there is no court appointment, third parties like carers have no legal right to insist on access. The guidance for social work records imply that access should be allowed, provided the department is satisfied the person seeking access is acting in the interests of the disabled person[16]. The guidance on health records is less clear and simply states that carers in that situation do not have a right of access under the Act but health professionals should consider whether informal voluntary access should be given[17].

MAKING A COMPLAINT

See Chapter 25

The law covering social work complaints specifically allows complaints to be made by anyone acting on behalf of a user (or potential user) of social work services[18]. Guidance makes it clear that this would include, amongst others, complaints made by carers[19]. No special powers

should be needed, even where the service user would not be able to authorise the person acting for them to raise the complaint.

There is no reason why a carer or any other concerned person should not use any of the other procedures outlined in Chapter 25 on behalf of someone who is unable to act on their own.

GOING TO COURT

See Chapter 26

Normally a lawyer cannot take up a court case for someone unless that person instructs them to do so. That can cause problems for people who might not be able to communicate with a lawyer. If a person becomes involved in a court case (eg, somebody sues them) and the court does not think they can instruct their lawyer, a **curator ad litem** can be appointed. This is someone appointed by the court (often another lawyer) who instructs the lawyer for the disabled person.

There is a bigger problem if a person wants to start a court case but they cannot give instructions to their lawyer. This might happen, for example, if the person has a claim for damages or might have a claim for **judicial review** to obtain services. The normal rule is that a curator bonis has to be appointed before the case begins so that the lawyer can be instructed[20].

The problem about this is that (unlike a curator ad litem) the curator bonis will still be in place after the case has finished. This can cause major problems, especially if the person does not have a great deal of money.

Recently, there has been a case where the court accepted that a curator ad litem could be appointed to start a court case instead of a curator bonis if this was required for "natural justice"[21].

A possible alternative might be for the carer or another concerned person to apply to be a tutor dative with power to raise a court action. The advantages over a curator bonis are that they could be given more specific power and would not need to stay in office beyond the court case.

Who can act

People who are relatives of, or care for, an incapacitated adult have no special legal authority to make decisions on their behalf. Sometimes they may be able to take certain actions (eg set up a standing order to pay bills) under the legal principle of "negotiorum gestio". However, the extent of this is not clear. This is a list of some of the appointments which can be made to take particular decisions.

Appointments	Who are they	Who appoints them	What powers do they have
DSS appointee	Any appropriate person - often a relative or carer	The Benefits Agency	Power to claim, collect, and spend welfare benefits
Hospital Manager	-	-	For residents of psychiatric and learning disability hospitals, they can administer patients' funds
Power of Attorney	Anyone chosen by the person (often relative or solicitor)	The person (before they become incapacitated)	Power to deal with financial affairs subject to any specifications in the deed appointing them
Curator bonis	Normally a solicitor or accountant but can be another suitable person, eg, a relative	Sheriff Court or Court of Session	Power to deal with all financial affairs
Tutor Dative	Normally a relative but can be any appropriate person	Court of Session	Depends on Court Order. Normally power to deal with personal decisions (eg, medical consent) but can also be given financial powers
Tutor at Law	Nearest male relative	Court of Session	Power to deal with both personal and financial affairs (this is a very rare appointment)
Mental Health Guardian	Almost always social work department or one of its staff	Sheriff Court	Power to: - require person to live in specified place - require person to attend for medical treatment and various other purposes - require person to see doctor or other specified person No power to give medical consent or deal with financial affairs
Curator ad litem	Usually a lawyer	Court of Session or Sheriff Court	Power to carry on legal proceedings on behalf of person

NOTES

1 For more detailed advice on the law, see Adrian Ward *The power to act*, and Ashton & Ward *Mental handicap and the law*. These texts focus on learning disability but contain a lot of useful information for other community care groups. For advice on financial management, see *Dementia and money matters – a guide for carers* available free to carers from Alzheimer Scotland – Action on Dementia. The law is currently under review by the Scottish Law Commission. See Discussion Paper 94 *Mentally disabled adults*. Firm proposals from the Commission are expected shortly.

2 Social Work (Scotland) Act 1968, s12A(1).

3 *Direction and Guidance on choice of accommodation* (SW5/93), para 13.

4 Reg 33 of the Social Security (Claims and Payments) Regulations 1987 (SI No 1968). The regulations do not prescribe who should be the appointee, but it is DSS policy that it should normally be a relative unless there is no one available or willing to act. The decision is made (at least in theory) by the Secretary of State. There is no appeal.

5 Mental Health (Scotland) Act 1984, ss36 - 59. For more information, see Blackie & Patrick *Mental health: a guide to the law in Scotland*, Chapter 3.

6 National Assistance Act 1948, s47 – see Blackie & Patrick, Chapter 2. This power and other emergency powers are also under review by the Scottish Law Commission. See Discussion Paper No 96 *Mentally disordered and vulnerable adults: public authority powers*. This also contains a very useful summary of existing powers.

7 Mental Health (Scotland) Act 1984. See Blackie & Patrick.

8 Mental Health (Scotland) Act 1984, s41(3).

9 Mental Health (Scotland) Act 1984, s92.

10 Relatives could apply for a tutor dative. It is not clear whether the local authority could. The Mental Health (Scotland) Act 1984 only gives the local authority the power to apply for a curator.

11 The case of *McLauchlin's Curator Bonis v Motherwell District Council* 1994 Scots Law Times Land Court & Tribunal, p31 ruled on the circumstances in which a curator bonis might seek to buy a council house on behalf of an incapacitated tenant.

12 Housing (Scotland) Act 1987, ss49 – 51.

13 For social work files see Scottish Office Circular SW2/1989 on *Access to personal files (Social Work) (Scotland) Regulations*, para 41. For health records, the authorisation should be in writing – see Access to Health Records Act 1990, s3.

14 *Access to personal files*, para 42.

15 Access to Health Records Act 1990, s3.

16 *Access to personal files*, para 42.

17 NHS in Scotland Management Executive *Access to Health Records Act 1990 – a guide for the NHS*, Chapter 3, para 8.

18 Social Work (Scotland) Act 1968, s5B(1).

19 Circular SW5/1991 *Local authority complaints procedures*, para 4.

20 *McGauchey v Livingstone* 1992 Scots Law Times 386. See Ashton & Ward, pp45 – 49 for a more detailed discussion of this issue.

21 *McKim's Curator v Collinge* (Greens Weekly Digest 1994 13 – 864), following *Moodie v Dempster* 1931 Session Cases p555. The case is discussed in SCOLAG July 1994 pp113-5. It was a judicial review of a decision to refuse a Social Fund payment to a disabled woman.

Confidentiality and access to information

This chapter looks at your rights in respect of information held about you, your rights to have it kept confidential, and your rights to have access to it.

CONFIDENTIALITY

Before you tell anyone about your circumstances you need to know that the information will be kept confidential. And generally, it will be. There are different codes of confidentiality for the different professions, but the duties they have are very similar[1].

We explain the rules in the health service and the rules for social workers. We also explain what you can expect from a voluntary organisation which may run supported housing, a drop-in centre or a befriending service. Private bodies, such as nursing homes or private therapists, have to keep information confidential, too.

We also look at the rare occasions when information will not be kept confidential and what you can do if confidential information about you is passed on without your consent.

The rules in this chapter cover all of Scotland. Your hospital or GP practice may have their own leaflet explaining their policy on confidentiality. You could ask for a copy.

The basic rule is that if someone receives information about you in a situation where it is expected that it will be kept confidential, it should be kept confidential, unless you agree that the information can be passed on.

MEDICAL CONFIDENTIALITY

The Scottish Office has prepared a Code of Practice for everyone in the NHS. This means not just doctors and nurses but porters, hospital managers and finance staff. The basic rule is that all information should be kept confidential. It should not be passed on unless you consent.

When can information be passed on?

Routine cases

- If you have agreed to the information being disclosed.

- **If other people need to know.** Information can be disclosed to others in the care "team" on a "need to know " basis.

  If other people, for example at a GP's surgery, are going to help with your care and they need to know details of your case, they can be told. If you have a carer who helps with your medication or personal care, they should be told whatever they need to know to help them care. You should be told that this will happen.

- **Non-medical staff in the health board or NHS Trust may need to see your records to help them manage the service** or to collect statistics, and your records may be seen by trainee doctors or nurses. But if you are not willing for them to be seen by a trainee, you should say so.

If you want someone else involved

Your case may be discussed with other people if you want this. You may want a friend or a member of your family or your carer to be involved. If you ask the doctors to discuss your care with them, they should agree.

But sometimes, because of confidentiality, doctors refuse to pass on information and they may refuse to discuss your case with someone even though you have asked them to.

The only time when this would be justified is if the doctors think that you are too ill to agree that someone else should have confidential information about you. In those circumstances, if they think it is not in your interests for the other person to know about your case, they may refuse to tell them.

If you want to make sure someone has the right to be consulted, you may want to appoint them your "**patient's supporter**" while you are well. See page 96.

- **The information may be used for medical teaching, research and /or audit.** Records may be made available on an anonymous basis, for teaching or research. If they are wanted for research, this would have to be approved by the local Ethics Committee. If you could be identified from the records, the doctors should ask your permission.

Unusual cases

- **If your consent cannot be obtained.** You may be too ill to say whether things should be kept confidential. If the doctor thinks it best, they may disclose the information to a relative or someone else. It would be up to the doctor to decide whether or not to do this, and no-one could force the doctor to tell them details except, perhaps, a **tutor dative.** See page 103.

- **If the information is required by law.** There may be a duty to report medical details under the law. Doctors have to notify the public health authorities of certain diseases and have to co-operate with Fatal Accident Inquiries, for example.

  A judge may order a doctor to answer a question in court. The law says that the doctor has to answer such questions, even though this would be a breach of confidentiality.

- **If it is in your interests.** The NHS Code of Practice says that information may be disclosed in the "best interests" of the patient even if the patient has refused consent. Unfortunately it does not give any examples of what kind of situations might justify this. It would be a very unusual situation and would require very careful consideration.

> **If you feel very strongly that there are certain people you do not want involved, you might want to tell your doctor this and get a note on your record. If you have a crisis card you might state on that the names of people you do not want involved.**

- **If it is in the wider public interest that the information should be disclosed.** A doctor can probably disclose information about someone if this is in the public interest, even though this may not be what the patient wants and not in the patient's interests.

There are no very clear rules about when this would be justified, as very few cases have come to court. The sort of situations where information might be passed on would be to try to stop a serious crime from being committed or to help detectives investigating a serious crime. If there was a risk of harm or serious injury to the patient or to someone else or a serious risk to public health, information might be passed on.

Breach of confidence: when can it be justified?

A psychiatrist was asked to examine someone who was appealing against his detention under the Mental Health Act in England. He decided that the man was very dangerous and should not be released. The patient dropped his case and so the psychiatrist's evidence was not heard.

The psychiatrist got in touch with the Secretary of State and told him how dangerous he thought the person was. The patient sued the doctor for breach of confidentiality. The court said that the doctor should not be criticised for what he did. It was in the public interest that a dangerous person should not be released from hospital[2].

SOCIAL WORKERS AND CONFIDENTIAL INFORMATION

The Government has drawn up a code for everyone working in social work departments. The rules apply to everyone employed in the social work department, to people supplying services under contract to the social work department, to social work volunteers and to paid carers[3].

The social work code says that all personal information should be regarded as confidential. Only in certain circumstances can it be disclosed without the client's consent.

When can information be passed on?

In some situations, information can be passed on about you. As with health workers, some of these are routine, others more unusual.

Routine cases

- Information about you can always be passed on if you agree.

- Information may be passed on so that social workers can carry out their jobs. For instance, finance staff may need information to work out how to charge you for certain services and social workers may need to co-operate with other professions to help you.

- Other agencies may be given information if they are working in partnership with the social work department.

- Volunteer carers may need to have personal information to help them look after someone.

Exceptional circumstances

- Information may have to be disclosed by law or social workers may have to answer questions in court or at a children's hearing.

- The code says it would be justified to pass information to the police if this would help prevent, detect or prosecute a serious crime.

- Occasionally, social workers may feel they have to alert the police to a person who is missing and is likely to be in danger.

- If disclosure was necessary to protect another person or to prevent a serious risk to public health, this would probably be allowed.

Social workers and confidential information

The social services department in a London borough told foster parents that they suspected one of their former foster parents of having abused children in his care. The allegations had never been proved and he sued them for breach of confidentiality[4]. The court said that he was right. The council had a policy of letting foster parents have full information about all the children in their care, but in this situation they had not given proper consideration to the effect the disclosures would have on the man. They could have warned parents without mentioning the man's name.

This case was about what information a person needs to know to help them act as foster parents.

The law seems to say that even if the rules say confidential information can be disclosed, the social work department must balance everyone's interests to decide whether or not to break confidentiality.

VOLUNTARY AND INDEPENDENT ORGANISATIONS

You may live in a private nursing home. Or you may visit a therapist or counsellor. Perhaps you go to a drop in centre run by a voluntary organisation or live in supported accommodation run by a housing association.

All these people should keep information about you confidential. It is only in very rare circumstances that they would be allowed to pass on information about you against your will.

If a voluntary or independent organisation working with the social work department receives personal information about you, they should keep it confidential. If they contract for services, the contract with the social work department will require them to keep their clients' personal information confidential.

They should have their own rules and procedures for dealing with confidential information[5], and should make sure that you have a copy.

REMEDIES FOR BREACH OF CONFIDENTIALITY

What can you do if personal information about you is passed on?

In the case of NHS staff, you would complain. For GPs you complain to the health board. In hospitals you complain to the general manager. If you are not satisfied you might want to take this further, to the health services ombudsman. Or you might want to complain to the health worker's professional body, if they have one. See Chapter 25 for further information about making complaints.

If the social work department was involved, you would complain through their complaints procedure (see page 126). If you are still unhappy, you might then to go to the local government ombudsman (see page 128). In the case of a voluntary organisation or housing association, they should have a complaints procedure you can follow. You may want to complain to the social work department if they are funding the voluntary organisation (see page 127).

The most difficult cases involve private organisations, such as private therapists or counsellors. They may be individuals who are self-employed, so you cannot complain to their employers. If they are members of a professional body, you can complain to it. If not, the only course open to you might be to take legal action.

If someone discloses confidential information about you unreasonably, you could take legal action against them. If they were found to blame, they could have to pay you damages to compensate you for any harm caused. This could include compensation for any mental distress you were caused. However this has very rarely been done in Scotland. You would need to seek legal advice. See page 153.

ACCESS TO RECORDS

Most patients and social work clients have the right to find out what doctors or social workers have written on their notes. What are your rights? And what if your records are wrong? Can you get them corrected? Are there any circumstances when you cannot see your records? This section tries to answer these questions.

It looks at the two main sets of records which may be kept about you: your medical records and social work records.

You have the right to see other records too, such as those of the housing department and the education authority. For further information see *What's on my record? A practical guide to your rights of access to personal information.* (Free from the Scottish Consumer Council.)

Access to medical records

Many doctors and health workers have always let patients see their records and talk over things which worried them. Now patients have been given the legal right to apply to see their health records by the Access to Health Records Act 1990.

Form appointing another person to have access to medical records

I hereby authorise .... (name)

of ....

.... (address)

to apply on my behalf for access to my health records, in accordance with section 3(1)(b) of the Access to Health Records Act 1990.

Name ....

Address ....

....

Signature ....

Date ....

Records covered by the Act

The Access to Health Records Act says patients can see records held by:

- doctors, including GPs, hospital doctors and doctors in private practice
- nurses
- community psychiatric nurses
- Mental Welfare Commission
- pharmacists
- dentists
- opticians
- health visitors
- psychologists, child psychotherapists and speech therapists
- art or music therapists
- occupational therapists
- physiotherapists

Who can apply for access?

You may apply yourself to see your records, or you may appoint someone else to do so.

If you want to appoint someone else, this has to be done in writing. We have included a form below, as the Act does not say how to do this.

> **If you know that you might want someone to have access to your records in the future, it is a good idea to send the form to your GP and perhaps to the hospital. It is important that your GP knows that when you signed the form you were well enough to appoint someone.**

If someone has been appointed by the court to manage your affairs, he or she will be able to apply for access. The legal representative of someone who has died, or someone with a claim arising from a person's death may apply. In certain cases parents will have the right to see their child's records, provided the child's right to privacy can be protected.

See page 102 for what happens when the person the files are about could not understand them or ask for them.

Applying for access

You have to apply in writing to the person who has your records. In the case of your GP, you would write to the surgery. In the case of a hospital it would be the health board or NHS Trust. The Mental Welfare Commission holds its own records. The records of community health workers, such as occupational therapists, are kept by the health board or trust.

Seeing your records

A person who had been asking to see his medical records since the 1960s took the health authority to court because they refused to let him see them. He argued there was a legal duty on on doctors and health authorities to show people records made before the Act came into effect.

The health authority said that it would be harmful to his health to let him see them. They offered to let a medical expert appointed by him see them instead.

The court said that the health authority were right. They were entitled to decide what was best for the patient. The patient should not be allowed to see his records. The health authority should decide what was best for the patient[6].

Fees

If you apply within 21 days of the record being made, no fee is payable. If you apply outside that period, a fee of up to £10 may be charged. It is up to the health professional to decide what to charge[7]. They may also charge copying fees and postage, if you want a copy.

When can access be refused?

You do not always have the right to see your medical records.

- You have no rights under the Act to information if it was recorded before November 1 1991 (the date the Act came into effect). (But see the case left.) The doctor must show you older information if it is necessary to explain any part of your record.

- If the record holder believes that showing you the record would be likely to cause serious harm to your physical or mental

They will probably have their own form for you to fill in. Or you can use the form opposite.

Remember to keep a copy of your application!

However a formal application under the Act may not be necessary. Many doctors and health workers have a policy of open access to records. This means that they will let you see your records anyway, if you ask. Always ask before you put in a formal application.

Gaining access

You will not necessarily see the whole record, particularly if it is very big or old. The holders can give you a copy or type out the appropriate bit for you to see.

If you want to have a photocopy to take away with you, you should ask. You may have to pay for this. You may want to take notes from your records and there is no reason why you should not be allowed to do this.

You must be shown recent records within 21 days of applying. (Recent records means records made within 40 days of your application.) If the records are older than this you must see them, or a copy, within 40 days.

If you cannot understand the record, perhaps because you cannot read the writing or because abbreviations are used which you don't understand, it must be explained to you.

Form of application for access to health records

To ....

....

.... (record holder's name and address)

I hereby apply for access to my health records in accordance with the Access to Health Records Act 1990.

or (if you are a representative applying on behalf of a friend or relative)

I hereby apply for access to the health records of

....

in accordance with the Access to Health Records Act 1990. I have been appointed by him / her under s3(1) (b) of the Act and I enclose a copy of his/her letter of appointment.

Records required for treatment for ....

....

at ....

.... Hospital / General Practice / Clinic

Records required in respect of treatment during the

period from .... to .... (dates)

Name ....

Address ....

....

Signature ....

Date ....

health or to that of anyone else, he or she need not disclose that bit of the record. The record holder does not have to tell you if he or she holds back part of the record in this way.

- If the record contains information about someone else who could be identified, you will not be entitled to see that part of the record, unless that person allows this or he or she is a health professional who has been involved in your care.

Correcting the records

If you think that any part of the record is wrong, you can apply to the record holder to have it amended. The law says the record should be changed if it contains anything "*incorrect, misleading or incomplete*".

For instance, the facts may be wrong, or it could miss out important facts. Or it could contain opinions which you think are misleading.

Complaint about access to medical records

To ....
.... (name and address of record holder.)

I, ... (name)

of .... (address)

hereby complain under the Access to Health Records Act 1990.

I applied for access to the health records

of .... (name of person whose records are to be seen) ("the patient")

on .... (date).
I am the patient*/I am authorised to act on behalf of the patient because I have been appointed by the patient in writing to apply on his/her behalf*/I am the parent/ guardian of the patient*/ the patient is incapable of managing his/her own affairs and I have been appointed by the court to manage those affairs*/the patient has died and I am the patient's personal representative*/the patient has died and I have a claim arising out of the patient's death.* (*delete as applicable)

The basis of my complaint is that you did not comply with the provisions of the Access to Health Records Act 1990 because

....
....(set out grounds for complaint)

I wait to hear from you.

....(Signature)
....(Date)

If the record holder changes the record, he or she must let you have a copy.

However the record holder may not agree to change the record. If this happens, he or she must at least make a note of your comments and give you a copy. The note should be kept with your records, so at least you will have your side of the story on the file.

There is no charge for this or for correcting records.

Complaints

If you think that someone has not done what the Act says they should do, you can complain.

First you must complain to the record holder. Then you must wait for their reply and then, if you wish, you can go to court to complain. There are very strict time limits for making complaints[8].

Complaint to the record holder

You must first put in a written complaint.

In the case of a hospital, you complain to the Unit General Manager. In the case of a health board or NHS Trust employee, you would complain to the health board or NHS Trust. In the case of a GP or the Mental Welfare Commission, you would complain direct to them.

If you want to complain, you must do this within 3 months of applying for the record or applying to have it corrected.

There is no form of complaint set out in the Act and these bodies may have their own forms. If not, you can use the form on the left.

Going to court

The record holder must reply within 3 months. The reply should state what action has been taken to comply with the Act, or if no action has been taken, why not.

If you are not satisfied with the reply, or if the record holder does not reply at all, you can go to court. You can go either to your local sheriff court or to the Court of Session in Edinburgh. Normally you would go to the sheriff court.

If you want to go to court, you must do this within one year from the date of the record holder's reply. If they do not reply you should go to court within a year of the date they should have replied[9].

If you want to go to court you may need legal advice. See page 153 about choosing a solicitor.

Access to records and human rights

Graham Gaskin had been in care as a child and wanted to find out about his early childhood and family life. He applied for access to his social work records. Various people named in the records did not agree to information being disclosed to him. The social work department did not give him the information. He complained and when that failed he went to the European Court of Human Rights in Strasbourg.

The court said that his human rights had been violated. He had a right to find out about his early life. They said there should be an independent appeal if people refuse their consent in such circumstances. The Scottish Office is currently looking into the implications of this case for Scotland[11].

ACCESS TO SOCIAL WORK RECORDS

Information you can see

Your right to see social work files is very similar to your right to see medical records. You have the right to see a copy of any personal information about you held by the social work department. This could relate either to information on your own file or on other people's files[10].

Information you cannot see

There are some situations where you cannot see the information written about you. You cannot see records in the following circumstances:

- You cannot see information recorded before April 1 1989, unless you need it to help you understand later records. (In certain circumstances you may be able to see older information: see box above.)

- You cannot see information about someone else unless they agree. This does not apply if the other person is a health worker, a member of the social work department or a paid carer. (But see box above.)

- You will not be allowed to see information if the social work department believes this would be likely to cause serious harm to your physical or mental health or to your emotional condition, or to that of someone else.

- If you are paid for your services by the local authority you will not be entitled to see your records. (So someone who is paid to care for a person will not be able to see what the social work department has written about them.)

- You cannot see the records kept by Reporters to children's panels.

- The records of social workers in prison and in the State Hospital cannot be seen.

- You do not have a right to see the records of voluntary or independent organisations, even if they are supplying services to the social work department, under this law. However, many such organisations will have a policy of allowing access to files.

- If the social work department holds information to help prevent or detect crime, it will not have to reveal this.

- They will not have to hand over certain records relating to adoption.

Who may apply for access

You may apply or, if you want, you can appoint someone to apply for you. You can use the form below to appoint someone.

The social work department will not allow your representative to see the information unless they are sure that you understood what you were doing when you signed the form. It might be a good idea to get your GP to witness the form if there could be any doubt about this.

Form appointing another person to have access to social work records

I hereby authorise ....
.... *(name)*
of ....
.... *(address)*
to apply on my behalf for access to my social work records.

Name ....
Address ....
....
Signature ....
Date ....

How to apply

The application has to be in writing. The social work department may have a form: otherwise just a letter saying you want to see the records should do. If you have difficulty in filling in the forms, a social worker should be able to help you.

If you are a carer or friend, you would have to say why you wanted to see the records.

The social work department may charge you for seeing the records. They are allowed to charge up to £10. Ask beforehand if there will be a fee.

Gaining access

The social work department must reply within 40 days. They should either give you the information or tell you that there is no information they have to supply. There may be information which they are not allowed to reveal. They will not tell you about this.

They must either give you a copy of the information or let you see it. They must explain anything which cannot be understood.

Getting the record corrected

If any facts on the file are wrong, you can apply to have them put right. If the social work department agrees to change the records, they will give you a copy of the corrections if you ask them.

If they do not agree to change the records, they should write down your objections and keep the note with the file. They must give you a copy of the note they make.

They must not charge a fee for this.

Complaints

If you have problems gaining access to your social work records, you may want to complain. You would begin by complaining through the social work department's complaints procedure (see page 126). If you wanted to take things further you would probably get in touch with the local government ombudsman (see page 128).

NOTES

1 For doctors, the rules are laid down by the General Medical Council in a book called *Professional conduct and discipline: fitness to practise* (paras 76 – 91). For nurses, there are rules laid down by the UK Central Committee for nurses. The UKCC has produced a very useful advisory paper, called *Confidentiality: an elaboration of clause 9 of the UKCC's Code of Professional Conduct*. For everyone (including doctors) who works in the Scottish National Health Service, there is a *Code of practice on confidentiality of personal health information* issued by the Scottish Home and Health Department. Unfortunately all the codes are slightly different. If you are a health worker and you do not know which code to follow you would have to get advice from your professional body.

2 *W v Egdell* [1990] 1 All England Reports page 835.

3 The rules are laid down in a *Code on confidentiality of social work records* issued by the Social Work Services Group (January 1989).

4 *R v Lewisham London Borough Council ex parte P* [1991] 3 All England Reports page 529.

5 A useful starting point for any organisation which has not, might be found in Louise Villeneau *Housing with care and support*, a MIND publication.

6 *R v Mid-Glamorgan Family Health Services and Another, ex parte Martin* Times Law Report 16/8/94.

7 If you think the fees charged are too high, you may want to complain. See Chapter 25.

8 The detailed rules are set out in the Access to Health Records (Steps to secure compliance and complaints procedures) (Scotland) Regulations 1991 SI 1191/2295.

9 Although the rules do not actually say what should happen in these circumstances.

10 See Data Protection Act 1984 (access to computer held records); Access to Personal Files (Social Work) (Scotland) Regulations 1989 (access to manual records); *Guidance to local authorities from Social Work Services Group* (Circular SW2/89).

11 Letter from Social Work Services Group, 27/3/92.

Community care and minority ethnic communities

INTRODUCTION

This chapter looks at the way in which the law says community care should work for people from black and minority ethnic communities. It also looks at what you can do if things go wrong.

LEGAL DUTIES OF LOCAL AUTHORITIES

Community care must be operated in a way which is non-discriminatory[1]. People from black and minority ethnic communities must receive equal access to services to the rest of the population. This applies both to NHS services and to services from social work departments and other organisations.

But, so far as social work departments are concerned, the law imposes a positive duty as well. Local authorities must make *"appropriate arrangements"* to ensure that they operate in a way which bears in mind the need to eliminate unlawful racial discrimination and to promote equality of opportunity and good relations between persons of different racial groups[2].

In other words, as well a negative duty not to discriminate, social work departments have a positive duty to see how they can use community care to reduce racial discrimination[3].

It is probably fair to say that the guidance from the Scottish Office does not really grapple with how local authorities can implement community care in a way which will reduce racial disharmony and promote a fairer society. It is, as we will see, more concerned with attempting to prevent discrimination in the provision of services.

The Commission for Racial Equality (CRE) has produced an internal document[4] which contains some far reaching and well thought out suggestions, but this is as yet unpublished.

It has been left to minority ethnic communities themselves to push for change and for local authorities to attempt to devise their own strategies.

We will look at how the Government says local authorities should consider the needs of people from the black and minority ethnic communities in the following areas:

- community care planning
- assessment and provision of services
- complaints

PLANNING COMMUNITY CARE FOR MINORITY ETHNIC COMMUNITIES

Planning is obviously vital. The Commission for Racial Equality says that local authorities should develop explicit and agreed strategies for including race equality initiatives in their community care plans, and that black and minority ethnic communities must participate fully in consultation and development of plans.

The guidance from the Scottish Office has given some suggestions. In its first guidance on community care planning the Government simply said that community care plans must set out what *"help for people from minority ethnic groups"* the local authority intend to offer[5].

The new planning guidance from the Scottish Office has gone further. It asked local authorities and their planning partners to *"have regard to the particular needs of cultural and minority ethnic communities groups"*. Community care plans should spell out how the social work department will meet the needs of ethnic and cultural minorities within the larger community care group[6]. So if part of the plan looks at help for elderly people, for example, that part should also should say how elderly people from minority ethnic communities would be helped.

Community care and minority ethnic communities

The latest circular from the Scottish Office, *Community care, the housing dimension*[7], says that planners must consult with organisations representing minority ethnic communities. Organisations representing users and carers should be included in the planning processes and this should include organisations representing minority ethnic communities[8].

Local authorities have to tell the Government whom they have consulted on their plans[9], so the Government will be able to monitor whether appropriate groups are being consulted. If the Government is unhappy about consultation with minority ethnic communities, it can issue binding directions to local authorities, telling them to consult with specific groups[10]. So if you feel your social work department is not doing enough, and it has not responded to your complaints, you could get in touch with the Secretary of State (see page 131).

You can find out what your local authority is doing by looking at its community care plan. Many plans show that local authorities are trying to implement racial equality policies. Some, particularly in the urban areas, are involving people from the minority ethnic communities in the planning of services. Others are monitoring the use of their services by people from the minority ethnic communities, to help in future planning.

ASSESSMENT AND PROVISION OF SERVICES

The Scottish Office guidance, *Assessment and care management*, confirms that decisions about what services people receive must not discriminate against people on the grounds of their racial background. The assessment process should be equally available to people from all racial backgrounds, and information about it should be available in languages other than English[11]. Anything less than this could be against the law.

In *Community care, the housing dimension*[12], the Scottish Office urges a flexible and sensitive approach in responding to the needs of minority ethnic communities including, for example, people's religious and cultural needs. Local authorities should take care to avoid even unintentional discrimination[13]. (The only way this can be done is by pursuing clear anti-racist strategies and staff education and training, although the Government does not specifically say this.)

The CRE would like to go further. They see a need for black and minority ethnic groups to become providers of services, not just for their own groups, but for the general population. Such imaginative measures could help to promote racial harmony, as required by law.

Many local authorities are now providing information in languages other than English, but certain authorities are still making no reference to equal opportunities in their community care plans. Others are going further, and are looking at ways of increasing the number of staff from the black and minority ethnic communities groups to deliver community care at all levels. Others see training as the key and are increasing training to staff at all levels to increase access to services by people from the black and minority ethnic communities.

COMPLAINTS

If the general population has a right to complain, complaints procedures must be equally available to members of the black and minority ethnic communities. Otherwise the social work department may be breaking the law by providing a discriminatory service.

But there is no specific requirement from the Scottish Office that local authorities should make details of their complaints procedures available in minority languages. They only have to *"consider"* whether to do so[14]. Again there is no duty to help with interpretation services should a person wish to make a complaint. Authorities are told they *"may particularly wish"* to do this[15].

Many local authorities are now setting up interpretation services and ensuring that leaflets are available in languages other than English.

DEALING WITH DISCRIMINATION

If you feel that any aspect of your social work department's community care procedures is discriminatory or non-accessible, you could complain to them, through the formal social work department's complaints procedure (see page 126).

If you feel that they are not consulting as they should with people from black and minority ethnic communities, you could complain to the Secretary of State.

If you experience discrimination in any other sphere of community care, you can complain to the organisation concerned.

The law and your rights to community care

If you are not happy about the replies you receive, you can take things further. You might want to complain to an ombudsman or you might want to contact the Commission for Racial Equality (see Chapter 25). Your area may have an organisation such as a Community Relations Council which can take the matter up.

There is a new law centre particularly for people of ethnic origin. They might be able to help. The address of the Ethnic Minorities Law Centre is 2nd floor, 41 St. Vincent Place, Glasgow G1 2ER. Tel: 0141.204 2888.

NOTES

1   Race Relations Act 1976, s20(1).

2   Race Relations Act 1976, s71.

3   Note that the duty under s71 extends to all aspects of the local authority's operations: they can all be measured against the yardstick of how far they seek to reduce racial discrimination.

4   *Community care: What are the implications for black and minority ethnic communities?* March 1993.

5   Scottish Office Circular SW1/1991 Annex, para 1(f).

6   *Community care planning* (Circular SW14/ 1994) Annex A, para 5.

7   Scottish Office Circular SW 7/1994.

8   See para 3.16.

9   *Community care, the housing dimension* Appendix to Annex 4, para 1(e).

10 s5A(3)(e) of the Social Work (Scotland) Act 1968, added by s52 of the NHS & Community Care Act 1990, gives the Secretary of State the power to specify whom local authorities should consult. See page 5 for directions.

11 Such clear guidance would be binding on the local authority. See page 145.

12 See footnote 7 above.

13 para 1.6.

14 Scottish Office Circular on *Complaints procedures* para 27.1. The practice guidance says special arrangements should be made for people where English is not their main language (para 2.3).

15 *Complaints procedures*, para 37.

Understanding contracts

INTRODUCTION

Some people describe community care as the "contract culture". What they mean is that no longer do things just happen: everything has to be written down and recorded, targets have to be set and results measured. Services are provided and paid for, just as we pay for goods at the supermarket.

While the Government has produced guidance for the people who will be selling and buying these services – social work departments, voluntary organisations and independent providers – there has been very little written for the consumer, the person who will use community care, the person for whom the services are bought, and who may in fact pay a great deal towards them.

This chapter aims to redress the balance. It tries to explain the kind of contracts you may be asked to sign and what you should do, both before and afterwards, when the contract is up and running.

WHAT IS A CONTRACT?

It is any agreement between two people which they wish to be binding. It does not have to be in writing, but obviously it is easier to prove what the agreement was if it is written down. Most of the agreements for community care will be in writing.

The word "contract" is sometimes used very loosely. It really means something that both sides must comply with. If one side does not, the other side can cancel the agreement, although they might have to give the person who is in the wrong a chance to put things right first. This kind of contract is binding. People cannot ignore what it says. It does not have to be written by a lawyer or to be in any special form. It could just be a letter to you saying what the terms of the agreement are, and you could sign, saying you accepted. That would be a contract, and the courts would enforce it.

However sometimes people use the word "contract" when they just mean something which

sets out what people would like to happen or will try to do. It can be helpful to write this down but it would not be binding.

If you are asked to sign a contract, make sure that you know whether it is a legally binding contract or not, and also make sure that the other person has the same understanding.

TYPES OF CONTRACTS YOU MIGHT BE ASKED TO SIGN

It could be:

- an agreement for housing (see Chapter 14)

- an agreement for community care services, such as a home help or respite care

- a discharge agreement, in which you agree a care plan with the hospital when you leave and they say what services they will provide. (This is the sort of agreement we were talking about above. It could be a contract or it could be just something both parties hope will happen.)

- an agreement for residential care. (It is important that you know whether this is intended to be a binding agreement.)

BEFORE YOU SIGN

- **You should read the agreement and make sure you understand it.** If there are any bits you don't understand these should be explained to you. Sometimes agreements are written in very technical language that is difficult to understand, but you should not sign anything you don't understand.

- **Make sure you know what signing something means.** Sometimes it means that you agree with what is in the contract or form. Sometimes it just means that you have been given a copy, but you might not agree with what it says. (For example, you might be asked to sign your community care assessment.)

- **You might want to get advice on the agreement from someone.** The person who gives you the advice should not be someone who is employed by the other party to the agreement. (See pages 160-162 for people who might be able to give you some advice.) You might want to get a solicitor to look at the agreement for you.

- **If you do not agree with something in one of the clauses of the agreement, or it would be difficult or inconvenient for you to do something in it, you should not just sign the agreement and hope it won't matter.**

  You should ask for an explanation of why the clause is there and ask whether it can be changed in your case. If you sign, you may then find it difficult to get the clause changed in the future, and, as we have said, if you cannot do what the contract says you should do, you could be at risk of losing your housing or the service.

  If you want to change anything in the contract, you might want to get help. See pages 160-162 for people who can give advice.

AFTER YOU HAVE SIGNED

- If something happens which doesn't seem right, for instance if a home wants to put up your fees, read the contract. It might say what should happen in that situation. Don't just put the contract away and never read it. It should have some of the answers. And remember that both you and the other party have to do what the contract says.

- If the other party says they want to change the contract, they can only do so if you agree. You should get advice on this if you are not sure.

> **REMEMBER: the contract is there for your protection. Read it and use it!**

WHEN SOMEONE CANNOT SIGN

A person cannot sign a document if, because of a mental disability, they are not able to understand what it means. It is not normally possible for someone else to sign a binding contract on the person's behalf, unless they have been given special legal powers. Chapter 20 explains more about this.

Community care plans

INTRODUCTION

The NHS & Community Care Act introduced a new requirement on local authority social work departments to produce a "community care plan". The idea behind this is that services should be better co-ordinated and more responsive to the particular needs of people in the local area. This chapter explains what the plan is and how it is produced. It also discusses how people might use the plan to improve the services they receive.

WHAT IS A COMMUNITY CARE PLAN?

From April 1992, every social work department has been obliged to *"prepare and publish a plan for the provision of community care services in their area"*[1]. The legislation does not spell out exactly what must be in the plan but the Government has issued guidance saying what they would expect to see[2].

The plan should cover the needs of elderly people, people with disabilities, people with learning disabilities or mental health problems, people with problems from drug and alcohol abuse, people living with HIV/AIDS and other progressive illnesses, and carers. It does not have to cover services for children, but should cover young disabled people[3].

The plan is not an end in itself. It should not solely consist of vague generalisations or statements of philosophy but should be a way of identifying local needs and proposing specific action.

These are some of the specific items which should be in every community care plan:

- any planning agreements or other statements (eg, hospital discharge protocols)

- the needs for each care group and how they are to be met by social work, health and housing departments. This should:

  - evaluate the extent to which services meet current needs

  - quantify and prioritise gaps and deficiencies

- the plan should concentrate on social, health and housing needs, but also touch on issues like transport, leisure, recreation, training and employment

- spell out from where the local authority intends to buy services

- explain how the local authority will meet the Government's objectives for community care (see page 1 for these)

- specify who has been consulted, what they said, and how it influenced the final plan[4]

The Government does not formally approve the plans but they do take an interest in what is in them. If you believe a plan is seriously defective and the local authority will not act, it may be worth taking this up with the Secretary of State, particularly if you can get the support of a campaigning organisation (see Chapter 25)[5].

HOW OFTEN ARE THE PLANS REVIEWED?

The Act only says that plans have to be reviewed *"from time to time"*. The guidance states that plans should be reviewed annually[6]. It was expected that each authority would bring out an updated plan every April, setting out their plans for the next three years. Already some local authorities have been unable to comply with this. The reorganisation of local government may cause further problems, and more guidance from the Scottish Office will be issued on this.

HOW IMPORTANT ARE THE PLANS?

The plans are very important for finding out what the local authority is doing and planning to meet a particular need. They provide valuable information in campaigning for better services. They are also taken into account by the Government in deciding how much needs to be spent overall on community care[7].

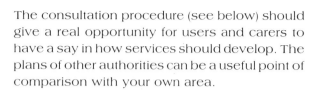

The law and your rights to community care

The consultation procedure (see below) should give a real opportunity for users and carers to have a say in how services should develop. The plans of other authorities can be a useful point of comparison with your own area.

In general, the plans are a statement of intention, not a legally binding document. A local authority is free to change its plans. Even if they did not live up to what they said they would do in the plans, this would not usually mean they had broken the law, although it would give ammunition for a campaign and possibly grounds to ask the Secretary of State to intervene.

There may also be some situations where what is in the plans could be legally important because it might create a legitimate expectation (see page 147).

This might help make a case for a judicial review of the council's actions. For example, if the plan said that people would get a particular type of assessment, someone who did not get that assessment could have a legal case. The same could apply to someone with a complaint which was not dealt with in the way set out in the plan. Another example might be where a particular service was stopped without proper consultation when it should have been possible to consult in advance using the community care planning procedure.

If you are concerned about a local authority's community care services or procedures, it is always worth checking what their plan has to say about the particular issue.

WHERE CAN I GET THE PLAN?

Local authorities are required to "*publish*" the plan. The Government expects the plans to be reasonably available to local people and to be written in a way which is understandable to the general public[8].

The plans are fairly lengthy and the authority may not be prepared to send a free copy to anyone who asks. However, it would be reasonable to expect organisations in the area which provide services or represent users to get a copy. Anyone else ought to be able to consult a copy without too much difficulty.

Any social work office or local library ought to be able to tell you where you can see the plan. If you have any problems ask your local regional councillor.

A number of local authorities have produced summaries of their plans which should be freely available. These are useful for general information but, if you have a specific concern, it is normally better to look at the plan itself.

Many service users would find it difficult to read a community care plan and groups representing users should encourage authorities to produce accessible versions (eg, in minority languages, on audiotape or video, simplified English).

HOW CAN I INFLUENCE THE PLANS?

The law requires consultation before a plan is issued or revised. The law specifies certain bodies which must be consulted[9]. The Government has issued a binding direction which adds to that list. They have also issued guidance on how the consultation should be carried out.

WHO MUST BE CONSULTED?

Health boards

All health boards in the area of the authority must be consulted. The social work department should consider what the health board is doing before drawing up its own plans and vice versa. The Government has strongly encouraged social work departments and health boards to produce a single joint plan for the areas they both cover[10] (see pages 76 and 122 for health board planning and planning agreements).

District councils

District councils in the region need to be consulted on the relationship between the plan and the housing in the area (see also Chapter 14). The proposals for local government reform abolish this requirement since the new single tier local authorities will deal with both housing and community care[11].

Representative user and carer organisations

The social work department must identify and consult with voluntary organisations which represent the interests of users of community care services and carers. Organisations representing carers of disabled children as well as adults are covered by this. The organisations may be national or local.

No particular organisation has a specific right to be consulted. However, a local authority which did not consult a particular organisation simply because it did not approve of the organisation's philosophy would not be complying with the intention of the legislation and could in an extreme case be acting unlawfully.

Service providers

Organisations which provide either housing or community care services in the area must be consulted. This includes housing associations, private care homes and charities, amongst others. Every organisation known to the authority to provide such services in the area should be consulted.

There is a separate requirement to consult any organisation which represents people who provide or may wish to provide community care services in the area and which writes to the local authority asking to be consulted[12]. This requirement seems to have been imposed because of a feeling that private sector organisations may not have had strong enough links with the local authorities in the past. Now a group of independent providers (eg, care home owners) can form a representative organisation and insist on being consulted.

WHO ELSE SHOULD BE CONSULTED?

The above list is a legal minimum. Other bodies have relevant interests and social work departments should consider whether they might also be involved in the consultation process[13]. Examples include:

- **Education authorities.** Although education is provided by the same local authority, the two services have not always worked well together. Consultation could be helpful to cover issues such as the needs for community care of school leavers and the provision of community education in places like day centres. The newly independent further education colleges may also have a role to play[14].

- **Employment and training agencies.** This could include the Department of Employment and Local Enterprise Companies.

- **Leisure and recreation services.** This is another area where the district council has an involvement.

HOW SHOULD CONSULTATION WORK?

The Act does not say how consultation should be carried out, but the guidance contains a number of points which local authorities should consider to make consultation meaningful[15]. Each community care plan must say how the authority proposes to consult with the bodies with whom it must consult[16].

The basic principle is that people should have a real chance to contribute. This means that people should have a chance to make suggestions at an early stage in the planning process, not be asked to "rubber stamp" a plan just before it goes to the printers. Some groups should be involved in advance discussions even before proposals are formally drawn up. People should have a reasonable time to respond.

The final plan should include statements on who has been consulted, the views expressed, and how they influenced the plan.

Consulting with the users and carers of services is particularly complex. Representative bodies need time to seek the views of their members. Sometimes the local authority may need to build up forums to represent particular groups of users and carers.

However, they should also attempt to consult users and carers directly. This may include things like public meetings but these may not be enough. It is often difficult for users or carers to attend such meetings or to put across their views in a way which could influence the plans themselves. Where meetings are held, it is important that people are notified and given a chance to prepare.

Consultation also needs to be tailored to the needs of users with communication or comprehension difficulties.

The assessment process may also be a way of influencing plans. The Government hopes that individual assessments will be a way of identifying the total need for services in an area. It might be possible to develop this so that people's comments on the services they would like to see for themselves could be included as part of the assessment process and fed into the plans.

CHECKLIST FOR ACTION

If you want to influence community care plans, these are some things you might do.

- Get the current plan. Consider whether you are happy with what it says about the services you are interested in. Are the proposals reasonable? Do they meet the need? Are they specific enough? Do they take account of what other people provide (or don't provide)?

The law and your rights to community care

- Check what the plan says about who has been consulted and how consultation is to be carried out. Have they consulted the right people? Have they involved users? What is the timetable for consultation? Are there ways you can be involved?

- Find out whether there are any organisations locally who might be trying to achieve the same things as you. This might include local disability forums or elderly forums, carers' groups, national charities or their branches, health councils and community councils. Find out if these organisations are involved in the consultation process and if they can represent your views. .

This process should give you some idea of what you want to say and how to get involved[17]. If you still don't think you have a chance to be involved, try to think what would need to happen to make consultation work, and suggest it to the local authority and any group representing people with your interests.

PLANNING AGREEMENTS AND JOINT PLANS

Although local authorities have to consult with other agencies before producing community care plans, the plans are mainly about the social work department's own services. Other bodies, such as health boards and housing departments, have their own planning procedures. They may

have different priorities and they may work to different timetables. This can mean that services are not well co-ordinated. Local authorities and health boards have a legal duty to work together (see page 77) but this has not always happened in reality.

Some attempts have been made to improve this as part of the community care reforms. In some areas, local authorities and health boards have got together to produce a single **joint plan**. This will include the community care plan which the local authority must produce.

A joint plan is not always possible but the government guidance expects health boards and local authorities to sign **planning agreements**[18]. These will be separate from the community care plan but will set out the ways in which the health board and local authority will work together to deliver community care. Planning agreements should specify who will do what, how much money will be spent over the next three years, and what standard of care is expected[19].

The consultation process for planning agreements is not as detailed as for community care plans. Nevertheless, you ought to be able to find out fairly easily from your local social work department or health board whether they have a planning agreement in place and how to see a copy. Some areas have set up regular meetings to consult the voluntary sector and these may be a useful way of influencing the planning agreements.

NOTES

1 s5A of the Social Work (Scotland) Act 1968 (inserted by s52 NHS & Community Care Act 1990).

2 Social Work Services Group Circulars: *Community care planning* SW1/91; *Community care plans: directions on purchasing* SW13/94 and *Community care planning* SW14/94.

3 *Community care planning* SW14/94 Annex A, para 4.

4 *Community care planning* SW14/94 Annex A. This list applies to any community care plans published after December 1994. Previously there was a more extensive list of contents (set out in Circular SW1/1991), including assessment arrangements, details of complaints procedures, etc. The Government now expects local authorities to publicise these in other ways.

5 You may want to copy any letter setting out your concerns to relevant civil servants, and campaigning organisations may be able to help you with this. Two parts of the Scottish Office with a particular interest are the Social Work Services Inspectorate and the Community Care Implementation Unit (see pages 137-138).

6 *Community care planning* SW1/91, para 1.4.

7 *Community care planning* SW14/94, para 16.

8 *Community care planning* SW14/94, para 11.1.

9 Social Work (Scotland) Act 1968, s5A(3).

10 eg, SW14/94, para 6 states *"the expectation remains firmly that joint plans will be the norm"*.

11 A circular entitled *Community care: the housing dimension* (SW7/1994) contains a great deal of information about how the Government expects planning to be co-ordinated between health, social work and housing bodies.

12 Local Authority Community Care Plans (Consultation) Directions 1993, issued with Social Work Services Group Circular SW4/93.

13 *Community care planning* SW1/91, para 7.1.

14 *Community care planning* SW14/94 re-emphasised the need to consult education authorities (para 2).

15 *Community care planning* SW1/91, paras 7.3 – 7.5. Consultation Directions SW4/93, paras 3 – 8.

16 Local Authority Community Care Plans (Consultation) Directions 1993.

17 You may also wish to read Alzheimer Scotland – Action on Dementia's useful booklet called *Having your say: planning dementia services – a guide for carers* 1992. Free to carers in Scotland, £3 to others.

18 *Community care planning* SW1/91, para 1.5.

19 See *Community care planning* SW1/91, para 5.4 for full list of contents.

Getting what you want without going to a lawyer

INTRODUCTION

In Chapter 26 we look at ways in which the law might be able to help you enforce your rights to community care services. This chapter looks at other methods of trying to enforce your rights.

Going to court is not something which many people want to do. So in this chapter we suggest other approaches which might be more practical and which make fewer demands on the person who has a complaint.

You might be able to use one or more of these methods first, and then if they fail, consider going to court.

This chapter should also be of interest to voluntary organisations which advise users of services. As we will see, it is often not possible for them to take out legal action on behalf of the people they represent; they may be able to use some of the suggestions set out in this chapter.

We list many bodies which can help; we would not suggest that you approach all of them! It all depends on what the problem is. You might find the table below helpful. We look at:

- complaining to the social work department
- the local government ombudsman
- the local government monitoring officer
- complaining to the Secretary of State for Scotland
- complaints about medical services
- the Mental Welfare Commission
- the Parliamentary ombudsman
- the Accounts Commission
- complaints about racial or sexual discrimination
- when the police should be involved

- when to approach the politicians: your local councillor or MP
- contacting the press

We also look at other bodies which have a role in community care. They do not have a part in formal complaints procedures, but if something is going wrong, you may want to get in touch with them. They are:

- the Scottish Health Advisory Service
- the Social Work Services Inspectorate
- the Community Care Implementation Unit

If you don't want to complain

Although we go on to describe a wide number of ways to take up a complaint, the majority of people who use community care services will never use any of them.

There is nothing to stop you saying you are unhappy about something without making a formal complaint. If you find it difficult to speak out or feel no-one will listen you, you could try to get an advocate. (See Chapter 19 and pages 160-162.)

However you should think about making a formal complaint in the following situations:

- if informal discussion and advocacy haven't worked
- if the matter is very important or urgent
- if you feel strongly that you have been badly treated

Complaining about social work services: who to complain to and how *(See also the table on page 143)*

Complaining about services provided	Stage One
	Social work department
	Service provider
	Registration and Inspection Unit
	Stage Two
	Local government ombudsman
	Mental Welfare Commission
Lack of services or delay	Stage One
	Social work department
	Stage Two
	Local government ombudsman
	Local government monitoring officer
	Mental Welfare Commission
	Secretary of State
Failure to provide statutory services	Local government monitoring officer
	Local government ombudsman
Services not properly planned / not value for money	Stage One
	Social work department
	Stage Two
	Local government ombudsman
	Accounts Commission
Abuse /fraud / assaults / other criminal offences	Stage One
	Social work department
	Registration and Inspection Unit
	Police
	Stage Two
	Social Work Services Inspectorate
	Mental Welfare Commission
Discrimination	Social work department
	Commission for Racial Equality or Equal Opportunities Commission
Government policies or guidance not being put into effect	Social work department
	Local government ombudsman
	Secretary of State
Need for a change in policy	Stage One
	Ask for a review
	Write to the Director of Social Work
	Stage Two
	Get in touch with councillor
	Tell press
	Secretary of State

COMPLAINTS TO THE SOCIAL WORK DEPARTMENT

If you are unhappy about any aspect of your dealings with the social work department, the first thing you should normally do is say so. You should complain. If, for example, you are unhappy about your community care assessment, or if any service you receive is unsatisfactory, the first thing to do would be to tell the social work department.

However, the fact is that complaints procedures are *not* widely used. Why? Sometimes people are unwilling to complain, thinking it might cause trouble. Some people do not think they will get a fair hearing. Others do not know that they have the right to complain. They may find it difficult to put their complaint in writing.

The Government has tried to deal with some of these problems in the new complaints procedures for social work departments which it introduced in the NHS & Community Care Act[1].

New rules for social work complaints

It has always been possible to make a complaint about social work services, and many of the departments had complaints procedures before the NHS & Community Care Act. But this Act laid down new requirements with which any complaints procedure must comply. Each local authority is free to set up its own ways of dealing with complaints, but they must comply with the legal requirements.

The rules are set out in two places:

- **Section 5B of the Social Work (Scotland) Act.** This says that all local authorities must set up procedures for people to make *"representations"* and complaints about the way in which the social work department carries out or fails to carry out its responsibilities.

  This applies to *all* functions of the social work department, not just to the way it runs community care[2]. So the same rules would apply if a complaint was being made about a child in care or by a person in prison receiving help from the prison social worker.

- **New directions issued by the Secretary of State[3].** As we saw on page 5, if the Secretary of State issues directions, local authorities must follow them. If your social work department's procedure does not comply, you should complain!

The directions said that all complaints procedures must contain the following elements:

- **People who might wish to complain or make representations must be told of their right to do so.** Departments may decide themselves what publicity they give to their complaints procedures, but they must do something. They might use leaflets, or they might put up posters. The guidance says that they should also consider making available leaflets in minority ethnic languages, Braille and cassettes.

  But leaflets alone are not enough. If it appears to social work staff that someone is dissatisfied with the service, the staff must ask the person if they want to make a complaint and if necessary, help them make it[4]. They should also consider what help they should give to a person who might need to use interpretation services or who might need an advocate to help with a complaint.

- **Complaints must be dealt with within a reasonable time.** Generally there should be a response within 28 days; if this is not possible, there should be a letter explaining why not[5].

- **Your complaint should not be investigated by the person you have complained about.** It should be someone different[6].

- **There is a right of appeal to a review committee, which must include at least one independent member.** If the person is dissatisfied with the department's response to his or her complaint, they have 28 days to complain to a review committee. The review committee has three members, at least one of whom must be independent, ie not employed by the local authority or by some other body which carries out social work functions, such as a voluntary organisation.

  The review committee reports back to the social work committee of the regional council. It should do this within 28 days. The committee then looks into the matter and should reach its decision and reply to the complainant within 28 days. If at any stage it is not possible to comply with these time scales, the complainant must be told.

- **If you cannot complain yourself, someone may do so on your behalf**[7]. This could be a relative, friend or carer (see Chapter 19).

- Complaints must be made in writing, but informal complaints can be dealt with too.

  There is nothing to stop you talking informally to staff about your concerns and the social work department may deal informally with the points you raise. However if you appear to remain dissatisfied, you must be told that you can make a formal complaint and should be helped to do this, if necessary[8].

Carers and complaints

The rules are not entirely clear about carers' rights to complain. Although a carer may complain on behalf of the person needing care, they have no right to complain in their own right, unless they can establish that they need a service from the local authority.

If a you are a carer and you disagree with an assessment, for example, you might not be able to complain in your own right, only as representative of the person who needs care. And occasionally your interests might not be the same. In practice this does not seem to be a problem. Most social work departments are allowing carers to use the complaints procedures.

Complaints by social work staff

The guidance envisages that, in exceptional circumstances, a member of social work staff could themselves complain. A user of services might specifically ask a social worker to put in a complaint for them, or a member of staff may know about some ill-treatment or abuse and believe that the abused person is reluctant or too frightened to complain. In such circumstances the staff member may even have a duty to complain on the user's behalf[9], particularly if it is not possible to deal with the matter through line management.

Complaints by children

There are special rules for complaints made by children. As well as the child themselves, their parent, any person having parental rights, a foster parent or another person whom the local authority considers has a sufficient interest in the child's welfare may complain for the child[10]. A child of sufficient age could also appoint someone to act on their behalf[11].

Services which are not provided by the social work department

As we saw in Chapter 1, one of the main changes brought about by community care is that the social work department is no longer to be the main provider of care services, but instead arranges for other organisations to provide care. If something goes wrong with a service provided by a third party provider, what can you do?

The way the system works is quite complicated. The social work department must tell you what arrangements it has made for making complaints about services provided by third parties under contract to the social work department.

If no special arrangements have been made, you may complain direct to the social work department about social work services you receive from someone else. But if you are told that the provider of the service will deal with complaints, you must complain to them. The social work department will monitor the way third party providers deal with complaints[12].

People living in residential care

If you are living in residential care arranged by the social work department, you can complain to the home owner about the way the house is run, but, if you were placed there by the social work department, you may also be able to complain to the department.

If you live in residential care you can also complain to the independent **Registration and Inspection Unit** at the social work department. You might wish to do this if there is some reason why you cannot complain to the home owners themselves. The home owners themselves may be the people who are at fault. Or if you feel things would get worse if the home owners knew you had put in a complaint, you can go direct to the body which registers the home.

Any complaint which you make to a home owner must also be passed on by them to the independent Registration and Inspection Unit[13].

Limitations of the complaints procedure

- A complaint may work well if a service you receive is unsatisfactory. But it may be less likely to bring results if you are unhappy with a decision which someone has taken about your case.

  You may be unhappy with the amount or kind of help the social work department have agreed to give you, for example.

  Making a complaint will not necessarily solve this. It will mean that your case is reviewed, and your concerns will be heard by the social work committee. If the decision was in accordance with the social work department's policy, your complaint may not succeed, although the review committee may ask the social work department to change its policy.

- **Your complaint might be so serious that you should go elsewhere – to the police, the Mental Welfare Commission, or to a lawyer.** Making a complaint might be too slow in an emergency.

- **The complaint will not necessarily solve everything.** You may still need to see your councillor or an MP or get help from the local government ombudsman or the Mental Welfare Commission. But many of these people prefer you to have made a complaint to the social work department before they become involved.

- **Even if the review committee agree with you, they cannot bind the social work department.** They can make recommendations but the social work department does not have to accept them. (But see page 146 for what happened to one council which did not accept what the review committee said.)

Further information

- Your local social work department should have a booklet about making complaints.

- If you receive services which are not supplied by the social work department, you should have been given an information booklet explaining the services. It should tell you how to complain.

- Your **local health council** can tell you who to write to at the health board if you want to complain about a nursing home.

THE LOCAL GOVERNMENT OMBUDSMAN

If you have complained to the social work department and are still dissatisfied, you should consider getting in touch with the local government ombudsman[14].

Bad management

The local government ombudsman is an independent official who investigates bad management or "maladministration" by local authorities. This includes regional and islands councils, which run social work departments, and district councils, which run housing departments. This will also include the new councils set up in 1996. He can also look into the affairs of Scottish Homes and the housing functions of new town development corporations.

If he finds that you have suffered injustice as a result of poor management, he may recommend ways in which the local authority can put things right, and he can recommend that they pay you compensation.

Two cases of bad management: delays

Mrs Young: A young woman became ill with a form of autism known as Asperger's syndrome. She was 19. She lived at home with her elderly parents, who looked after her. When her health deteriorated, the social work department were asked to assess her needs. They received no response and wrote again, saying her needs were urgent. The family complained to the social work department and to the local MP. Miss Young (not her real name) was finally assessed six months after her family first asked for this.

The ombudsman said the delay was unacceptable and could have had tragic consequences as Miss Young's condition was getting worse all the time. Now she was attending a day centre she was getting much better. He said that the Council should pay compensation to Miss Young's sister for her time and trouble in making the complaint and that £600 compensation should be paid to Miss Young[15].

Mrs Black: Mrs Black (not her real name) had been ill for some time and had been in contact with the social services department about adapting her home. Later she had a stroke and needed a downstairs bathroom and toilet. The council did not visit until a year later, because of staff shortages. She had to wait two and a half years before the work was done. She complained to the ombudsman.

The ombudsman said this was an unacceptable delay. The social services department should have come to assess Mrs Black's needs within about four or five months. The ombudsman recommended that the department look at their procedures to make sure such delays did not happen in the future and recommended that they pay compensation of £250 to Mrs Black[16].

What is bad management?

The law does not define what it means by "maladministration". Any bad management would do. Incompetence, delays, unreasonableness, giving wrong information, acting in bad faith or failing to act within the authority's own policy guidelines would all count.

Matters he cannot investigate

It is very important to understand that the ombudsman can only criticise the local authority if something they did was wrong in some way. You may not like what a local authority decide to do, and he may agree with you, but if the decision was properly taken and there was no bad management, the ombudsman cannot get involved.

But bad management can cover all sorts of things, such as not taking all the relevant facts into consideration, not giving you a chance to make your case, and not following government guidelines, so if you think something is wrong, you should always contact the ombudsman.

He cannot investigate if:

- the matter arose more than 12 months before you contact him (unless there are special circumstances)
- you have not complained to the local authority itself first
- you have a right of appeal under statute against the decision of the local authority[17] or you could have gone to court to enforce your rights, *unless* it is not reasonable to expect you to take out legal proceedings because of particular circumstances[18]. (This is a very important restriction on his powers and we will look at in more detail below.)

> **There are other cases too which he cannot investigate, which are not relevant to this book. However it is always best to put your complaint in, even if you are worried that he might not be able to help. Even if he cannot help, he may be able to suggest other things you can do.**

The courts and the ombudsman

We will see in Chapter 26 that if a local authority does not carry out its duties under the law, it may be possible for a person to go to court to enforce their legal rights.

But there may be all sorts of reasons why someone might not want to go to court, and they may not even know that they could do so. Judicial review, for example, is not a familiar procedure, even to many lawyers. Would someone who did not want to go to court be able to go to the local government ombudsman instead?

This question has not come before the courts in Scotland, but it has been considered in England[19]. While this English decision would not bind the Scottish courts, there is no reason to think that they would decide the matter differently.

The court said that if the local government ombudsman thought that a case raised legal issues which could be decided by the courts under the judicial review procedure[20], the ombudsman should not investigate the case. The ombudsman should not take on the case even if it was not clear whether legal action would be successful.

What this might mean is that if a local authority is in clear breach of its legal duties under one of the statutes we have mentioned, the local government ombudsman might not be able to help.

However there may be another approach to the problem.

The law says that the local government ombudsman can look into someone's case if *it is not reasonable to expect the person to exercise his or her legal rights.*

Is it reasonable to expect people with disabilities or people who are ill or vulnerable to take out court cases? Whilst some people may feel strong enough (both physically and emotionally), is it reasonable to expect this of them?

The local government ombudsman might well take the view that, in all the circumstances of the case, it would not be reasonable to expect the complainant to go to court. He would then be able to help.

If you feel that you have a case, but you do not feel able to consider going to a lawyer, you should ask the local government ombudsman to look into your complaint. See Mr Ford's case on page 130, for someone who did.

What can the local government ombudsman do?

- **Perhaps the main thing that helps is having someone on your side.** He will investigate and call for papers from the local authority. He will usually write to the Chief Executive and ask for an explanation, or he may talk to the local authority staff.

    It is surprising how often things get cleared up when an independent person can

---

The ombudsman looks at community care

Mr Ford (not his real name) complained to the ombudsman. He had been in a psychiatric hospital for six weeks and he said that his local social work department in Tower Hamlets in London did not give him the support he needed when he left.

The ombudsman said that Mr Ford was right. The social work department should have assessed his needs under the NHS & Community Care Act. There should have been more co-operation between the hospital and the social work department before Mr Ford was discharged. When he was back home, his GP should have been consulted.

The social work department managed his case badly and that caused Mr Ford worry and stress. The ombudsman recommended that they pay Mr Ford compensation of £550 for the delay and trouble caused him. He told them to carry out a community care assessment for Mr Ford[21].

---

negotiate on your behalf. The present local government ombudsman is very proud of his ability to arrange informal settlements, and he sees this as one of his most important functions. In 1993/94, 183 cases were dealt with in this way. Over 900 complaints were sent to the ombudsman[22].

- **If he decides that you do appear to have grounds for complaining and the matter cannot be resolved informally, he may carry out an investigation.**

  This may take several months, so going to the local government ombudsman is not necessarily a quick remedy. He then publishes a report, which does not name you, but which explains whether he thinks you have suffered injustice because of the local authority's bad management.

- **His report may call on the local authority to take further action.**

  He may recommend that the local authority pay you compensation[24]. Or he may recommend that the local authority supply you with the service you have been asking for. The authority then has to tell him what they propose to so.

  If they do not comply with his recommendations, he can then issue a further report saying that the local authority has failed to comply with his recommendations.

- **However, the local government ombudsman cannot force a local authority to act if they decide not to do so, and neither can the person who complains.**

  Some people think this is a very unsatisfactory solution and argue that the local government ombudsman is "toothless". However most local authorities do carry out the local government ombudsman's recommendations. If they do not, there will be increasing pressure to give him more "teeth".

Further information

For more details about the local government ombudsman, see *Having an argument with your council, Scottish Homes, New Town? Call in the referee*. A free leaflet issued by him.

The local government ombudsman is at 23 Walker Street Edinburgh EH3 7HX. (Tel: 0131.225 5300)

Withdrawal of services criticised by ombudsman

Barbara Quick (not her real name) received psychotherapy which was paid for by the London Borough of Brent. The council decided to stop the funding even though the therapist said that stopping it too quickly could be very damaging to Ms Quick.

Ms Quick carried on with the psychotherapy, but was unable to pay the therapist. She complained to the council and to the local government ombudsman.

The ombudsman said that what the council did was wrong. The council should have assessed her needs. They should have seen if the health authority would help with the costs.

He ordered the council to pay Ms Quick's debt to the psychotherapist and to pay her compensation of £1250 for the distress caused her[23].

The ombudsman criticises complaints procedures

Four people got in touch with the local government ombudsman because they were unhappy about the way in which Strathclyde Regional Council had handled their complaints about social work services.

The ombudsman found that the social work department had not yet implemented a proper complaints procedure as they were required to do under the NHS & Community Care Act. (See page 126.)

Whilst he had some sympathy with the social work department and felt that changes to the whole complaints procedures were necessary, the local government ombudsman ordered that three of the people complaining should receive compensation of £200 and the fourth should receive compensation of £1000 because of the council's bad management[25].

LOCAL GOVERNMENT MONITORING OFFICER

Duties

Local government monitoring officers make sure that local authorities comply with the law[26]. If they believe that anything their local authority is doing is illegal they must report this to the council. They should also prepare a report if there are questions of bad management. The council will then have a chance to put things right before there is a complaint to the local government ombudsman (see above).

Contacting the local government monitoring officer

If you think that a local government department is doing something which against the law or which is bad management, you can contact the monitoring officer. So if a social work department refuses to supply you with services which the law says they must supply, or refuses even to give you an assessment, for example, or if there are excessive delays, you could ask the monitoring officer to intervene.

You can phone or write to the monitoring officer. Keep a copy of any letter you write, and a note of any phone call.

If the reply from the monitoring officer is not helpful, you could then go to the local government ombudsman or even think of taking legal action.

Further information

District and regional councils each choose their own monitoring officer. It is usually either the Chief Executive or the head of the Legal Department. If you phone up the enquiries office at your council offices, they will tell you who the monitoring officer is.

COMPLAINING TO THE SECRETARY OF STATE FOR SCOTLAND

If you feel that a local authority is not implementing community care properly, or is even not complying with its legal duties, you could complain to the Secretary of State.

Powers and duties of the Secretary of State

The Secretary of State is responsible for monitoring the progress of community care and can issue directions to local authorities if they are not complying with policy guidelines[27]. The local authorities have to do what the directions say.

The Secretary of State can hold an enquiry into the way a local authority is carrying out its functions[28]. If he holds an enquiry and finds that the local authority is not carrying out its legal duties, he can order the local authority to do so, and if necessary he can get a court order forcing them to do so[29].

So if you think a local authority is not carrying out its legal duties, you could ask the Secretary of State to take action for you.

The advantages of going to the Secretary of State

- It costs you nothing (except the price of a stamp).

- You will not have to take on a stressful court case.

- It might be possible for your name to be kept out of it. (Some people worry that if they complain things will get even worse.)

- Someone else does the work: once you have written your letter, everything else will be done by the Scottish Office.

- It does not prevent you from using other remedies. You could still bring a legal case, either at the same time as you write to the Secretary of State, or later, if the Scottish Office decides not to become involved[30].

- Anyone, not just the person with the complaint, can go to the Secretary of State to complain. The complex rules about who has the right to sue in the courts[31] do not apply here. This might be an appropriate method for a voluntary organisation to use to ensure that the law is enforced on behalf of its members[32].

The disadvantages of going to the Secretary of State

- It all depends on how seriously the Secretary of State regards the matter. He is in control of what happens. You cannot force the Secretary of State to take your case on, as the rules give him discretion whether or not to do so[33].

- The procedure for local enquiries is cumbersome and slow. This would not be the method to use if you need a quick response. The decision of the Secretary of State about whether to become involved would probably take some time, too.

- The Secretary of State may be reluctant to become involved if the complaint is basically about resources, since the council might blame the Government for not giving them enough money.

How to make a complaint

Simply write a letter to the Secretary of State. If you believe that a local authority is not carrying out its legal duties, your letter should:

- state what the legal duty is

- explain the way in which you claim that the local authority is not complying with its duties (with copies of any relevant documents which are evidence of this) *and*

- ask the Secretary of State to carry out an enquiry, and if necessary, take enforcement proceedings against the authority

Further information

You can write to the Secretary of State for Scotland at St Andrews House Edinburgh EH1 3DG.

Jane Brown wrote to the Secretary of State

The Secretary of State for Scotland
St Andrews House
Edinburgh EH1 3DG

11 May 1994

Dear Secretary of State

RIVERDALE REGIONAL COUNCIL

I am writing to you about the care my brother, Graham Brown, receives from our local social work department. My brother has a learning disability and is 21 years of age.

Page 25 of *The care maze* by Colin McKay and Hilary Patrick says that under s11 Mental Health (Scotland) Act 1984, the council should provide him with training or occupation during the day.

Since my brother left school, he has never had a place at a day centre or adult training centre. The council say that, because he has very special needs, there is a five year waiting list.

I have complained to the social work department, but they have said there is nothing they can do because of lack of resources.

I enclose copies of my letters to the social work department and their replies.

I am writing to ask you carry out an enquiry to look into the matter, and, if necessary, to take legal proceedings against the social work department to make sure that they carry out their legal duties. I am told that you can do this under s211 Local Government (Scotland) Act 1973.

Please let me know if I can give you any further information.

Yours sincerely

Jane Brown

Jane Brown

COMPLAINTS ABOUT MEDICAL SERVICES

You may have a complaint about a medical service you have received. You may be unhappy with your GP, an occupational therapist or with out-patient services at the hospital.

You will have to follow one of the procedures for making NHS complaints. There are different procedures for complaints about doctors, complaints about hospital services and complaints about community medical services. Moreover, what form of complaint you make often depends on what has gone wrong.

Complaints about hospitals

The Secretary of State has issued directions to the NHS about how to handle complaints about hospitals[34]. These are less detailed than the directions to social work departments.

The directions say all health boards must have a procedure for dealing with complaints and they must publicise this procedure. All patients and staff should know about the procedure. Details should be in the hospital's information booklet.

There must be a nominated member of staff to receive and deal with complaints. That person must investigate complaints and report back to the board and the complainant.

The person complaining should be kept informed of progress and how long the investigation should take. Anyone who has been a patient can complain. They can appoint someone to act for them. Where the patient has died or is unable to act for him or herself, a relative or representative can make a complaint. This procedure could be used if, for example:

- you were not treated with respect and courtesy

- the organisation in the hospital was poor (eg, appointments were cancelled or you were kept waiting)

- the services were poor (eg, the food!)

Complaints about clinical judgement

There is a separate procedure for this type of complaint[35]. It should be used where you feel:

- a doctor (or dentist) has made the wrong diagnosis

- you have not been given the right treatment

The basic procedure is that the consultant involved in the case will look into the complaint.

They will normally offer to meet the person complaining within a few days of the complaint. The health board will write to the complainant giving a response. If the complainant is not happy, he or she can say so. The doctors and administrators should look at it again. They may arrange for the case to be reviewed by two independent medical specialists. The specialists should speak to the complainant and report back to the health board. The board then write back to the complainant.

The problem with this procedure is that it is not always easy to know whether your complaint relates to "clinical judgement". The patient often has no idea what decisions contributed to a problem and who took them. In that case, you could use the general hospital complaints procedure. If the problem turns out to be about clinical judgement, the health board should initiate the relevant procedure.

Complaints about GPs

If you don't feel able to resolve a complaint by discussions with your GP, it should be sent to the health board. It will be looked into by a body called a "Service Committee"[36]. This is made up of doctors and lay people. The Chairperson will look into your complaint and decide if it is worth investigating. If he or she thinks it is not worth looking into, you will be given a chance to send in a further statement. If it is to be looked into, the GP will be asked to comment.

The Committee will look at the papers. They will either report to the board or decide to have a hearing. This will be in private and you would be given a chance to put your case and the GP can respond. The Committee will then report to the health board. The board will write to you. If you are not happy, you can appeal to the Secretary of State[37].

Your initial complaint should normally be sent in within 6 weeks of the problem causing the complaint. Late complaints may be allowed, but there is no guarantee.

The health service ombudsman

The health service ombudsman (his formal title is the Health Service Commissioner for Scotland) can look into maladministration by health boards and **NHS Trusts** (see page 129 – "*What is bad management?*" for an explanation of maladministration).

He can also investigate complaints that a health board or NHS Trust has not provided a service it should have, or that there has been a failure in the service.

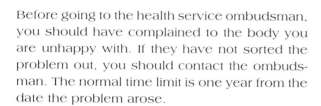

Before going to the health service ombudsman, you should have complained to the body you are unhappy with. If they have not sorted the problem out, you should contact the ombudsman. The normal time limit is one year from the date the problem arose.

The way the health service ombudsman works is similar to the local government ombudsman (described above). He will not normally look into clinical decisions or complaints about GPs[38].

See page 85 for an important case involving the English health service ombudsman.

Professional bodies

Most professionals within the NHS are members of individual professional bodies who set standards and are responsible for disciplinary procedures (for example, the General Medical Council for Doctors)[39]. If you feel a health professional may have failed to behave properly or competently, you can report the matter to the professional body. Your local health council can help with information.

Committees of Enquiry

Occasionally, the Secretary of State will set up a Committee of Enquiry to look into a problem in the health service. This is only likely to happen if there is evidence of a serious failure in a service.

Complaints and legal action

The NHS complaints procedures and the health service ombudsman are not set up to resolve legal disputes. If you threaten legal action or it looks as if you might have a legal claim, the complaint will probably be held up and may not be fully dealt with. This is because the NHS and its staff will not want to make any admission which may be held against them in court.

If your complaint is a serious one, it would be a good idea to see a lawyer first to decide whether you want to pursue legal action. You will have to consider what you want to get out of any action. If you just want an apology, a complaint would be better. If you want compensation, you may need to go to court. (The table on page 143 discusses this in more detail).

Conclusion

Making complaints in the NHS is very complex. The Government has said it will try to simplify this[40]. In the meantime, if you want to make a complaint, you will probably need advice. You could go to a Citizens Advice Bureau or your local health council. It may be that in fact you have legal remedies because of the negligence of a health professional, in which case you would need to see a lawyer.

Alternatively you might be best to contact the health service ombudsman, the Health Service Commissioner for Scotland.

Further information

The Further Reading section contains details of further information about making medical complaints. See, in particular, *Patients' rights*, which explains some of the ways in which NHS complaints can be made, *How the Health Service ombudsman can help you* from the health service ombudsman for Scotland (See page 161) and *A way through the complaints maze* by the Scottish Association for Mental Health.

THE MENTAL WELFARE COMMISSION FOR SCOTLAND

If you need community care help because of mental health problems or a learning disability, you can contact the Mental Welfare Commission if you do not get the help you need.

Duties and role

The Mental Welfare Commission for Scotland is an independent watchdog which was created under the Mental Health (Scotland) Act to protect the interests of everyone who has either mental health problems or a learning disability, if they are unable to do this for themselves[41].

Unlike its English counterpart (the Mental Health Act Commission), it can look into the care people get both in hospital and in the community. With the coming of community care, this is going to become more and more important.

The Commission visits housing, employment and day services projects, to find out about good practice and to see what is lacking. But it also has a more specific role in hearing complaints from people who are not receiving the help they need.

It has the legal duty to investigate wherever it appears that someone is either:

- being ill treated
- not receiving adequate care or treatment
- being detained improperly *or*
- at risk of losing their property[42]

Contacting the Mental Welfare Commission

If you do not receive the community care services you need, you could ask the Mental Welfare Commission to carry out an investigation, as you would not be receiving *"adequate care or treatment".*

Anyone can bring a case to the Commission's attention. You could contact them, and so could a member of your family, a friend or neighbour, or a voluntary organisation working with you. If someone other than the person concerned makes a complaint, the Commission will usually want to try to persuade the person to agree.

You should generally try to do what you can in your own area first. The Commission will usually say that it would like you to make a formal complaint to the social work department or hospital before it will become involved. But this should not stop you from contacting the Commission or for asking for advice. The Commission may be able to help you make a complaint.

Powers of the Mental Welfare Commission

What can the Mental Welfare Commission do? It cannot force anyone to do anything. If it decides there is cause for concern, it will tell the hospital management or the social work department involved. Often this is enough to improve the situation.

It may also tell the Secretary of State. He has the power to insist on change. Sometimes it tells the press the results of its findings, and this can lead to political pressure for change. It also highlights important issues in its Annual Reports. In its 1993 report it made several criticisms of how community care was developing.

The Mental Welfare Commission has a very important role in monitoring whether community care works. If you have tried what you can locally and are getting nowhere, or if you need help and advice, you should get in touch with it. Remember it can only investigate cases where there is some *"mental disorder"* involved. This includes mental health problems, learning disability and dementia.

Further information

The Mental Welfare Commission is at 25 Drumsheugh Gardens Edinburgh EH3 7RB. (Tel: 0131.225 7034) There are several free leaflets about its work which they will send you.

THE PARLIAMENTARY OMBUDSMAN

The Parliamentary ombudsman has a role very similar to that of the local government ombudsman (see above). But he looks into bad management by Government departments, rather than by local authorities. Among the departments he can investigate are the Scottish Office, the Department of Social Security and some functions of Scottish Homes.

As with the local government ombudsman, the Parliamentary ombudsman is interested in any matters which could be regarded as mismanagement: serious delay, unfair discrimination, failing to give proper advice or failing to consider someone's case properly.

The main difference from the local government ombudsman is that members of the public cannot approach the Parliamentary ombudsman direct. You have to ask an MP to refer the matter to him[43]. The MP decides whether or not to refer you on to the ombudsman.

The Parliamentary ombudsman criticises the DHSS

A man who was deaf applied to his local social services department for equipment to help him use the telephone. He was turned down because the department said he did not fit their criteria of someone who "needed" a telephone. (See *page 23.*)

The British Deaf Association wrote on his behalf to the then Secretary of State for Health and Social Security asking him to investigate whether the local authority was in breach of its statutory duties. They had to wait three years for a reply.

The ombudsman said the delay by the Department of Health was inexcusable. The Department apologised to the man and gave assurances that they had improved their procedures. The ombudsman did not award any compensation[44].

Bad management by central government

One of the things the Parliamentary ombudsman can do is recommend compensation.

Some people who had suffered from the delays caused when Disability Living Allowance was introduced went to the Parliamentary ombudsman. He said the delays had been unjustified. He told the Department of Social Security to compensate them and they did so[45].

Further information

There is a leaflet called *Can the Parliamentary ombudsman help you?* It is free from the Parliamentary ombudsman's office at the House of Commons Palace of Westminster London SW1A OAA. (Tel: 0171.276 2130)

THE ACCOUNTS COMMISSION

The Accounts Commission is an independent body which attempts to monitor whether local government achieves value for money. It audits local authority accounts and it advises on efficiency and good practice. It was set up by the Local Government (Scotland) Act 1973.

It is interested in community care. In 1994 it published a report criticising local authorities' community care plans.

It is unlikely that you will ever have to get in touch with the Accounts Commission. But they do occasionally get reports from members of the public asking them to investigate spending by a local authority[46].

Further information

The Accounts Commission is at 18 George Street Edinburgh EH2 QU. (Tel: 0131.477 1234)

RACIAL OR SEXUAL DISCRIMINATION

As we saw in Chapter 22, you have a right to receive community care services in ways which do not discriminate against you on grounds of either your race or your sex. If you think you have been discriminated against, you should complain.

Further information

In the case of racial discrimination, contact the Commission for Racial Equality, Hanover House 45/51 Hanover Street Edinburgh EH2 2PJ. (Tel: 0131.226 5186)

The Equal Opportunities Commission is the body which deals with sex discrimination. It is at Stock Exchange House 7 Nelson Mandela Place Glasgow G2 1QW (Tel: 0141.248 5833)

THE POLICE

Sometimes going through complaints procedures is too slow. If you think that a criminal offence has been committed, you can go straight to the police. If you think someone is being sexually abused or assaulted, or defrauded of their money, for example, you might want to tell the police straight away.

This is especially important if there is any risk that evidence might be lost if the police do not investigate immediately.

GETTING HELP FROM YOUR LOCAL COUNCILLOR OR YOUR MP

Some people would put this at the top of their list.

A sympathetic district or regional councillor can be very effective in getting action from the housing department or social work department. They can also agitate for political change, so that departments will actually change their policy.

Remember to go to the right councillor! For social work and education it is the regional council. For housing, leisure and recreation and most planning issues it is the district council. (After April 1996 it will all be part of one council.)

The first person to contact is normally the councillor for the area where you live. However you might also want to contact the councillor who is the chair of the relevant committee (eg, the social work committee).

MPs can also put pressure on local authorities to reconsider their decisions. If you have a complaint about the Scottish Office, another Government department or an agency such as the Benefits Agency, your MP would be the person to approach. They can take matters up for you with the relevant department or Government minister. If they are very concerned about a problem affecting their constituency, they may even raise it in Parliament.

We have seen that you have to go though your MP if you want the Parliamentary ombudsman to look into poor management by a Government department.

Further information

Many councillors hold surgeries where you can go and put your case. There will usually be details in your local paper. The enquiry office at your district or regional council office or local library should also be able to tell you when surgeries are held. You can write to councillors at the district or regional council offices.

MPs also hold surgeries. The local office of their political party or your local library would be able to tell you when surgeries are. You can also write to your MP at the House of Commons. The address is House of Commons, Palace of Westminster London SW1A OAA.

TELLING THE PRESS

If you have a story of wrongdoing to tell, the press may well be interested. Nobody likes bad publicity. An article in the papers might get things done. You can get wide publicity for your case.

But it may backfire. You must be careful that you don't disclose confidential information. If anything you say is untrue, you could be sued for defamation. You could make people very angry and run the risk of being victimised. You might find that the publicity affects your private life. You cannot guarantee that the press will tell your story accurately.

You need to be sure you know what you are doing before you get the press involved. You should try to talk it over with someone you can trust. See page 160-162 for people who might be able to help.

THE SCOTTISH HEALTH ADVISORY SERVICE

Role and duties

This service reports on hospitals and nursing homes for long-stay patients. It used to be called the Scottish Hospital Advisory Service. It inspects hospitals for people with mental health problems, learning disabilities, old age or physical disabilities. It also inspects nursing homes, if health boards purchase places there[47]. It is different from the Mental Welfare Commission,

because it is not an independent body but is part of the NHS.

It visits hospitals and nursing homes and meets with staff and patients. It then reports to the Secretary of State and the health board concerned. Its reports are made public.

Contacting SHAS

The Scottish Health Advisory Service does not have a procedure for dealing with complaints from individual members of the public (although when it meets patients it may inevitably hear complaints). If you are a member of staff in a hospital or nursing home, you can request a private interview with inspectors if you have a concern about patient care or the management of the organisation.

If you are unhappy about the conditions in a nursing home or a NHS long-stay ward, the Scottish Health Advisory Service would not be the first or only people you would contact. However you may want to send them a copy of any complaints you do make, if only for information.

Further information

The Scottish Health Advisory Service is at Trinity Park House, South Trinity Road Edinburgh EH5 3SE. (Tel: 0131.552 6255) There is a free leaflet about its work. If you want copies of any of its reports, these can be bought from SHAS.

THE SOCIAL WORK SERVICES INSPECTORATE

Duties of SWSI

This body, which was set up in April 1992, is part of the Scottish Office. Its job is to advise the Secretary of State for Scotland on how his policy for social work services in Scotland is being achieved[48]. It monitors the performance of individual social work departments and sees, among other things, how far they meet the aims set out in their community care plans and the needs of their local population.

It can inspect residential or other premises run by local authorities and by voluntary and private organisations[49]. It can carry out spot checks.

Dealing with complaints

The Scottish Office has said that the Inspectorate will not handle individual complaints[50]. It is not intended to be a channel for the public to make their dissatisfactions known. However, the Inspectorate has the legal power to interview people who live in the premises it inspects and to investigate any complaints they may have[51]. If people wish to complain, therefore, they can ask to speak to an inspector.

The law does not say that the Inspectorate *must* hear complaints, but it says that it *may* do so. The Inspectors are given a *discretion*. The general law says that it is not permissible for them to decide in advance how they will exercise that discretion. This is called "fettering" their discretion, and the courts would be likely to disapprove of any policy decision that the Inspectorate would never look at individual complaints.

If you are living in premises being inspected by someone from the Social Work Services Inspectorate you can ask to see an inspector in private to tell them about any complaints you have. If you are living in premises which you think ought to be inspected, you should write to the Secretary of State.

Further information

If you want the inspectors to investigate something, you should write to the Secretary of State at St Andrews House Edinburgh EH1 3DG.

THE COMMUNITY CARE IMPLEMENTATION UNIT

This is part of the Scottish Office. It is meant to help the various bodies in community care work together. It works with the health boards, social work departments and housing agencies.

It is a small unit which does not cover every aspect of community care and it was not set up to respond to individual complaints. However if there is a general problem in one of the areas they are interested in, it might be worth letting them know.

Their main areas of work are:[52]

- community care planning
- the reduction of long-stay institutions
- staffing issues (eg, training)
- sharing information and good practice

Further information

The Community Care Implementation Unit are currently at 43 Jeffrey Street Edinburgh EH1 1DG.

Writing a letter of complaint

It is not always easy to know what to say when you are making a complaint. You need to include your name, your address, the date, and brief details of your complaint. If you want to send copies of any letters or papers, you should always take copies and keep the originals.

It is very important that you keep copies of every letter you write and of every reply you receive. Your local library should have photocopiers.

If you need help in writing, get in touch with one of the organisations on pages 160-162.

Mary Black wrote to complain to her social work department

15 Sunnytime Avenue
Summertown
Lowland KZ2 4BJ

15 July 1992

To: Complaints Officer
Lowland Regional Council
Border House
BIGTOWN BG1 2BC

Dear Sir

I am writing to complain about the way you have handled my mother's case.

On April 2 1991 wrote to you saying I thought she needed a home help. On June 15 I got a letter saying you could not visit her at the moment.

On September 1 1991 I wrote again. She has had a fall and cannot get out to shop. I am doing it, but it is very difficult. I did not get a reply to that letter.

I enclose copies of my letters. Can you please look into her case?

Yours sincerely

Mary Black

Mary Black

The law and your rights to community care

NOTES

1   s52 introduced a new s5B into the Social Work (Scotland) Act 1968.

2   s5B(1).

3   Social Work (Representations Procedure) (Scotland) Directions 1990. Enclosed in Scottish Office Circular *Complaints procedures*, which also contains guidance on how to operate the new system.

4   Directions, para 1.

5   Directions, para 9.

6   See *A right to complain*, practice guidance from the Chief Social Work Adviser, the Scottish Office.

7   s5B(1) and (2). Complaints can only be made on behalf of people who have a need for social work services.

8   Direction 7.

9   See *A right to complain*.

10 s5B(4).

11 Although the Directions do not specifically say so.

12 Directions, para 10.

13 See Chapter 7.

14 The post was created by s21 of the Local Government (Scotland) Act 1975.

15 Report on Investigation No.93/C/05 into a complaint against Sheffield City Council.

16 Report on investigation No.91/C/3108 into a complaint against Wirral Metropolitan Borough Council.

17 None of the community care acts give you a legal right to appeal. There are rights of appeal under the Education (Scotland) Acts.

18 Local Government (Scotland) Act 1975, s24(6).

19 *R v Local Commissioner ex parte Croydon London Borough Council* [1989] 1 All England Reports page 1033.

20 See page 144.

21 Investigation No.92/A/1374 from the local government ombudsman in England, 21 Queen Anne's Gate, London SW1H 9BU.

22 *Annual report of the local government ombudsman 1993/4.* (Available from HMSO.)

23 Investigation No.93/A/0523 from the local government ombudsman in England, 21 Queen Anne's Gate London SW1H 9BU.

24 s29(3).

25 Report of the local government ombudsman's investigation of a complaint against Strathclyde Regional Council. (Case no. 1157.)

26 The law says that every local authority must appoint a monitoring officer – Local Government and Housing Act 1989, s5.

27 See 5.

28 Under s6A Social Work (Scotland) Act 1968, the Children Act 1975 and s123 of the Mental Health (Scotland) Act 1984.

29 Under powers given to him in s211 Local Government (Scotland) Act 1973. He may also ask the court to make such other orders as it may think fit. This could, perhaps, include a request for compensation for any injured parties.

30 See *Walker v Strathclyde Regional Council* (1986 Scots Law Times, page 523) where a complaint to the Secretary of State under the Education (Scotland) Act did not prevent the complainer from later going to judicial review.

31 See pages 147-148.

32 It was used to enforce tenants' rights to buy their council houses under the Housing (Scotland) Act 1987. Following local enquiries in Stirling and Dundee, both housing authorities agreed to implement the sale of council houses in their areas.

33 However, if the Secretary of State acted very unreasonably, for example by refusing even to look into the question, it might be possible to obtain judicial review of his or her decision! *R v Kent County Council ex parte Bruce* Times Law Report 8/2/86. Or you could complain to the Parliamentary ombudsman.

34 NHS Hospital Complaints Procedure Act 1985 Direction 1991. Issued with NHS Circular SOHHD/DGM (1991) 74, 19/9/91. The directions are made under s1 of the Hospital Complaints Procedure Act 1985.

35 NHS Circular No 1981 (GEN) 43 30/11/81.

36 NHS (Service Committees and Tribunals) (Scotland) Regulations 1974. NHS leaflet SCP1, *Complaints by patients against family doctors, dentists, chemists, or opticians in the NHS.*

37 See NHS leaflet SCP2, *Appeals against decisions of health boards.*

38 The ombudsman can be contacted at Ground Floor, 1 Atholl Place, Edinburgh EH3 8HP (Tel: 0131.225 7465).

39 General Medical Council, 41 Hallam Street, London W1N 6AE. (Tel: 0171.580 7642).

For nurses - UK Central Council For Nursing, Midwifery and Health Visiting, 23 Portland Place, London W1N 3AF (Tel: 0171.637 7181).

For other health professionals - Council for Professions Supplementary to Medicine, Park House, 184 Kennington Park Road, London SE11 4BU.

40 See *Being heard.* Report of the Wilson Committee into NHS Complaints, May 1994. You can get a copy from the NHS Management Executive, Room 51, St. Andrews House, Edinburgh EH1 3DG (Tel: 0131.244 5026).

41 Mental Health (Scotland) Act 1984, s3.

42 Mental Health (Scotland) Act 1984, s3(2)(a).

43 This would normally be your own MP. However if your own MP is unwilling to take this on, you can approach another MP, perhaps one who has an interest in that sort of matter. If they are also unwilling to take the matter on, you can, as a last resort, go direct to the Chairman of the Select Committee in Parliament which monitors the Parliamentary ombudsman and ask him to refer the matter to the ombudsman. Write to: The Chairman, Parliamentary Select Committee for the Parliamentary Commissioner for Administration, Palace of Westminster, London SW1A 0AA.

44 Case No. C656/87 in Sixth Report of the Parliamentary Commissioner for Administration Session 1987-8, Volume 3, page 29.

45 Special report of the Parliamentary Commissioner for Administration: *Delays in handling disability allowance claims.* (6th Report of Session 1992/3.) Copies of Annual Reports can be obtained from HMSO or consulted in reference libraries. Complainants' names are not published.

46 Under s101 Local Government (Scotland) Act 1973 any person interested can inspect local authority accounts and if they have an objection, they can request a hearing with an auditor. For further details see *Stair Memorial Encyclopaedia of the Laws of Scotland*, Volume 1, para 343.

47 This means that the majority of nursing homes are not inspected by SHAS: that is up to the health board which registers them.

48 At the time of writing, the precise role of the Inspectorate is still being developed in consultation with interested bodies. See *Inspection of social work services in Scotland: a consultation document* published by the Scottish Office in April 1993.

49 See s6 Social Work (Scotland) Act 1968 as amended by the NHS & Community Care Act 1990.

50 Consultation document, para 50.

51 Social Work (Scotland) Act 1986, s2C(a).

52 Full details are in a letter from the Scottish Office Social Work Services Group dated 10/8/93 to Directors of Social Work and Housing and General Managers of Health Boards.

When things go wrong – how the law might help

INTRODUCTION

In this book we have tried to tell you what the law says community care should be like. We have also explained the way in which the Government says it should work and have explained the good practice guidance which the Scottish Office has sent out to local authorities.

Most of community care law is found in Acts of Parliament, directions from the Secretary of State and guidance from the Secretary of State to local authorities (see Chapter 1). Cases which other people have brought to court help explain the rules.

But what if things don't happen as this book says they should? What can you do if people don't carry out their legal duties?

In this chapter we explain what you can do if things go wrong and people do not do what the law says they should. This chapter looks at remedies using lawyers and the courts. In the previous chapter we looked at other ways of making complaints.

Of course, if things do not happen as this book says, the first thing you should do is tell the person who is responsible. If a social work department says you do not need an assessment, tell them you do. Tell them you have a book which says the law is that you are entitled to one.

If you cannot afford to pay for your home help, tell the department you want to appeal. Say this book says you can. (See Chapter 4.)

But what if that doesn't work? You may want to take things further. You may want to get legal advice.

In this chapter we look at some of the legal remedies which you might be able to use.

Even if you do not think you want to take legal action you should read this chapter. It might help you in your negotiations with the local authority if you can say you are thinking about going to see a solicitor. Sometimes this can persuade people to think again.

Many people do not want to take legal action. They may not want compensation, but just an explanation of what went wrong or an apology. In these circumstances there might be other remedies which would be more effective. The previous chapter looked at remedies which do not involve going to a lawyer. You may need help to choose the appropriate course of action. (See the tables on pages 125 and 143.)

Warning! Because we are explaining quite complicated legal remedies, some of this chapter is quite difficult. You might want to read just this Introduction and the final section, *Going to a solicitor*.

Will going to a lawyer make things more difficult?

Some people worry that things might get worse if they start rushing off to their lawyer insisting on their rights. It might all become too confrontational.

Not all lawyers work like this, however. Some are skilled in negotiation and can help get the two sides talking and sorting things out.

The law can be used as a tool. A lawyer can tell you what your rights are and whether there is anything that can be done. If your social work department is not complying with its legal duties to you, you should be able to suggest this reasonably to them without prejudicing your relationship with them.

In fact none of what we are suggesting should be taken as an attack on local authorities. Many local authorities argue that the Government has not given them enough money to make community care work properly. If people know about their legal rights to community care services, it may help local authorities when they ask for money from central government.

What do you want? *(See also table on page 125)*

Before you follow a particular course of action, you should try to decide what you want from it. The following list might help. You might need more than one remedy. Generally you can use one or more of the procedures at the same time.

Remedy required	Possible courses of action
An explanation	Ask the person themselves If they won't explain, complain
An apology	Ask for one Complain Ombudsman
Getting someone to do something / coping with delays	Complain Ombudsman Mental Welfare Commission Councillors / MPs Secretary of State Legal action
Financial compensation	Legal action Ombudsman
Punishment of the offender	Complain Notify their professional body (if they have one) Tell the police
A confidential enquiry	Tell the Mental Welfare Commission Ombudsman Scottish Office
Publicity for your case	Legal action Tell the press
Review of a decision	Ask for a review Complain Involve local councillors / MPs
Change in policy for the future	Involve local councillors / MPs Tell the press Complain Tell the Scottish Office

In this way you can help the social work department to provide what they want to provide: a better service.

Possible legal remedies

In this chapter we look at five different types of legal remedies which might be useful.

The first is **judicial review**. Basically it means asking the courts to rule whether what a public authority did was lawful. If they decide it is unlawful, they may order the authority to comply with the law and perhaps give you compensation.

Next comes a little known process: **asking for an order to carry out statutory duties**. If the court finds that a public authority has not fulfilled its legal duties, they can make an order saying it should do, and can even fine it if it does not comply.

If you are more concerned about financial compensation for what has gone wrong in the past, you might want to **sue for breach of statutory duty**. This is a way of asking for damages if a public body did not carry out its duties under the law.

The law and your rights to community care

The next topic we cover is negligence. If someone who should take care does not do so and you are injured or damaged (either physically or mentally) as a result, you might be able to sue for negligence.

Finally, we look at breach of contract. What do you do if you have an agreement with someone and they do not keep their side of the bargain?

Courts say man needs carer

A disabled man in Hereford applied for judicial review to force his local authority to provide him with a carer. The County Council settled the action out of court, agreeing to pay the man compensation of nearly £8000 and to provide him with a carer[2].

---

ested in whether they made the right decision.

They will only intervene if what the authority did was unlawful. They will not set aside a decision which was properly taken, even if they might not agree with the decision themselves.

It is very important to understand this. You cannot use judicial review to appeal against a decision which you do not like, unless something about the way the decision was made was unlawful.

These are the types of conduct which the courts might say were unlawful.

- **Not carrying out duties under an Act of Parliament.** For example, if a social work department does not provide a service it is under a legal duty to provide, such as after-care or services under the Chronically Sick and Disabled Persons Act, or does not make a community care assessment.

- **Unreasonable delay in carrying out legal duties.** For example, delay in providing the services a social work department is legally obliged to provide under the Chronically Sick and Disabled Persons Act or the Mental Health (Scotland) Act or delay in making an assessment of your needs.

- **Not complying with the procedure laid down in a statute or in Scottish Office directions and possibly not acting in accordance with government guidance.** (For directions see page 5. For guidance see box opposite.) An example would be if a local authority did not consult properly on its community care plans or did not operate its complaints procedure according to the rules.

JUDICIAL REVIEW

All public authorities have to comply with the law: both the general law and also any special laws, such as the community care laws, which apply specifically to them. The courts have the power to supervise the activities of all public bodies which carry out duties under statute, to make sure that they act in accordance with the law[1].

If you want the court to do this, you send in a petition for judicial review to the Court of Session in Edinburgh.

What kind of bodies might be subject to judicial review?

- doctors, health boards and NHS Trusts
- local authorities operating community care
- housing and education departments
- the Mental Welfare Commission and the ombudsmen (see Chapter 25)
- the Secretary of State for Scotland and the Scottish Office
- the Department of Social Security

What kind of conduct would be investigated?

The Courts are only interested in whether the authority has kept the law. They are not inter-

---

After-care to be provided by law

A man who was a patient in Broadmoor Special Hospital was discharged by a Mental Health Review Tribunal, which said the health authority must make proper arrangements for his care and supervision in the community.

The health authority decided not to provide the supervision and kept the man in Broadmoor. The Court said that they had a legal duty to give him after-care under the English Mental Health Act and they must try to make the necessary arrangements[3].

Government guidance: how binding is it?

We saw on page 6 that the Government has the power to give guidance to local authorities. The Government has issued a great deal of guidance, over forty circulars since community care began. How binding is guidance? Do social work departments have to do what it says?

If you look at Scottish Office circulars you will see that they contain different kinds of information, not all of which could be described as "guidance". Some is purely historical or explanatory. The circular might describe the new system, or the old one it replaces, or might try to give the background or thinking behind the new circular. That part would be read for information only.

Distinguishing between information and guidance

There are really two types of message in most circulars. There will be a mixture of suggestions of what might be a good idea and also some fairly direct and uncompromising statements about what the Government expects to happen in the future.

For an example of a suggestion, see the circular on *Care programmes for people with mental illness*. It refers to the need for daytime activities for people living in the community. It says that "*....the provision of daytime activities for people discharged from hospital which would contribute towards such people leading ordinary lives, will often be an important requirement as well.*"[4].

Whilst this is clearly an expression of hope from the Scottish Office that daytime activities will be provided, it is expressed rather in the same way as we express the hope that our children might tidy their bedrooms, not, perhaps, with any great expectation it will be done.

Contrast this with part of the circular on assessment. It says "*Users and carers should be informed of the conclusions of an assessment.*"[5]

The Government seems to be saying that it expects that social work departments will do this. This looks like an instruction from the Government to social work departments.

So not every word of the circular will be guidance which the social work department would have to follow. The suggestion in the first case might be a good idea, and a social work department may well try to do this, but it would not feel it had to. It could decide whether to take up the idea.

Clear guidance

But what if the guidance does say very clearly that a social work department must do something?

In the circular on discharge of patients from hospital the Scottish Office says that "*health boards and social work departments must ensure... a system for establishing individual care programmes for people with a long term mental illness.*"[6]

The assessment guidance says that "*assessment systems should ensure the participation of the individual and his or her carer*"[7].

Is the social work department free to disregard this guidance, or should it do what the Secretary of State says? And what could you, a member of the public, do if you were affected?

Legal interpretation of guidance

There have been very few cases before the Scottish courts explaining the legal status of guidance. There have been some cases looking at the duties of local authorities to consider the guidance given to them in homelessness cases. But the duty of housing departments is different.

Housing authorities are told that when they operate the homelessness laws they must "*have regard to*" guidance from the Secretary of State in Codes of Practice[8]. The courts have said that this means that they must consider what the Secretary of State has said but that they can then make their own minds up.

But the duty under the Social Work (Scotland) Act is different. Social work departments must "*act under the general guidance*" of the Secretary of State. This is stronger wording than used in the Housing (Scotland) Act. It seems to mean more than simply considering the guidance and then making their own minds up.

Baroness Blatch, the English minister who spoke for the Government in the House of Lords during the passage of the NHS & Community Care Bill said in the House of Lords that "*guidance is expected to be followed*".

All guidance issued by the Secretary of State must be taken into account by social work departments. If guidance is very clear and unambiguous and suggests a direction in which social work departments should move, they should generally try to move in that direction. And, as we have seen, if a social work department does not follow guidance from central government, the government could issue a direction compelling them to do what it wants.

If a member of the public felt they had suffered because clear Government guidance had not been followed, they might want to take legal advice.

Not following guidance

Mr William Hargreaves took his local social services department to court because they were not providing the respite care for his sister which he thought she needed.

His sister had learning disabilities and had previously had six weeks away from home, which she liked. The social services department wanted her to stay at home and go to an adult training centre with home support.

The court said that the department had not taken into account Ms Hargreaves' wishes when they offered the respite care. The social worker had not tried to find out what she wanted and had only listened to him. They were wrong to think that the two views would coincide.

They had not followed Government guidance. Their decision was unlawful. They should reassess her needs and pay Mr Hargreaves' legal costs[9].

(But guidance should be taken in context. When a local authority refused to register a child minder because she would not agree that she would not smack children she was looking after, the court said that was illegal. The council had taken the Government guidance out of context[10].)

- Acting unreasonably, in a way no reasonable authority would have done. (This might sound difficult to prove but it is more than just clearly absurd decisions.)

The courts will act if, for example, irrelevant matters have been taken into account. For example if your assessment of needs was tailored to meet what the social work department could provide this would be unlawful, because what they have on offer is legally irrelevant to what your needs are.

The courts would also say it was unreasonable if relevant matters were not taken into account. (For instance if a social work department did not consider the carer's position when deciding what services to offer a disabled person.)

- Acting on the basis of factual information which was inaccurate

- Exceeding the powers given to you by statute. Doctors who were obliged to discharge a patient under the Mental Health Act (Scotland) were not allowed to hold him under any other pretext[13].

- Not acting in accordance with "natural justice". Natural justice says people should be given a chance to put their case and to be heard. It says that people should not be judge in their own case: someone impartial should decide. Appeals and complaints procedures should be fair and unbiased.

Authorities ignoring relevant facts

Case 1 Vulnerable young people: A homeless young woman of 16 took her district council to court under the homelessness laws. The law said they should consider whether she was *"vulnerable"*. If so, she would be entitled to extra help (see page 70).

The court said the district council had not considered this properly. They had not given enough attention to the reports they got from the social work department.

The council was asked to reconsider her case and give her compensation for the emotional distress she was caused. They had not taken into account all the relevant considerations when they made their decision[11].

Case 2 Residential care: A man with Down syndrome in Avon took the County Council to court over their decision to place him in a cheaper residential home than the one he thought he needed. The court upheld his case; he should go to the home that best met his needs[12].

The court criticised the social services department for two main reasons. Firstly they failed to take account of the man's own wishes about the type of care which would suit him. Secondly they also failed to take sufficiently seriously the recommendations of the complaints review which had reported to them.

The courts criticise restrictive contracts

Private home providers took a social services department in England to court because their standard form of contract was too harsh and restrictive. No home owner could sign it. The Court said the council had acted unreasonably. If they went ahead with their contract, there would be no private homes in the area, and this would defeat one of the aims of the community care laws[14].

- **Making decisions in advance so that they cannot give your case their full consideration.** For example if a social work department said that it would not make telephones available to disabled people unless they were housebound. By doing this, it would have made a decision in advance about what people might *"need"* under the Chronically Sick and Disabled Persons Act (see page 21). This is called "fettering your discretion".

- **Acting in bad faith, or showing bias, or acting maliciously or dishonestly.**

- **Not acting in accordance with the body's own publicly stated policy or with a regular, known practice** (eg in a Patient's Charter or in a housing department's allocations policy). This is known as the doctrine of **legitimate expectation.**

Advantages of judicial review

- For a legal procedure it is relatively cheap, speedy and efficient. (It may take as little as 6 weeks to get a case to court, and in an emergency even less. However many cases will take longer than this.)

- Legal aid might be available.

- The court can make a wide range of orders. It can set a decision aside; stop the authority doing something; tell them to do something; explain what their legal duties are; order them to stop doing something they are doing and/or compensate the complainant for loss suffered because of the authority's failure to comply with the law.

So, if a social work department fails to provide you with after-care under the Mental Health (Scotland) Act (page 24), the court might order them to give you after-care for a certain period and compensate you for their failure to provide it in the past.

Or if a social work department assesses your needs without consulting you or your carer (see page 14) the court might say that the assessment is invalid and tell them to do a new assessment.

Disadvantages

- It can only be used if the initial decision was unlawful: it cannot be used if the decision or action was lawfully taken.

- It is almost impossible for you to do it yourself: you would need a solicitor.

- The case has to go to the Court of Session in Edinburgh, not the local Sheriff Court. If you do not live in Edinburgh, your solicitor would then have to get an Edinburgh solicitor to take the case to court. This adds to the cost if you cannot get legal aid.

Natural justice and home closures

Residents of a residential care home took the local authority to court when the home was closed without consulting them. The court said that the local authority did not act fairly. People should be told of the possible closure and given time to put forward their objections[15].

- It is still an unfamiliar procedure: not many people (including many lawyers) know about it. But it is not complicated, and any lawyer who does litigation (court work) could do it. You might want to contact an advice agency or relevant voluntary organisation to see if they can give you the names of any lawyers who have experience of judicial review cases.

- It can only be used by the person affected themselves: not by a voluntary body campaigning on their behalf. This is because of a very complex legal rule which effectively says that only the person with a personal interest in a case can sue. (See page 148.)

When can judicial review be used?

- **You should generally have used all the remedies available in the statute first.** If a statute gives you the right to appeal against a decision made by a public authority, you generally have to do this before you can go to judicial review. We look at this in more detail below.

Who can sue for judical review?

In 1987 Age Concern Scotland tried to take the Department of Health and Social Security to court to discover whether its way of making cold weather payments to elderly people was illegal. The court threw out their case because it said that Age Concern itself was not personally affected by the Department's decision[16].

(A self help or users' group may be able to sue, because their members would be personally interested in the decision. Otherwise a voluntary organisation would have to fund an individual claimant as a "test case". The test case would then establish the law for other people as well.)[17]

* It should not be used where the primary remedy of the individual is under the "private" law.

Judicial review is a "public" law remedy. If what you want is really no different from what you would seek against another private individual, judicial review is not appropriate.

For example, if an authority was negligent or failed to carry out its duties under a contract with you (see below), you would not go to judicial review. Although the other party to the dispute is a public authority, you would take out an ordinary civil action. Judicial review cannot be used if a social work employee wants to question action taken under his or her contract of employment.

Judicial review and other remedies

We saw above that you cannot use judicial review if the statute lays down other ways for you to make a complaint. The statute might provide a method of appealing against decisions taken, for example.

(In planning matters a person who is unsatisfied with a planning decision can appeal against the decision to the local authority and then to the Secretary of State. There are similar provisions in the education system. You would be expected to use the appeals procedure before you had any chance of going to judicial review.)

None of the acts we have been talking about in this book gives you the right to appeal against decisions you are unhappy with. But there are various ways in which you can complain. Firstly there is the new complaints procedure which was put in place by the NHS & Community Care Act (see page 126). Secondly, if you are unhappy with decisions of a local authority, you can ask the Secretary of State to intervene (see page 131).

Does the rule about using up all available statutory remedies mean that you have to make a complaint and /or go to the Secretary of State before you go to judicial review?

Complaints procedures

There is no clear cut answer. Some experts say that you should go through the social work department's complaints procedure first. Others say that it is not so simple as that. It all depends on the facts of the case and your own individual circumstances. In particular, if your case is urgent and the complaints procedure might be too slow, it might be reasonable for you to go to judicial review. If a complaint would not give you the help you need, judicial review might be appropriate.

Some people argue that the complaints procedure is not a statutory "remedy" anyway. As we saw on page 128, the review body cannot *order* the social work department to act. It can only make recommendations.

There has not yet been a case in Scotland to clarify the point. In the meantime, the best advice is: get advice. If your solicitor thinks there is a good reason why the decisions of the local authority should be judicially reviewed, he or she will apply for you[18].

Complaints to the Secretary of State

The Social Work (Scotland) Act says that the Secretary of State can direct social work departments how to carry out their functions. The Secretary of State can organise inspections and carry out public enquiries into social work services. (See page 131.)

Does this mean that you must first apply to the Secretary of State to review the local authority's action before you can apply for judicial review? Do you have to use that statutory remedy before you can go to court?

So far the answer has been no. The fact that you can apply to the Secretary of State to investigate should not stop you from applying for judicial review[19].

Summary

If you think a public body has not carried out its duties according to the law you might want to consider judicial review.

Legal cases are extremely valuable, because they make the law clear for other people too. For example, we said on page 25 that we do not know exactly what kind of after-care a social work department should provide to people who have mental health problems. A court case might make this clearer.

You may not be sure whether judicial review is the right thing to do, or whether you should use a complaints procedure or write to the Secretary of State. If so, you should seek advice. See pages 160-162.

ORDER TO CARRY OUT STATUTORY DUTIES

If someone is not carrying out their legal duties, you can apply to the Court of Session for an order compelling them to do so[20]. You could use this remedy against a local authority (including a social work department), a health board, a doctor who has legal duties under the Mental Health (Scotland) Act and possibly even the Secretary of State for Scotland[21].

The application is to the Court of Session in Edinburgh, and uses the judicial review procedure.

How does it differ from judicial review?

- The Court may impose conditions on the order and can even impose a fine or imprisonment if the authority does not comply. This could not be done under judicial review.

- It is only available if there is a clear statutory duty and the authority has refused or delayed to perform the duty without good reasons. (These are narrower grounds than those available for judicial review.)

- The rule about exhausting all statutory remedies (see page 147) does not apply. This could be quite an important difference. You can apply for an order even though you have the right to appeal, complain or go to the Secretary of State[22].

- You must know exactly what you want the authority to do and spell this out in your petition to the court. (For example you might be requesting an assessment of needs, or a disabled person's assessment, or the provision of a service under the Chronically Sick and Disabled Persons Act.) Under judicial review, you ask for specific remedies but you can also ask the court to make such further orders as it thinks fit.

What kind of duties will be enforced?

How can local authorities comply with their duties under Acts of Parliament if they do not have enough money? Would the courts make an order even if it was physically impossible for an authority to do what the law says?

It all depends on the precise wording of the statute. You have to look at the kind of duty the law imposes. The law may give the authority a discretion, a power or a duty to act.

Discretion

If the statute gives a *discretion* to the local authority, they do not *have* to supply the services. A statute may say the local authority must supply "such services as they think fit", or make "such provision as they consider to be adequate".

In those circumstances we say that the statute gives them a "discretion". They can decide what services to supply and what is adequate. On the whole the judges will not interfere with the decision they take. We saw how this works in s12 of the Social Work (Scotland) Act (See page 20). (But see page 147 for how they must exercise their discretion.)

Power to act

Sometimes a statute gives an authority the *power* to supply services, but not the *duty* to do so. Section 13B of the Social Work (Scotland) Act says the social work department "may" make arrangements to help prevent illness and to care for people suffering from illness.

This section gives social work departments the *power* to act, but it does not mean that they have a *duty* to do so (unless the Secretary of State orders them to do so, which this Act gives him the power to do).

Duty to act

On the other hand, some acts impose a very clear legal duty: for example, the duty to provide after-care, to assess people's needs, and to supply welfare services to people who need them. (See Chapter 3 for the full list.)

In those cases the local authority *must* comply with their legal duties. The acts say this. The local authority "*shall*" provide services or "*shall*" make arrangements. The language is clear. Lack of money would not be a defence.

However if an authority cannot carry out its legal duties for reasons beyond its control, then it would have an excuse.

Failure to carry out legal duties

In 1986 Strathclyde Regional Council were taken to court for not supplying education to children during the teachers' strike. The Court said they were not to blame. It was physically impossible to supply education if they did not have any teachers[23]. However they were told they must make efforts to deal with the situation.

Summary

If an Act of Parliament imposes a very clear cut duty on a local authority and it has not done what the act says, or has delayed unreasonably, then you can go to court for an order requiring them to comply with their legal duty.

It has recently been used in several homelessness cases. In one case it was used to order a district council to provide the applicant with temporary housing[24].

However it is not the procedure to use if you want to question a decision which was properly made. It cannot be used to appeal against a decision if there is no right to do so under the law[25].

ACTION FOR BREACH OF STATUTORY DUTY

If a public authority has not carried out its duties under an Act of Parliament, you can take out proceedings for judicial review or for an order compelling them to do so.

Another thing you could do is sue the authority for breach of statutory duty. Perhaps this will seem little different to the non-lawyer. But it is. It is not asking for things to be put right for the future. It is asking for financial compensation for what has gone wrong in the past.

You would be saying that you had suffered "injury" because the authority has not carried out its legal duties, and you want damages. If you can prove your case, you would receive com-

pensation for the injury caused to you. This might include money lost, physical injury or emotional stress and worry.

Advantages

- It might be possible to have the case heard in the Sheriff Court rather than the Court of Session. The general rule is that it should be heard in the Court of Session. But in at least one case, where the local authority did not deny the claim, the matter was dealt with in the Sheriff Court[26].

- Legal aid should be available if you have a good case.

Disadvantages

- It is not an easy case to argue. See below for some of the problems.

- You can only ask for compensation, not some of the other orders you might require. It is not the right remedy to use if you want to get the authority to start providing a service for you. All you could hope to get is compensation for what they failed to give you in the past.

When can you sue for breach of statutory duty?

The rules are very complicated, but basically they say you can sue if you can show that:

- **There is a clear statutory duty.** If the authority has a discretion whether to act, you will not be able to sue. (See page 149 for duties and discretions.)

- **The authority failed to carry out the duty and as a result you suffered "injury".** (This term is wide enough to include psychological damage[27].)

There are also very complicated legal rules which decide whether or not the statute gives legal rights to members of the public so that they can sue if the statute is not complied with[28]. Basically there are two tests: You have to look at the purpose of the act. You also have to see whether the act has penalties for non-performance.

Carer sues for breach of statutory duties

Mr Hargreaves in Yorkshire sued his local social services department for breach of their statutory duty under the Chronically Sick and Disabled Persons Act. They agreed his sister needed respite care but refused to meet the whole cost. He had to make up the difference. He was awarded £60.33, the money he had lost.

Purpose

The court will look at why the act was passed. Who was supposed to benefit? If the act was intended to benefit a certain class of persons, such as homeless people or disabled people, and you are one of the class of people intended to benefit, you may be able to sue.

Penalties

If the statute has penalties for non-performance, such as fines or disqualification of directors, the court would say that an individual does not have the right to sue. The penalties are the remedy which should be used.

Summary

This is the remedy to use if your main aim is compensation for failure to supply a service, not to obtain a service in the future.

Penalties in an Act bar personal claims

The Disabled Persons (Employment) Act 1944 says that firms of a certain size must make sure that at least 3% of their work force are registered disabled people. Very few firms actually do what this Act says. The Act says that employers who do not comply can be prosecuted. Members of the public who might want to sue are not able to, because the Act contains penalties for non-performance.

SUING FOR NEGLIGENCE

Negligence is about people who do not take care when they should. The law says that if someone does something for you in a situation where they should take care and they do not take care, they should compensate you for any loss or damage you suffer as a result.

There are all sorts of situations when a claim for negligence might arise under community care. These are just a few examples:

- where a doctor treats a patient or decides to discharge a patient

- where a nurse or care assistant looks after someone

- where a local authority assesses someone's needs

- where someone gives someone else legal or financial advice. It could be a lawyer or a welfare rights worker or a voluntary advice agency

- where a carer takes someone for an outing or gives them their medicine

Proving negligence

If you think you have suffered as a result of someone's carelessness or negligence, there are three things you have to prove:

- that the person had a duty to take care

- that they did not take care

- that, as a result, you suffered loss

The duty to take care

Whenever someone puts himself or herself in a position of taking responsibility for someone else, they have a duty to take care.

It could arise in any of the circumstances we mentioned above. A doctor treating a patient must take care. A bus driver carrying people back from a day centre must drive carefully. If someone asks you for advice, you must take care that you consider all the facts of the case. If you are looking after someone in a residential care home, you must be careful to avoid accidents. A hairdresser coming to the home must be careful about the chemicals they use.

Wherever someone *takes responsibility* for another person, the law says they should do so carefully. If they are careless and as a result the other person is injured or suffers psychological damage, they may have to compensate him or her.

The duty to take care: child abuse

The law is not always clear about when there is a duty to take care.

A child sued the social work department because they did not take action when she was at risk, despite the fact they had been warned she was in danger. She suffered years of abuse.

In another case, a psychiatrist wrongly diagnosed that a child was being abused by someone in her home. She was taken away from her mother.

The courts said that it would not be in the public interest if social work departments could be sued in the courts if they failed to take proper care when they were carrying out their child protection duties[29].

These cases, which were heard in England, could have a very dramatic impact. At the time of writing, they are being appealed to the House of Lords.

Failing to take proper care

Generally the courts will say that the person should have taken "reasonable" care. Accidents will happen and if a "reasonable person" could not have prevented it, the courts will not hold the person liable. In other words, you have to prove that the other person was at fault.

If an expert is involved, such as a doctor or a lawyer, they will be judged according to what a "reasonable" expert would have done. A consultant psychiatrist will be judged according to the standards of a "reasonable" consultant psychiatrist.

The courts have said that a professional person should only be found to blame if they did what no "reasonable professional" in that situation would have done. This means that it would not be enough for you to get another expert along to say that they would not have done what the professional defending the case had done. You have to get an expert to say that no-one would have done what the defender did.

Loss or damage suffered

You have to show that you have suffered loss. It could be financial loss, or personal injury, or psychological damage or trauma.

If all these three elements are present you may be able to sue for negligence.

Advantages of suing for negligence

- If you want financial compensation for damage you have suffered, you might want to sue for negligence: if the damage is great, you might be awarded a large sum.

- Legal aid should be available if you have a good case.

Disadvantages

- It could be very slow.

- It could turn out to be quite a stressful business. You have to keep a close eye on what is going on; it is not possible to leave it all to your solicitor. The solicitor will need to get information from you and answers to questions which come up. There will be a great deal of correspondence to and fro and the solicitor will need to know your views.

SUING FOR BREACH OF CONTRACT

If you have an agreement with another person and they do not do what it says, you have various legal rights. One of the things you may do is sue for breach of contract. If you suffer any loss as a result of the breach of contract, you have the right to sue. You may be able to recover damages both for financial loss and for disappointment and hurt feelings[30].

What kind of contracts apply?

The rules apply to any agreement which two parties have which they intend to be binding on them. This could include:

- a tenancy or supported accommodation agreement or a contract to go into residential care

- an agreement to provide you with a home help (the local authority may want you to sign a contract)

- (possibly) a care plan which you have on discharge from hospital, if you and the hospital sign. It would all depend how it was worded

(See Chapter 23 for more details about the kind of contracts which could be involved.)

Advantages of suing for breach of contract

- It is the method to use if you want someone to comply with their agreement with you or to get compensation for their failure to do so.

- It could be used even if the person was not negligent.

- Generally you would need legal advice, and legal aid should be available. You could do it yourself in the Sheriff Court if the amount involved was less than £750. (See *A Guide to small claims in the Sheriff Court*, free from all Sheriff Courts: ask at the Sheriff Clerk's office.)

- You should get legal aid if you have a good case.

NOTE – If you are providing community care services or advice, you might be worried that you could put yourself in a position where you could be sued for negligence. You should check this with your employer. Your employer may need to get insurance to cover negligence claims.

Disadvantages

- As for negligence: see above.

- It would not be something you would rush into. If someone breaks their contract with you, it is better to give them a chance to make amends before you start legal action (eg, write a letter saying that you will start legal action if they do not remedy the situation within, say, 7 days.)

GOING TO A SOLICITOR

If you think you need legal advice, how do you get it? How do you choose a solicitor?

You may not need to go to a solicitor's office in your high street, or at least not at first. Among the other places you could try are:

- your Citizens Advice Bureau, who may be able to talk to a solicitor for you or may even run a legal service, where you can have a free interview with a solicitor

- one of the organisations listed on pages 160-162. A few of them have lawyers on their staff who can advise, or even take on your case

- a Community Law Centre, which will have particular experience of dealing with local authorities

- the Legal Services Agency (see page 162)

- a welfare rights advice centre. (However many of these are run by the local social work department. If your claim is against the social work department, you may want to go somewhere else for advice.)

Choosing a solicitor

If you want to go to a solicitor, how do you choose one? Personal recommendation is the best thing. But a solicitor who is good at house buying will not necessarily be good at court work (litigation). So if your case might involve court work, you need to get the name of some-one who does that. The Law Society of Scotland has a list of people whom it has recognised as specialists in particular areas of the law.

You may get help from one of the organisations listed on pages 160-162. They may be able to suggest someone.

If you think you may qualify for legal aid to help with the legal costs, you need to check that the solicitor does that kind of work.

Some solicitors give a free first interview, to see if they think you have a case. At that interview you can decide, too, whether you like the solici-tor and whether you think he or she seems efficient.

However, your case may not be dealt with by the solicitor you see at that meeting. It is quite likely that a more junior solicitor (usually called an "assistant solicitor") will take the matter on. But a partner will remain in overall charge, and you can get in touch with the partner if you are not satisfied with the way your case is being handled.

If at all possible, before you agree to start a legal case, you should get an idea of what it might cost you. If court action is involved, it is almost impossible for the solicitor to say what it will cost, because they do not know how long it will take. However they should be able to tell you their hourly rate. You should get them to agree that they will not let the fees pass a certain amount without coming back to you.

For further information see *Getting the best from your solicitor*, published by the Scottish Con-sumer Council[31].

SUMMARY

- If you feel a public authority has not taken decisions about you properly you should consider judicial review.

- You should get advice if you are not sure whether to put in a formal complaint first.

- If the local authority has not complied with a clear legal duty, you might want to get an order compelling them to do so.

- If you want compensation for someone's failure to act in accordance with the law, you could sue for breach of statutory duty.

- If someone has made a decision about you or treated you without proper care, you might be able to sue for negligence.

- If you have an legal agreement with someone and they are not doing what it says, you could sue for breach of contract.

NOTES

1 This chapter deals with the system in outline. For a very clear guide for non-lawyers see Tom Mullen *A guide to judicial review in Scotland*, available from Shelter Scotland.

2 *Community Care* magazine 24/10/91, page 1.

3 *R v Ealing DHA ex parte F* Times Law Report 24/6/92. For the Scottish duty to provide after-care, see page 24.

4 para 2.3.

5 para 5.9.

6 *Guidance on care programmes for people with a mental illness including dementia,* (Circular SW 1992/1) Annex A, para 2.1.

7 *Assessment and care management* (Circular SW11 1991), para 5.3.

8 s37 Housing (Scotland) Act 1987.

9 *R v North Yorkshire County Council ex parte Hargreaves* Times Law Report 9/11/94.

10 *Sutton London Borough Council v Davis* Independent Law Reports 17/3/94.

11 *Kelly v Monklands District Council* 1986 Scots Law Times, page 169.

12 *R v Avon County Council ex parte M* [1994] 2 Family Court Reports 259.

13 *B v F* 1988 Scots Law Times, page 572, House of Lords.

14 *R v Newcastle upon Tyne City Council ex parte Dixon,* Independent 21/10/93 and *R v Cleveland County Council ex parte Cleveland Care Homes Association,* Independent 30/12/93.

15 *R v Devon County Council ex parte Baker and Another* and *R v Durham County Council ex parte Broxson and Another* Times Law Reports, 21/1/93.

16 *Scottish Old People's Welfare Council, Petitioners.* 1987 Scots Law Times, page 179.

17 In England the rules are better. Anyone with a "sufficient interest" can sue. In 1985 the Child Poverty Action Group were able to sue on behalf of claimants affected by a decision of the Secretary of State. *R v Sec of State for Social Services ex parte CPAG* Times Law Reports 8/8/85.

18 There may be circumstances where you do not have to use all the available remedies first. This is discussed in an article by Neil Collar in the *Journal of the Law Society of Scotland* in August 1991, page 299. You could point this article out to your solicitor.

19 See *Wilson v Independent Broadcasting Corporation* 1979 Session Cases at page 360 where the court said that applying to the Minister was very different from going to court. It was not so readily available a remedy, it was not so speedy or effective, nor was it so independent as an appeal to the court. If Parliament wanted to exclude the courts' jurisdiction, they should have made that clear.

20 s45 of the Court of Session Act 1988 (used 5 times between 1868 and 1972).

21 *Carlton Hotel Co. v Lord Advocate* 1921 Session Cases 237 (see page 249).

22 *T Docherty Ltd v Monifieth Burgh* 1971 Scots Law Times, page 13.

23 *Walker v Strathclyde Regional Council* 1986 Scots Law Times, page 523.

24 *Galbraith v Midlothian District Council* 1979 SCOLAG, page 122.

25 *Mackenzie v West Lothian District Council* 1979 Session Cases, page 433.

26 *Purves v Midlothian District Council* 1986 SCOLAG page 144. (This differs from the case of *Brown v Hamilton District Council* 1983 Scots Law Times, page 397 which first said that this was a matter for the Court of Session.) In this case, there was more work for the Court to do. The district council challenged the complaint and the Court had to decide whether it had failed to comply with the homelessness laws.

27 In *Mallen v Monklands District Council* 1986 Scots Law Times, page 347, the claimant was awarded damages for the emotional distress caused her by the district council's failure to comply with its duties under the homelessness legislation.

28 For a more detailed discussion, see Cross *Local Government Law* paras 10.30 – 10.34. An English law book, available in law libraries.

29 *M and another v Newham London Borough Council; X (minors) v Bedfordshire County Council* Times Law Report 3/3/94.

30 For a straightforward and readable guide to the rules, see *Contract* by Stephen Woolman, a Scottish advocate. Published by Greens Law Publishers.

31 Available from Kelso Graphics, The Knowes, Kelso, Roxburghshire TD5 7BH (Fax: 01573.226225)

When things go wrong – how the law might help

The law and your rights to community care

Glossary

In this glossary we define some of the technical terms we use in the book. To help you identify terms we have included in the glossary, the first time they appear in each chapter they are typed in **bold** type like this.

Advocate	Someone who helps another person to speak up for themselves or have their wishes considered. See Chapter 19.
After-care services	Help from social work departments for someone who has mental health problems or a learning disability. A person may have a legal right to after-care. See page 24.
Appointee	See **DSS appointee**.
Benefits Agency	The body which deals with benefit claims and payments on behalf of the **DSS**.
Care gap	Before 1993, social security benefits often did not meet the total cost of residential care. The difference became known as the "care gap". It is still a problem because the money going to social work departments to pay for community care is based on the old levels of social security benefits.
Care management	The way the social work department organises the care you receive. See Chapter 2.
Care plan	A written statement (usually from the social work department or the NHS) setting out what help a person needs and how it will be organised. It may follow a **community care assessment**.
Community care assessment	The way in which the social work department is supposed to work out what services you need and how to provide them. See Chapter 2.
Community care plan	A plan prepared and regularly reviewed by the social work department showing how it will organise community care in its area. See Chapter 24.
Charging Order	The mortgage which the social work department can put on your house if you fall behind in your residential care fees. See page 56.
Crisis card	A card, a bit like an organ donor card, which says what should happen if you are in some sort of emergency. Crisis cards are beginning to be used by some people with mental health problems and also by carers.
Curator ad litem	A person appointed by the court to carry on legal proceedings on someone's behalf if they are unable to do this themselves. See page 103.
Curator bonis	A person appointed by the court to manage someone's property and money affairs. See page 103.
Disabled person	A person who is entitled to a **disabled person's assessment**. This means a person who is chronically sick *or* disabled *or* has mental health problems *or* has a learning disability. There is no legal definition of these terms.
Disabled person's assessment	An assessment of a person's need for services under the Chronically Sick and Disabled Persons Act. See page 16.
Discharge protocol	A procedure to set out what should happen to make sure services are in place before someone leaves hospital.

Discretion	If the law says somebody "*may*" do something or "*has the power to*" to something then they have a discretion or a choice. They can decide whether or not they should do it. The courts will not usually interfere with how somebody exercises their discretion.
Discretionary trust	A trust where the trustees who are in charge of the money can decide themselves when and how to pay any money over to the person the trust is for.
DSS	The Department of Social Security, the body which makes the benefit rules.
DSS appointee	A person appointed to collect someone else's DSS benefits.
Domiciliary care	Care provided in a person's own home (eg home helps).
enduring Power of Attorney	See **Power of Attorney**.
Fundholder	See **GP fundholder**.
Future needs assessment	The assessment which is made when a child with a **Record of Special Educational Needs** is about to leave school. See page 17.
Guardianship	See **mental health guardianship**.
GP fundholder	A family doctor who has been given a certain sum of money to buy services for patients direct from health **providers**.
Health board	The body which arranges the planning and purchasing of health care. See page 75.
Incapax	A Latin term describing a person who, in the eyes of the law, is unable to take decisions for themselves.
Judicial review	The courts have the power to investigate claims that a public body has not complied with the law when carrying out its duties. The court action is called judicial review. See Chapter 26.
Interdict	A legal remedy which a person can use to stop someone else from behaving in a way which is unlawful.
Legitimate expectation	If a public body does not act in accordance with its own policy or with what it has said publicly, people may be able to ask the courts to investigate whether it has acted unlawfully. See page 147.
Liable relative	Because by law a man is supposed to give financial support to his wife and a wife to her husband, if either of them goes into residential care, the social work department and the Benefits Agency may expect the other spouse to contribute towards the costs of the care, depending on their resources. The spouse who is liable to pay is called the "*liable relative*". See page 48.
Local health council	Local health councils are independent bodies which try to protect the interests of users of health services. They can help with information and are very useful if you want to make a complaint about NHS services. See under Health Council in the phone book.
Means testing	Doing a detailed assessment of a person's financial circumstances as part of offering them a service or calculating their entitlement to benefit.
Mental health guardian	A person appointed by the court to protect the welfare of a vulnerable adult. For powers, see page 103.
Mental health officer	A social worker who has special experience and training in mental health issues. They should also know about learning disability and dementia. They have a special role under the Mental Health (Scotland) Act.
Negotiorum gestio	A rule of law which says that in certain circumstances a person may be able to manage another person's financial affairs if the other person is unable to do this themselves. The person who does this is called a "negotiorum gestor". See page 103.

NHS Trust	Most hospitals in Scotland are now owned and run by NHS Trusts. They were set up following the NHS & Community Care Act. Many community health services are also run by NHS Trusts.
Notional capital	Money which the DSS or social work department assume you have when carrying out means testing, even though you do not have it (eg money you gave away to avoid charges).
Nursing home	A care home employing nursing staff and registered with the health board. See page 39.
Ombudsman	A watchdog who monitors the performance of a public body. There are ombudsmen for local government, the health service and national government.
Person in need	A person who may be entitled to help from the social work department under the Social Work (Scotland) Act. See pages 2 and 3.
Personal allowance	The amount of money you are supposed to be left with for your own personal use out of welfare benefits or after paying for your residential care.
Power of Attorney	A document someone can sign to give another person power to manage some or all of their financial affairs. If the power is made after 1991 it may be an enduring Power of Attorney, in which case it will continue in effect even if the person making the appointment loses mental capacity.
Preserved rights	People who were living in residential care when the community care changes came in (March 31 1993) can in most cases still have their fees paid by the Department of Social Security. See Chapter 12.
Purchaser and provider	Under the NHS reforms, one body or person decides what services the community needs and it buys them. This is the purchaser. Health boards and GP fundholders are purchasers. Another body employs the staff and sells the service to the purchaser. This is the provider. NHS Trusts are providers. In social care some social work departments are becoming the purchasers and charities and the private sector are often the providers.
Record of Special Educational Needs	A document which the education authority draws up for a school child with special needs. See page 17.
Residential care	Care in a home which is not a hospital but which has staff whose job is to look after people who need extra help.
Residential care home	A care home which is registered with the social work department. See page 39.
Resource transfer	The shift of money from the health service and the DSS to social work departments to help develop community care services.
Respite care	Someone else taking over the caring, to give the carer a break. Respite care may be arranged in the person's own home, with another family or in residential care or a hospital.
Social work department	The department of the local authority which is responsible for arranging community care. Until 1996 this is the Regional Council. After April 1996 it is possible that some local authorities will not have separate social work departments, but they will still have all the responsibilities for community care which we set out in this book.
Statutory complaints procedure	By law all social work departments have to set up a way of making complaints about services. See page 126.
Transitional protection	When benefit rules change, the Government often phases this in so that people who came under the old system do not lose out at once. This is called "transitional protection".
Tutor dative	Someone appointed by the Court of Session in Edinburgh to take decisions on behalf of someone who cannot take decisions for themselves. Tutors are usually appointed to deal with personal matters, such as medical decisions, but they are sometimes given financial powers too. See page 103.

Helpful names and addresses

Charities – Information, Support and Services

(National organisations can often supply details about local groups)

Age Concern Scotland	113 Rose Street, Edinburgh, EH2 3DT (Tel: 0131.220 3345).
Alzheimer Scotland Action on Dementia	8 Hill Street, Edinburgh, EH2 3JZ (Tel: 0131.225 1453). (24 hour Dementia Helpline on Freephone 0800.317817)
Carers National Association	11 Queens's Crescent, Glasgow, G4 9AS (Tel: 0141.333 9495).
Children in Scotland	Princes House, 5 Shandwick Place, Edinburgh, EH2 4RG (Tel: 0131.228 8484).
Disability Scotland	Princes House, 5 Shandwick Place, Edinburgh, EH2 4RG (Tel: 0131.229 8632).
Disablement Income Group (Scotland)	5 Quayside Street, Edinburgh, EH6 6EJ (Tel: 0131.555 2811).
ENABLE	6th Floor, 7 Buchanan Street, Glasgow, G1 3HL (Tel: 0141.226 4541).
Manic Depression Fellowship	Charlie Reid Centre, 19 Elmbank Street, Glasgow, G2 4PB (Tel: 0141. 248 3234).
National AIDS Helpline	0800.567123.
National Schizophrenia Fellowship (Scotland)	40 Shandwick Place, Edinburgh, EH2 4RT (Tel: 0131.226 2025).
Royal National Institute for the Blind	9 Viewfield Place, Stirling, FK8 1NL (Tel: 01786.451752).
Royal National Institute for Deaf People	9 Claremont Gardens, Glasgow, G3 7LW (Tel: 0141.332 0343).
Scottish Aids Monitor	26 Anderson Place, Edinburgh, EH6 5NP (Tel: 0131.555 4850).
SACRO	31 Palmerston Place, Edinburgh, EH12 5AP (Tel: 0131.226 4222).
Scottish Association for Mental Health	Atlantic House, 38 Gardner's Crescent, Edinburgh, EH3 8DQ (Tel: 0131.229 9687).
Scottish Council for Single Homeless	9 Forrest Road, Edinburgh, EH1 2QH (Tel: 0131.226 4382).
Scottish Council for Spastics	22 Corstorphine Road, Edinburgh, EH12 6HP (Tel: 0131.337 9876).
Scottish Council for Voluntary Organisations	18/19 Claremont Crescent, Edinburgh, EH7 4QD (Tel: 0131.556 3882).

The law and your rights to community care

Scottish Down's Syndrome Association	158-160 Balgreen Road, Edinburgh, EH11 3RU (Tel: 0131.313 4225).
Scottish Drugs Forum	5 Oswald Street, Glasgow, G1 4QR (Tel: 0141.221 1175).
Sense Scotland	5/2, 8 Elliot Place, Glasgow, G3 8EP (Tel: 0141.221 7577).
Shared Care (Scotland)	123 Duncan Crescent, Dunfermline, KY11 4DA (Tel: 01383.622462).
SKILL: National Bureau for Students with Disabilities	336 Brixton Road, London, SW9 7AA (Tel: 0171.274 0565).

Official Bodies

Accounts Commission	18 George Street, Edinburgh, EH2 2QE (Tel: 0131.477 1234).
Commission for Racial Equality	Hanover House, 45 Hanover Street, Edinburgh, EH2 2PJ (Tel: 0131.226 5186).
Commissioner for Local Administration in Scotland (*Local government ombudsman*)	23 Walker Street, Edinburgh, EH3 7HX (Tel: 0131.225 5300).
Convention of Scottish Local Authorities	Rosebery House, 9 Haymarket Terrace, Edinburgh, EH12 5XZ (Tel: 0131.346 1222).
Equal Opportunities Commission	Stock Exchange House, 7 Nelson Mandela Place, Glasgow, G2 1QW (Tel: 0141.248 5833).
Health Service Commissioner for Scotland (*Health service ombudsman*)	Ground Floor, 1 Atholl Place, Edinburgh, EH3 8HP (Tel: 0131.225 7465).
Mental Welfare Commission for Scotland	25 Drumsheugh Gardens, Edinburgh, EH3 7RB (Tel: 0131.225 7034).
MPs	You can write to your MP at the House of Commons, London, SW1A OAA (Tel: 0171.219 3000).
Parliamentary Commissioner for Administration (*Parliamentary ombudsman*)	House of Commons, Palace of Westminster, London, SW1A OAA (Tel: 0171.276 2130).
Scottish Federation of Housing Associations	38 York Place, Edinburgh, EH1 3HU (Tel: 0131.556 5777).
Scottish Health Advisory Service	Trinity Park House, South Trinity Road, Edinburgh, EH5 3SE (Tel: 0131.552 6255).
Secretary of State for Scotland	The Scottish Office, St Andrew's House, Edinburgh, EH1 3DG.
Social Work Services Inspectorate	43 Jeffrey Street, Edinburgh, EH1 1DG (Tel: 0131.556 8400).

Professional Bodies

British Association of Social Workers	28 North Bridge, Edinburgh, EH1 1QG (Tel: 0131.225 4549).
British Medical Association	3 Hill Place, Edinburgh, EH8 9EQ (Tel: 0131.662 4820).
Law Society of Scotland	26 Drumsheugh Gardens, Edinburgh, EH3 7YR (Tel: 0131.226 7411).
Royal College of Nursing Scottish Board	42 South Oswald Road, Edinburgh, EH9 2HH (Tel: 0131.662 1010).

The law and your rights to community care

Royal College of Psychiatrists, Scottish Division	9 Queen Street, Edinburgh, EH2 1JQ (Tel: 0131.220 2910).

Advice and Representation Services

Child Poverty Action Group	Citizens Rights Office (*information for advisers only*), 1-5 Bath Street, London, EC1V 4PY (Tel: 0171.253 6569, Mon-Thurs 2-4pm).
Citizens Advice Scotland	26 George Square, Edinburgh, EH8 9LD (Tel: 0131.667 0156).
Disability Alliance ERA	1st Floor East, Universal House, 88-94 Wentworth Street, London E1 7SA (Tel: 0171.247 8763, Mon & Wed 2-4pm).
ENABLE Legal Services	6th Floor, 7 Buchanan Street, Glasgow, G1 3HL (Tel: 0141.226 4541).
Ethnic Minorities Law Centre	41 St Vincent Place, Glasgow, G1 2ER (Tel: 0141. 204 2888).
Legal Services Agency Mental Health Legal Representation Unit	Fleming House, 134 Renfrew Street, Glasgow, G3 6ST (Tel: 0141.353 3354). *and* 18 Walker Street, Edinburgh, EH3 7LP (Tel: 0131.225 2343).
Scottish Association of Health Councils	18 Alva Street, Edinburgh, EH2 4QG (Tel: 0131.220 4101).
Scottish Association for Mental Health	Atlantic House, 38 Gardner's Crescent, Edinburgh EH3 8DQ (Tel: 0131 229 9687)
Scottish Child Law Centre	4th Floor, Cranston House, 104/114 Argyle Street, Glasgow G2 8BH.
Scottish Consumer Council	Royal Exchange House, 100 Queen Street, Glasgow, G1 3DN (Tel: 0141.226 5261).
Scottish Council for Civil Liberties	146 Holland Street, Glasgow, G2 4NG (Tel: 0141.332 5960).
Shelter Housing Law Centre	18 Walker Street, Edinburgh, EH3 7LP (Tel: 0131.225 2343).

User organisations and networks

Barnardo's Advocacy Service	235 Corstorphine Road, Edinburgh, EH12 7AR (Tel: 0131.334 9893).
Scottish Advocacy Workers' Forum	c/o Barnardo's Advocacy Service, 235 Corstorphine Road, Edinburgh, EH12 7AR (Tel: 0131.334 9893).
People First (Scotland)	11 St Colme Street, Edinburgh, EH3 6AG (Tel: 0131.225 4606).
Scottish Users' Network	Box SUN, SCVO, 18/9 Claremont Crescent, Edinburgh, EH7 4QD.
Values Into Action	Stella Morris, 12 Bullers o' Buchan, Cruden Bay, Peterhead, AB42 7NS (Tel: 01779.812819).

(National advocacy organisations can often supply details about local groups.)

Further Reading

This list gives a general guide to some of the main publications which may be of interest to community care service users and advisers. It is not intended to be a comprehensive bibliography.

General

Jim McKenny et al, *National Welfare Benefits Handbook* (Child Poverty Action Group, London, 1995) ISBN 0-946744-69-6

Richard Poynter, and Clive Martin, *Rights guide to non-means-tested benefits* (Child Poverty Action Group, London, 1995) ISBN 0-946744-70-X

Judith Paterson, *Disability Rights Handbook* (Disability Alliance ERA, London, 1995) ISBN 0-946336-67-9

Social Work Services Group, *Thinking about moving into a care home?* (HMSO, 1995)

Rosemary Bland, *Residential care – is it for me?* (HMSO for Age Concern Scotland, 1987) ISBN 0-11-493412-6

*Barbara Meredith, *The community care handbook* (Age Concern England, 1993) ISBN 0-86242-121-7

*Michael Mandelstam, with Belinda Schwer, *Community care practice and the law* (London, 1995) ISBN 1-85302-273-X

Challenging community care decisions – a briefing paper by the Public Law Project (UNISON/The Public Law Project, London, 1994)

Patients' Rights: GP and hospital services (Scottish Consumer Council and Scottish Association of Health Councils, 1992)

Learning Disability

Adrian Ward, *The Power to Act* (ENABLE, Glasgow, 1990) ISBN 0-9506697-7-6

Gordon Ashton, and Adrian Ward *Mental Handicap and the law* (Sweet & Maxwell, London, 1992) ISBN 0-421-42000-6

Mental Health

John Blackie, and Hilary Patrick, *Mental health: a guide to the law in Scotland* (Butterworths, Edinburgh, 1990) ISBN 0-406-16777-X (Out of print but available in libraries)

Dementia

Dementia, money & legal matters: a guide for carers, (Alzheimer Scotland – Action on Dementia, 1995) ISBN 0-948897-20-1

Having your say: planning dementia services – a guide for carers (Alzheimer Scotland – Action on Dementia, 1992)

Education

Graham Atherton, *In special need* (HMSO, for Scottish Consumer Council, Edinburgh, 1989) ISBN 0-11-493423-1

Linda Kerr, Liz Sutherland, Joyce Wilson, *A special partnership* (HMSO, for Children in Scotland, 1994) ISBN 0-11-495237-X

Housing

Himsworth, CMG, *Housing law in Scotland* (Butterworths, Edinburgh, 1994) ISBN 0-406-02979-2

* Applies to English law

Scottish Office community care circulars and directions

Circulars

Title	Circular No	Date
Certification of the blind and partially sighted	NHS 1986 (PCS) 35 SWSG 8/1986	8/12/86
Guide to the Act	SW6/90	1/10/90
Introductory circular	SW8/90	30/10/90
Provision of aids, equipment and home adaptations for disabled people living at home	SDD 40/1985	
Inspection of establishments	SW9/90	30/10/90
Mental Illness Specific Grant	SW10/90	30/10/90
Commencement Order	SW2/91	7/1/91
Community care planning	HHD/DGM(91)1 SW1/91	7/1/91
Complaints procedures	SW5/91	20/2/91
Bridging finance scheme	HHD/DGM/(91)17	8/3/91
Housing and community care	ENV/8/91	28/3/91
Assessment and care management	SW11/91 HHD/DGM(91)40	17/6/91
Progress (Community care in Scotland)	HHD/DGM(91)59	8/7/91
A right to complain: complaints procedures in social work departments (Practice Guidance)		8/91
Care management and assessment: summary of practice guidance		18/9/91
Bridging finance scheme	HHD/DGM(91)89	18/10/91

Commissioning and purchasing	SW19/1991	22/11/91
Monitoring and evaluating community care	SW21/1991 NHS SOHHD	31/12/91
Health Board involvement with voluntary and private sector care	HHD/DGM(92)1	20/1/1992
Bridging finance scheme	HHD/DGM(92)8	23/1/1992
Guidance on care programmes for people with a mental illness, including dementia	SOHHD DGM 1(92)9 SW1992/1	7/2/92
Implementing the Government's community care reforms	CCIU	7/9/92
Joint purchasing, resource transfer and contracting: arrangements for inter-agency working	CCIU MEL(92)55	15/9/92
Resources for 1993-94	SWSG	2/10/92
Mental Illness Specific Grant		23/10/92
Independent Living Arrangements from April 1993	SW7/1993	31/3/93
Liaison between the Benefits Agency and social work departments	SW8/1993	31/3/93
Local authorities' powers to make arrangements for people who are in independent sector residential care and nursing homes on 31 March 1993	SW11/1993	7/4/93
Bridging finance scheme 1993/94	MEL(93)67	14/5/93
The needs of people with alcohol and drug problems within community care	SW14/1993	20/7/93
Monitoring/evaluation of community care policy	SWS16/1993	5/8/93
Choice of accommodation – cross border placements	SW6/1994	6/5/94
Community care: the housing dimension	SW7/1994	8/94
Public awareness and local discussion	SW8/94	
Community care planning	SW14/1994	11/11/94

Directions and regulations

Title	Circular No	Date
National Assistance (Assessment of Resources) Regulations 1992 – Regulations and Guidance	SW13/92	31/12/92
Community care plans: Directions on consultation	SW4/1993	26/3/93
Directions on choice of accommodation	SW5/1993	17/3/93
National Assistance (Sums for Personal Requirements) Regulations 1993	SW6/1993	31/3/93
National Assistance (Assessment of Resources) (Amendment) Regulations 1993: Regulations and Guidance – Amendment 1	SW13/1993	21/6/93
Health and Social Services and Social Security Adjudications Act 1983 s21-24: Orders and guidance	SW/15/1993	23/7/93
National Assistance (Assessment of Resources) (Amendment No 2) Regulations 1993: Regulations and Guidance – Amendment 2	SW1/94	21/1/94
National Assistance (Assessment of Resources) (Amendment) Regulations 1994. Regulations and Guidance	SW4/1994	9/5/94
Community care plans: Directions on purchasing	SW13/94	2/11/94
National Assistance (Assessment of Resources) (Amendment No. 2) Regulations 1994: Regulations and Guidance	SW15/94	30/11/94

Table of Statutes

The law and your rights to community care

Index

The law and your rights to community care

languages, other, information in, 115
learning difficulties, where, 83
legal right to, where need of services, 3, 10, 15, 18, 50, 69, 70, 81, 150
local authority and private care assimilated, 59, 60
mental disorder, where, 81
"mobility", excluded from, 66
mortgage, outstanding, 52
movement and preserved rights, 61, 62
need,
    criteria, 23, 130
    definition, 2, 3, 10
    disagreement over, 23
    effect of, 14
    established, position where, 5, 10-12, 14
    medical and social care distinguished, 84
    priority over services availability, 12
    provision possibility irrelevant to, 146
    refusal to meet, 23
    where specialised, 15
new, on carer giving up, 33
non-cooperation, where past, 11
notification of, 15, 18, 23
ordinarily resident, as basis for payment, 11
participation by user and carer, 15, 16, 145
person responsible for, 15
preference, respect for, 42, 44
racial background, irrelevant, 115
refusal of, 10, 11
reluctance of person concerned, 99
representative present at, 97
respite care, see respite care,
review, provisions as to, 15, 23
screening, preliminary, 11
services offered after, 14
service, where not available, 11
specialised services needed, 11
transitional protection after April 1993, 60
welfare benefit, inclusion of, 65
Assessment and Care Management, 115
assets,
    charge on person receiving, 56
    disposal of, 54 et seq.
Attendance Allowance, 30, 37, 40, 53, 66, 67

bad management,
    central government, by, 135, 136
    meaning, 129, 133
bankruptcy, 57
bathing, help with, 8, 84, 85
behavioural problems, 90
Blind and Partially Sighted Persons, Register, 20, 27
blindness, Blindcraft factories, 15, 27, 90, 94, 126
"board and lodging allowances", 61
braille, complaints procedure in, 126
British Deaf Association, 135
budgeting, 8, 29

capital,
    Income Support, and, 48, 59
    "notional", 55

care,
    April 1993, significance of, 38
    assessment of need, see assessment.
    community, in, arguments for, 1
    continuing, need of, 84, 85
    facilities/services, registration and inspection, 5, 9
    home, at, excessive cost, 30
    long stay, NHS reluctance to provide, 38
    nursing, 8
    reform, need for, 1
    relatives, financial involvement of, 38
Careers Service, 93
"Care Gap", 38
carer,
    assessment, involvement in, 16, 32, 35
    care, inability to give full, 31
    Carer's Premium, 33, 37, 65, 66
    complaints by, 33, 34, 102, 127
    Council Tax, and, 33
    death of,
        emergency residential care, 14
        tenancy, where, 70
    disabled,
        children, of, 120
        person, and needs of, 16
    fellow occupier enters residential care, 33
    files, access to, 102, 111
    future, ability to continue in, 32
    giving up, and reasons for, 33
    groups, 34, 120
    home care services, not liable for, 30
    homeless housing, priority for, 71
    hospital discharge, consultation on, 82
    housing, medical, services help with, 32
    Income Support, receiving, 33
    Invalid Care allowance, 33, 37, 66
    needs of, 1, 16, 18, 32
    paid, not to see records, 111
    provision, enforced, of, 144
    residential/nursing care, contributions to, 33
    respite care for, 8, 16, 32, 35
    supporter, as, 96
    tenancy of deceased, taking over, 72
    views of, consideration of, 14, 15, 99
Carers (Recognition and Services) Bill, 16, 32
Caring for people principles, 1
cash emergency, in, 21
charities,
    payments in kind by, 48
    training and employment schemes, 93, 94
Chief Adjudication Officer v Palfrey and others, 58
Children (Scotland) Bill, 3
Children's Panels, Reporters to, 111
children/young persons,
    after-care, 4
    assessment,
        chronically sick, disabled, 4, 17, 120
        full, requested, 17
        not entitled to, 3
        review of, 17
    complaints by, and on behalf of, 127

The law and your rights to community care

The law and your rights to community care